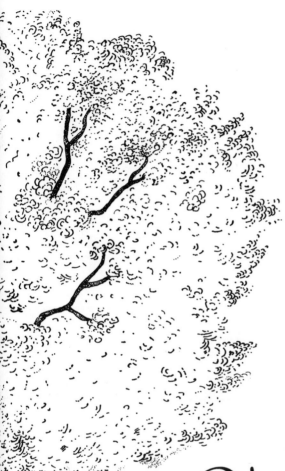

Maggie's

FARM

MAGGIE BEER

Illustrations by Jiri Tibor Novak

A Rathdowne Book
Allen & Unwin

In memory of my parents

© Maggie Beer 1993
Illustrations by Jiri Tibor Novak

Design and layout by P.A.G.E. Pty Ltd, South Melbourne, 3206, Victoria

Cover image: Hans Heysen, Australia 1877–1968, *Autumn Fruits*, oil on canvas 69.8 x 85.1cm,
Art Gallery of South Australia, Adelaide, William Birkinshaw Wilkinson Bequest 1928

First published in 1993

A Rathdowne Book
Allen & Unwin Pty Ltd
9 Atchison Street
St Leonards NSW 2065, Australia

National Library of Australia
Cataloguing-in Publication data:

　　Beer, Maggie.
　　Maggie's Farm

　　Bibliography.
　　Includes index.
　　ISBN 1 86373 425 2.

　　1. Cookery, Australian. I. Novak, Jiri Tibor. II. Title.

641.5994

Printed in Australia by Southwood

10 9 8 7 6 5 4 3

Contents

The starting point for this book was the collection of my weekly columns in the Adelaide *Advertiser*. I was asked to write the column, and later the book, not so much for my ability as a writer but as a cook who was happy to share her knowledge with others.

There is not one way only of doing anything in life, and especially cooking. Here I share with you my love of food, my experience and my way of doing things in the kitchen. For those with more formal training, some of my methods may appear suspect, but to me the proof is in the pudding! My ideal is to encourage you to make the most of the food the seasons bring. Good food can be very simple and at the same time give great pleasure.

ACKNOWLEDGEMENTS

The greatest thanks of all are due to my husband Colin who has been my rock and supporter through the good and the bad, and to those two infuriating and wonderful daughters of mine, Saskia and Eliette, my thanks for their love and belief in me.

The loyalty and co-operation of my staff and suppliers has always been exceptional and their input into the restaurant over the years has been one of its great strengths.

I want to thank my fellow team members of the 1991 Seppelts Menu of the Year Competition, captained by Nigel Hopkins of the *Advertiser*, led by Urs Inauen, with Tom Milligan and Cheong Liew. The teamwork, and the sharing of knowledge and fun we all had preparing for the competition, and then taking our menu to New York, was the experience of a lifetime.

The loyal support of the customers of the Pheasant Farm has given me so much pleasure over the years and enabled us to win the Remy/*Gourmet* Restaurant of the Year Award in 1991. It certainly changed my world but has not changed how I feel about pleasing those people who believed in us, awards or not.

A special group of customers are the Wednesday Table, led by Sir Lunchalot Bob McLean and Rod Schubert, artist and guru of the valley. The characters of the Barossa Valley winemakers made a stimulating table for anyone in the trade who was visiting and added a feeling of expectation to Wednesday trading.

Tony Love of the *Advertiser* convinced me to write the original columns and I am grateful to him for that chance to share my love of food with a wider audience.

I cannot finish without mentioning my publisher, Julie Gibbs, who coerced me into this book with a throw-away remark! I certainly found fitting work on the book around the frenetic pace of the restaurant very demanding, but without her encouragement I could never have done it. Thank you.

Maggie Beer

Introduction

M
Y HUSBAND, COLIN, and I began farming pheasants some
eighteen years ago. At the time, we had no thoughts of
opening a restaurant. We bought a vineyard in the
Barossa Valley when we left Sydney to 'live in the
country'. Colin was originally from an area near the
Barossa Valley and was happy to return, as he didn't
enjoy city life. I, on the other hand, was a city girl but the
Barossa felt like home the minute I arrived. It was not
until Colin won a Churchill Fellowship to go on a
learning tour of Europe and America that we formalised
the Pheasant Farm and it became the dominant factor in
our lives.

We had been rearing pheasants for four years before
the Fellowship was awarded, but always with the same
problem: we would make sales but rarely get repeat
orders. It took us a long time to realise that the basic
problem was that people did not know how to cook
pheasant. Most people referred to (European) cook
books, which told them to cook the pheasants for 40
minutes to 2 hours—of course, the birds came out dry,
tough and utterly detestable. (These days, I would bake a
prepared pheasant for 10-15 minutes in a very high

oven.) There were many reasons for this difference: the European bird was wild and of indeterminate age, and it was also important whether or not it had been hung.

While in Scotland on the tour we visited a turkey farm that called itself a 'farm shop'. It sold its products direct to the public from the farm site, preparing everything imaginable from turkey—turkey breast, turkey roll, turkey giblets, turkey necks. We decided that this would be our model—a direct marketing chain from farmer to table.

As cooking had always been a passion in my family, it seemed natural that I would become the cook; Colin would undertake to increase production from what might have been called a 'hobby' to a full-scale farm. And so it all began.

It sounds easy, but pheasants are very hard to rear. There was one disaster after another—birds that were cannibalistic or suicidal, birds that were bad mothers, and inbreeding, just to name a few.

So, as well as selling fresh whole pheasants, I made pates, terrines and cooked take-away pheasant, stuffed and roasted quails, pickled quail eggs and fresh-baked bread. People used to bring a bottle of wine and picnic on the grass, or treat it as a high-class take-away. I talked to people about how to cook the birds if they bought them fresh, and supplied recipe sheets for them to follow. I think I charged the grand sum of $1.00 per bird to cook and dissect. We also supplied salads, tables and glasses—the public loved it.

The farm shop lasted for only nine months—we were working too hard for too little money as our prices were ridiculously low. We decided to go the whole hog and open a restaurant. The audacity of it— we were miles off the beaten track, on one of the worst roads in the state! The restaurant was a success from the beginning but it took ten years of trading before we were even moderately successful in terms of our monthly overdraft. In those early days, we had a simple 'table d'hôte' menu where I cooked pheasant every day as a fixed menu and in as many ways as I could think of.

Eventually, taking on another chef to help, we expanded to an à la carte menu and I tried to ensure that the food would be simple and of the region. I knew that the only way was to be as fussy as possible about each small issue and everything was done 'à la minute'. This was a nightmare really, and that people coped with the delays can only be put down to their being a loyal lot and having an exceptionally tranquil place to sit and contemplate. I can tell you, the kitchen wasn't tranquil—

simple food it may have been but my emotional temperament (highly strung, my mother used to say) has always made hard work of it!

Fashion in food has never been of much interest to me. My cooking has developed from my own very personal style and will obviously not suit everyone. I cook without any schooling in the matter, which enables me to develop my natural skill—an instinct for food. I cook from the heart, unhampered by rules and dietary guidelines. Flavour has always been my driving force—gutsy, flavoursome, simple food.

The success of my restaurant owes much to the food culture of the Barossa Valley, which is the one place in Australia where there is a strong peasant culture and food heritage. According to Michael Symons in *One Continuous Picnic*, the 'peasant base' helps explain the actual importance of food in daily life in countries such as France. In the Barossa, as in Europe, peasants and farmers grew food primarily for themselves, so they not only learned about quality from their parents, but were also eating their own produce—so of course they cared. Large-scale farming tends to reduce the farmer's interest in his or her product.

One reason that the Barossa food heritage is so strong is that it was settled by a group of small land-owners united by their churches. There were thirty-odd Lutheran churches in the Valley, many of the families having emigrated from Germany to escape religious persecution. There was also German migration to the Darling Downs in Queensland and to Hahndorf in South Australia, but there were fewer people involved and they were not so closely tied to their parcels of land.

Moreover, the Barossa is a wine area (tobacco was originally grown here but it failed), so the tradition of feasting to celebrate the vintage has been very important here and, of course, has led to South Australia's biennial Vintage Festival.

Most of the small land-holders were, and still are, almost self-sufficient, naturally hard-working and incredibly resourceful people. The Barossa has a wealth of food resources, from vines, fruit trees and almonds to the wild olive trees growing on the side of the road. All of these foods are in harmony with the South Australian climate, and have been established for 150 years. There are few places in Australia where the early white settlers took such advantage of the climate and worked with it rather than against it. We certainly reap the benefits today and have a richness of supply no matter the season.

I have been lucky enough to take the best of this peasant culture and use it in an 'Australian' way, for example with my gum-smoked kangaroo, where, in the Barossa tradition, I smoke a readily-available game meat. It is also the Barossa way to utilise every part of the animal so I often have offal on the menu. It was that principle which inspired our pate, which is now sold all over Australia.

The restaurant has benefited from having our own produce—pheasant, quail and guinea fowl—supplemented with local fare, including hare shot in the vineyards, pigeons from local farmers and yabbies from the dams. My base is regional, yet when I started I knew nothing about this term—it was simply the logical way to proceed.

As an untrained cook with nothing more than a love of and instinct for food (inherited from my father rather than my mother, who couldn't boil an egg when she married), it was obvious that I needed to learn as much as possible about my product so that my farmer, who happened to be my husband and partner, could set about giving me the standard of food I required. This is, of course, what should be happening everywhere—that direct link between farmer and consumer. There is much knowledge to be shared, but it is only when consumers demand quality that they will have an impact on producers. Consumers may feel apathetic because they think they can't make a difference to the situation. But it is in these economic times, particularly, that they should encourage producers or farmers to learn more about their products and improve them. How many people understand the pleasure of an apple picked straight from the tree, rather than from cold storage? How many know how a juicy, ripe pear tastes compared to a brick-hard, green one? And as for tomatoes, they are a complete subject in themselves. People who have grown these foods in their back yards understand, and so does a small band of producers across the country. Look at Stephanie Alexander's book *Stephanie's Australia—Travelling and Tasting*; that book is truly about the coming of age of eating in Australia and a celebration of these producers of quality food.

Many people are turning from other, more pressured ways of life to some kind of farming because of the satisfaction they get from it and their passion for food. It is, however, a hard vocation, and producers of quality products should be rewarded financially for the extra care and attention they give to provide a top product. Very few people understand how hard the work is and the frustration when a season fails through no fault of the farmer's. Encouragement should be freely given to support these producers: we'll all be the richer for it, especially those of us who have access to the direct link between farmer and table.

We have to remember that growers of food are retail-driven: that is, they grow for the public what they are told the public wants—'good-looking food'. But what is the use of a tomato or strawberry that looks wonderful but tastes of nothing? The public can demand something different. The more everyone learns about food—about how good, how simple, how inexpensive food can be when bought at the right time of the year—the more pleasurable the whole eating experience will be.

TOWARDS MY OWN MEDITERRANEAN CUISINE

GOOD COOKING is about balance and produce, and really good cooking is about small details. Mediterranean food gives us all of this, in simple, uncomplicated food which is full of flavour. It is not only a cuisine using lots of olive oil and wine, it is the food of the sun.

The Mediterranean climate is not limited to the fifteen countries that border the Mediterranean sea; Koppen's classification draws a line through South Australia, parts of south-western Australia and western Victoria, as well as the southern tip of Africa, California and Chile. So in South Australia we have the natural advantage of a climate to grow Mediterranean produce, and we are not limited by the arid conditions of the Mediterranean region—we have the advantage of good pasture as well.

I am convinced that Mediterranean food is a great example for living. Not only is it healthy, it tastes wonderful. Because of our climate, the Mediterranean diet is the most obvious one for us to pursue and has put us well on the way to establishing an identifiable cuisine of our own.

My expansion from straight game to Mediterranean food came about from searching out local produce and starting to look at the balance of my food. Game is mostly eaten in colder climates, served with fairly traditional, heavy sauces. I made sure my entrees were almost always made up of pastas, vegetables, salads or fish so that people wouldn't have an overkill on game and feel the worse for it. Polenta and couscous became staples on my menu, teamed with the main courses—not because I was trying to cut down on the meat component but because I was trying to cut down on the richness of my food.

To give a quick example, the entrees on my menu this week were:
- Leeks and garlic with wild olives
- Raw salmon with cucumber and chives

- Tart of goat's cheese, caramelised onions, oregano and prosciutto served with rocket
- Pumpkin and sage ravioli
- Globe artichoke risotto
- Duck egg pasta with smoked kangaroo (the one exception)

On my main course menu of six different dishes, at least three (kid, squab and kangaroo) would be treated in simple Mediterranean style, while the others could be classified as more French in origin (chicken, salmon and pheasant).

My region is rich in food. There are the vines, of course, which are the soul of the Barossa Valley, but there are also the almond orchards and wonderful stone fruits where the growers I have dealt with for years will ripen the fruit on the tree for me. There are wild fig and quince trees everywhere and, in fact, I am more passionate about quinces and figs than any other fruit. We are about to plant a quince orchard of 200 trees. The desserts at the Pheasant Farm are almost always fruit-based according to local availability and my own preference.

We can't get salmon locally, and I am happy to bring that in from Tasmania, but we do have St Vincent's Gulf nearby, where we get the amazing blue swimmer crabs, razorfish and garfish. As we are a wheat-growing area we are lucky enough to have excellent hard flour which is fantastic for pasta and bread.

Within a 32 km radius, we have a kid farm, quail and pigeon farm, yabbies in the wild, pine forests that give us wonderful mushrooms in the autumn, and the adjoining region of the Riverland where citrus abounds. The fresh herbs I love to cook with have had to be introduced to the Valley as, aside from a rosemary hedge, they were not to be found. The enthusiastic gardeners of the Valley have quickly taken them up.

It has seemed only natural to me to use the wealth of my region, to follow the seasons of my local food to make the heart of my menu and then add to that the best Australia has to offer.

When we started, the only olive oil I knew of was that bought at chemist shops. Indeed, it had the same connotations as castor oil. Little did I know what a profound effect olive oil was to have on me and my life. My discovery of olive oil was simply to do with flavour. I found an Italian farmer at Angle Vale with a sign out on the road saying 'Olive oil and almonds for sale'. I stopped to buy it and loved it and set about using it with a vengeance. I nearly lost most of my winemaker customers who, being friends, used to say things like 'Should we call it the "Olive Oil Restaurant" now?' These same people now eat the food as a matter of course.

The uses in my mind for olive oil are never-ending and, on average, we would use 15-20 litres a week in the restaurant kitchen. This covers cooking, marinating, making mayonnaises and vinaigrettes, tossing it in pasta, making cakes and storing foods. I'm not averse to rubbing the odd bit on my skin from time to time and my younger daughter sometimes massages it into her long, very curly hair when it becomes dry.

One of my heroes is the visionary Philip Muskett, who wrote *The Art of Living in Australia* in 1893 as Surgeon-General of New South Wales. This book is still as fresh and alive as if it had been written yesterday. In 1893 Muskett advocated the planting of Mediterranean vegetables and following the diet trends of the Mediterranean rather than those of cold-climate countries. It has taken us 100 years to begin this development and to realise what can be done with our country. We are finally taking advantage of our climate and working with it rather than against it. Regionalism and climate go hand in hand, and we in South Australia are finally making fuller use of this principle. Mediterranean food is simple, gutsy and full of flavour and it suits our lifestyle. With education and enthusiasm we can emphasise the fun and joy that such good, simple food can bring to our lives.

RESTAURANTS

MOST CHEFS WILL tell you that there have to be reasons other than financial for running a restaurant: the love of food, the excitement of the buzz of activity, the camaraderie, the feeling that you are actually helping in a small way to shape the destiny of food, giving people pleasure... If you get hooked on it, a restaurant can give you so much satisfaction that you keep going despite the odds.

On the other hand, the actual physical and mental work of running a restaurant is tremendous. It never lets up, and you are judged on every performance even though you are only human and cannot work to your full potential all the time. The more you strive for perfection the greater the toll, but you do it because you believe in it. The burn-out rate in the industry is a real issue—I can tell you I'm getting too old for it!

A huge amount of education is needed to make people more aware of all aspects of food and the food experience. One area to be covered is understanding dining and its etiquette: letting a restaurant know when you are late, cancelling if you have changed your plans, treating the staff as you would want to be treated, and setting out for the night in a highly expectant mood, leaving your fights at home—bad moods filter through a restaurant like wildfire. The public should know how hard it is to run a restaurant, although constructive criticism (politely given) always has a place.

When you go out to dinner at a restaurant, ask questions of the staff. To enjoy the experience of dining out, you need to be relaxed about it, and the easiest way to become relaxed is to ask when you are not sure of something. Good front-of-house people always enjoy making dining a special experience for you—they enjoy their job so much more if you have a good time.

I do not for a moment believe that good food is limited to restaurants but they are the most immediate way to bring new foods and trends to the public's attention, and to promote excellence as a benchmark for everyone to strive for. Good food is not necessarily complicated: in fact, the best food is often very simple. However, it seems that people need to reach a certain level of sophistication before they can perceive this.

Restaurants are also important because so few people in Australia learn about food from their parents, either because food isn't important to them or because of the pressures of modern life.

Before you begin

LIFE IS TOO SHORT to eat bad food (as it is to drink bad wine). Good food need only be simple and fresh. And it is the sharing of food and friendship around the table where everyone is relaxed that is the most important thing.

As Marion Halligan says in *Eat My Words*, 'Dinner parties were foisted upon us in the fifties', where the idea was to outdo the last occasion. In these hurried days where so many of us live in households where both partners work, there is hardly the time for going to all the trouble and fuss of putting on a show.

It is useful to look at other cultures where food is an important element. If you were asked to dinner by a Greek or Italian friend it would be to share their table; that is, their favourite dish would be cooked for you and you would all sit at the table in their home with just another place added.

Look at what is available in the markets before you decide what to cook. Don't set your heart on exotic dishes such as guinea fowl with crab apples if guinea fowl and crab apples are not in season. You will buy best by buying locally and seasonally—you just need a little bit of thought and inspiration. If you need a nudge in the area of inspiration, buy a book such as the *English Cook's Calendar* by Frances Bissell or *The Independent Cook* by Jeremy Round, *The Seasonal Kitchen* by Perla Meyers, *Ma Cuisine des Saisons* by Georges Blanc and the Australian *Four Seasons of Food and Wine* by Elise Pascoe.

Demand more of your greengrocer, butcher and fishmonger by asking questions if you are unsure of how to tell quality. The more knowledge you have, the more discerning you'll become, the more you'll enjoy the pleasures of preparing food at its best, and the more the greengrocer, butcher or fishmonger can communicate the needs of the public back to the grower, farmer or fisherman. The food chain has to be improved for quality to filter through to everyone, and things will only improve if the consumer demands it!

Go to the trouble of planting a few herbs in your garden, even if they are in terracotta pots. Fresh herbs are so wonderful in food and take such little care. They seem to tell you when they need watering and can so often save the culinary day. There are many to choose from but I recommend starting with the staples—rosemary, sage, thyme, parsley and basil for the summer. Once they become established, you can plant different ones next year. I promise you'll never regret the little trouble of planting them compared with the end result!

―――――――

KITCHEN EQUIPMENT

- Make sure your kitchen is equipped with good, sharp knives. My preference is for Dick knives. The best all-rounder is a small chef's knife. I also have a small paring knife and a thin-bladed boning knife. For working with fish and removing the sinews in game, a thin flexible fish knife is necessary. A top-quality serrated carving knife can be used for carving and slicing bread. Have on hand several smaller, cheaper serrated kitchen knives for cutting tomatoes and peeling fruit.
- A pastry brush with proper bristles.
- A good-quality pepper grinder to grind coarsely.
- At least two potato peelers—for when one is in the washup!
- A nutmeg grater.
- Three kitchen serving spoons.
- Three slotted kitchen serving spoons.
- Stainless steel ladles—one small for individual serves of sauces and one large for soups.
- Three to four pairs of tongs—shorter ones for better hand control.

- Whisks of several different sizes—one very tiny for vinaigrettes, one small yet solid and one medium-sized and strong. If they are too large they will be too heavy to use. Buy commercial whisks, not toy ones!
- Wooden spoons—at least small, medium and large.
- Spatulas for scraping ingredients out of bowls.
- Plastic pastry cutter for making pâté brisée.
- Large wooden chopping board.
- Fine conical hair sieve.
- Chinois (larger conical sieve).
- Colander.
- Dutch oven with lid or a similar very heavy pot for braising and pot roasting.
- Stainless steel pots with heavy copper bases, in various sizes.
- Baking trays—one small and one large of light gauge with 1 cm sides, and one small and one large of heavy gauge with 2 cm sides.
- One large and one medium non-stick pan.
- Good kitchen scales.
- Rolling pin—I have one with ball bearings in it!
- Flan tin with 6 cm high sides and a removable base.
- Expandable cake tins—one size does all!
- Lots of stainless steel bowls that fit inside each other for easy storage.
- 2 spring-form pans—one small, one large.
- Food processor.
- Kenwood mixer for making cakes—if you have one you may like to buy the purée and mincer attachments.
- Pasta machine—the Imperia brand also has the optional extra of an attachment for ribbon pasta.

LARDER ESSENTIALS

HOW RICH IS your larder? Organisation and forward planning are the most important features of a full larder. Not everyone has the time or resources for some of the things suggested, but you might find the ideas valuable.

Perhaps there is a family member who has given you that special pot of jam or pickled cherries to personalise your collection of food—just the thing for when you come home late and tired from work or friends arrive unexpectedly. Such items in your larder mean that you can produce food with a minimum of effort and a maximum of style.

I offer these suggestions as a base to work from for last-minute ideas. Of course, nothing replaces carefully-planned, well-balanced meals but at least this list will ensure you are never caught short!

STAPLES

Black and **white peppercorns** and a grinder.

Salt—there is none better than Maldon sea salt flakes. They are visually attractive and not as strong as normal table salt.

Bread (see page 23)—An essential part of life. Keep interesting loaves in the freezer or good, strong flour to make your own. Don't forget yeast. You can make pizza as well.

Butter Resolve never to buy salted butter. More sauces and dishes are ruined by salted butter than almost anything else. I am not talking about salt from a health standpoint—important as that is, it is for experts in other fields to tackle. I am talking about balance in a dish. It seems to me that quality control of salted butter is far from perfect—you will often find batches of butter which have been excessively salted. At the very least, buy low-salt butter, available in almost every brand. I prefer unsalted butter but many people don't like it: when we served premium unsalted butter in the restaurant, customers would butter their bread and then sprinkle on salt! My compromise is to buy low-salt butter for normal use and unsalted butter for special dishes (especially desserts).

Potatoes—particularly the waxy variety. They make wonderful roesti or potato casseroles.

Rice—Ferron riso superfino carnaroli (my favourite rice—it is expensive but worth it for a superior risotto) or arborio for risottos. Long grain or brown rice for cooking by the absorption method.

Pasta—bought fresh, then frozen for emergencies. Italian packet pastas, particularly Cipriani, are a wonderful indulgence. They cook in just a few minutes and are fit for the most discerning palate.

Lentils and **couscous**—add to a dish of lamb shanks or pork hocks left all day in the crock pot while you are at work. Toss some bacon and shallots into the lentils and serve. A wonderful winter's dish!

Pinenuts, almonds and **walnuts**—very versatile, adding crunch to both hot and cold salads. They can be puréed with parsley or basil, with a little garlic and olive oil, to produce pesto to serve with pasta.

Puff pastry—keep in the freezer. Home-made is best! You can make a tasty rissole with mince, onions and lots of flavourings wrapped in thinly-rolled puff pastry and baked as a large sausage roll. Also useful for making quick cheese straws to go with drinks.

Good coffee makes such a difference. Search out coffee merchants who will be happy to let you taste or ask your favourite coffee shop about their preferred blend and supplier.

Olive oil of different grades (see page 200)—a tin bought from the supermarket if you need bulk amounts and, for special things such as vinaigrettes and drizzling over pastas, a bottle of Coriole virgin olive oil, Joe Grilli's, or a flagon of Greenfield's from Angle Vale, or from roadside stalls at Virginia.

Capers—or caper berries in a small pickle jar. Those imported from Italy and packed in salt are my favourites. Rinse well before use. Great for an antipasto plate or for accompaniments to fish or rabbit. A necessary ingredient for tapenade (a paste of olives, capers and anchovies).

Stocks (see page 17)—keep in the freezer for soups, sauces and risottos. Freeze different quantities and different strengths, such as an ice cube of very reduced stock for throwing into a sauce. You can make vegetable soup in a flash or, if you buy some mushrooms on the way home and use your rice and some onions, a wonderful mushroom risotto in half an hour.

Cheese—fresh Parmesan is a must. Australian Parmesan is inexpensive but if you can, try Parmigiano Reggiano. Buy it in a whole piece and keep it well-sealed in the refrigerator, grating it just before you are going to use it. Mozzarella cheese is another must, for impromptu pizzas. Goat's cheese balls kept in olive oil and herbs in the refrigerator can be melted on pieces of crusty bread crisped in the oven, and served with tapenade or just slices of fresh tomato.

Olives (see page 196)—either picked from the side of the road or bought from a good Italian deli together with pickled artichokes and aubergines. Try Vari's Grocery, on The Parade, Norwood, in Adelaide; The Lygon Food Store, on Lygon Street, Carlton in Melbourne; or Santoro on Parramatta Road, Leichhardt in Sydney. All of these are easy to do yourself in season and keep in the pantry.

Sun-dried tomatoes (see page 140)—very simple to make in our South Australian climate, particularly if you plant Roma tomatoes. They are so adaptable, I don't know how we ever did without them, but don't be tempted to use them in everything. Great in fresh pastas, as part of an antipasto, with dishes such as the goat's cheese one described above, in stuffings, filled with capers and served with anchovies, or simply tossed into a salad.

Anchovies—I couldn't live without them. I prefer the Western Australian ones sold in a jar, Bella del Tindari anchovy fillets in oil. Use them in pastas and salads, as a compound butter with olives to serve with kangaroo, or in stuffings (such as for whole squid) with lots of sweated onions and chopped parsley. Use scraps of puff pastry, roll out with anchovies and Parmesan, and bake into sticks.

Prosciutto and **pancetta**—buy from a good Italian deli. Prosciutto is the uncooked, unsmoked leg of pork, dry salt cured and air-dried. It takes one year to cure. Pancetta is the belly of pork made into a roll and cured as for prosciutto but taking only three months to cure. Especially good with pasta, game and chicken dishes.

Free range eggs (see page 64)—they make a wonderful omelette teamed with fresh herbs from the garden or mushrooms or cheese, served with a salad.

Vegetables—you can't do without shallots, garlic and brown onions. Green vegetables should be a daily proposition.

Vinegars—different vinegars for different uses (as for olive oil). Buy local rather than imported brands if you can. Yalumba and Coriole wineries make superb red wine vinegar, now available in specialty shops. Quality sherry or champagne vinegars are worth having on hand as well as fruit vinegars, which are very simple to make yourself when berries are in plentiful supply.

THE SPECIAL THINGS YOU CAN MAKE AND HAVE ON HAND:
Mustard fruits (see page 138)—made with fresh stone fruits such as plums, peaches and apricots (or dried apricots if you are impatient). Terrific with cold, smoked or boiled meats or hot quail.

Pickled quinces—to serve with pickled pork.

Mustards—made yourself from mustard seed. They are inexpensive and satisfying.

Chutneys—made from ripe fruit or tomatoes. Serve with cold meats or give an instant boost to a sauce or curry.

Home-made tomato or **grape sauce**—they make sausages a worth-while experience!

Preserved lemons (see page 94)—hold for a couple of months and use as an accompaniment to slowly-braised meats or couscous.

Prunes or **dried fruits** in tokay or port, or cumquats in brandy—to give sweet-tooths an instant fix.

Ice-cream (real vanilla)—to serve with prunes, dried fruits or cumquats for a special dessert to round off an impromptu meal. (Note that ice-cream really is best the day it is made as freezing diminishes the flavour.)

TECHNIQUES

TRY TO MASTER what I consider the two most important principles of cooking: (1) the resting of meat after cooking and (2) pan frying techniques. These two principles seem to be unfamiliar to many, but don't feel alarmed if you are among them—I have seen lots of professional chefs who do not understand their importance either.

The resting of meat applies to all poultry, game, roasts, pan-fried meats and barbecues. It involves, very simply, cooking at a high temperature (in most cases) and then allowing the meat to rest for approximately the equivalent of its cooking time. For example, I roast a pheasant for, say, 12 minutes and then I rest it for 12 minutes. I barbecue a piece of kangaroo for 6 minutes and I rest it for 6-10 minutes. Whether it is a saddle of lamb or a fillet of beef, the same applies. Resting the meat before carving allows it to relax and keeps in the maximum amount of juices. You will be surprised at the heat that is retained in the resting period. The perfect situation is to serve without reheating at all—if you insist on having 'hot' food, you will be sacrificing moistness and flavour. It is also important to use a very sharp knife to carve hot meat.

Pan frying or sautéing gives a delicious flavour and is often used for simple, easy-to-prepare food but in my experience it is the most often abused principle of cooking. Firstly, choose the right kind of pan—an appropriate size and an appropriate type of pan for the piece of meat to be sealed. For example, for sealing steak or kangaroo I keep black iron pans, but I would never use them for a cream sauce. I find a simple, non-stick pan the most fail-safe or, if you are lucky enough to have one, copper.

Secondly, use butter, or butter and a little oil (this is less likely to burn), and heat the pan to very hot and the butter to nut-brown before placing anything in it. Only use enough butter to give a light film over the pan. Do not allow the butter to be a poaching vehicle, as your meat will become grey and insipid. If you are frying, say, two chicken breasts, the important thing is to place them in the hot brown butter and then regulate the heat of the stove so the butter stays sizzling and nut-brown. Do not allow the butter to burn and your meat will be sealed perfectly. Always cook the first side just a little longer than the second side. The tricky part comes when you wish to fry a whole dish of meat for a casserole or curry. Only fry a small amount at a time and, when that nut-brown condition is attained, remove from pan and strain juices into a bowl to add to the sauce later. Wipe the pan out and begin again until all the meat is done.

Pot roasting is also a valuable cooking method (particularly for old game). I use a very heavy enamelled oval dish with a lid. I brown the meat or poultry very gently to seal with chosen herbs (and vegetables), add about half a cup of good quality stock, and cover. Continue cooking in the oven or on top of the stove at a very low temperature. The meat juices will break down into protein concentrates, move to the pot edges and make a wonderfully reduced glaze. If the juices are too reduced and caramelising (near to burning), just add a little extra stock. If on top of the stove, a simmer pad will keep the heat in check.

Stocks

IT CANNOT BE repeated too often that good cooking requires good stocks. Stocks are the heart and soul of a good kitchen and are required for many dishes—there is no substitute for a good stock. A properly prepared stock can completely change a dish and lift it out of the mundane and into the realm of the exceptional. They are not just used for sauces and glazes but also for making risottos, polentas, soups and pot roasts. Food fashions change and although reduced stock sauces may seem old hat to some, I personally can't imagine not using them in much of my own cooking—a good stock is completely indispensable to me.

Often when I am making veal stock I recall the following incident: Some years ago the famous French cook and author Madeleine Kamman came to the Barossa Valley to give the first cooking school ever held at Yalumba. Di Holuigue of The French Kitchen in Victoria was hosting Madeleine's tour of Australia. Ahead of time Di sent me Madeleine's menus so that I could choose which class she would conduct here. I chose one that incorporated a very exciting dish with a rack of veal that required a veal stock. A very exacting teacher, Madeleine sent me her specific requirements for a veal stock. The purchasing of the veal saddles and veal bones was not easy in those days so advance notice had to be given to the butcher. I handed the job to my second year apprentice at the time with strict instructions to follow the recipe to the letter and the resultant stock was wonderful. The problem was that all the veal saddles, breast, shins and bones had been used for the stock and there was no meat left to cook for the class! Di had to tear around visiting Melbourne butchers on the Saturday afternoon just 2 hours before her flight to Adelaide to remedy the situation. The class was a fabulous success despite the first disaster and Madeleine Kamman stays firmly entrenched as one of my first choices of cook book writers. Many of these tips I have absorbed over the years have been derived from her book *In Madeleine's Kitchen*.

Some general hints about making stock:

- Use at least fifty per cent bones and fifty per cent meat; up to two thirds meat if you have it available.
- Vegetables are as important as the meat. The onions should be the ordinary brown variety; white and red onions are too sweet. I just cut my onions in half and add them unpeeled. Carrots should be used with discretion because of their high sugar content. I cut a whole quorm (head) of garlic in half and throw it in without peeling. Leeks add something to a stock but can be extravagant, so use only the light green and 3 cm of the dark green, keeping the white for another dish.
- Never use tired old vegetables in a stock.
- Never let a stock boil as it will become cloudy.
- Use a tall, heavy stockpot so that evaporation is slow.
- Cool the stock rapidly after cooking by placing in a sink full of cold water.
- Strain the stock through a fine mesh strainer or several layers of cheesecloth.
- Use white wine for its flavour and because acid will work on the bones to release a maximum of gelatine.
- Stocks are perfect for freezing. Veal and chicken stocks will last in the freezer for up to 3 months.
- If you do not have a freezer, reduce the stock to a glaze and keep it in the coldest part of the fridge. This will have to be reboiled for 5 minutes every 5 days to keep it.
- One litre of water yields about 3 cups of stock.

T HIS BASIC veal stock can be used for cooking oxtail or enriching a steak and kidney pie or can be reduced up to seven eighths to be a demi-glace, often called for in a recipe to give a concentrated flavour to a sauce.

VEAL STOCK

1 kg veal breast	*4 leeks (reserving the white parts*
1 kg veal bones (veal breast is	*for a vegetable dish)*
probably the most economical	*10 stalks parsley*
piece to buy for the meat ratio	*1 bay leaf*
and the knuckle is the best bone)	*3 sprigs fresh thyme*
1 cup dry white wine	*1 tin Roma tomatoes (optional)*
4 medium onions	*approximately 4 litres water*
2 medium carrots, chopped roughly	

Have the butcher cut the veal meat and bones into chunks. Remove any visible traces of fat. Roast the bones, meat, carrots and onions in flat oven dishes in a very hot oven until golden brown, turning several times to avoid burning or catching. This will take 40 minutes to 1 hour. (If you use the stockpot to brown the onions and carrots there will be the chance that you will take them too far and if the vegetables or meat are burnt the stock will be bitter. If this happens try adding a touch of honey to the finished product.)

Transfer the meat, onions and carrots to the stockpot and deglaze the roasting pan with white wine. Reduce and scrape well into the stockpot. Add the leeks, herbs and tomatoes and cover with luke-warm water.

Bring the stock carefully to the boil and simmer for 4 to 5 hours. Remove any scum as it appears during the cooking. The roasting of the bones first ensures that less skimming will be necessary.

My friend and Adelaide cook Cath Kerry advises not to overcook your stocks so that they taste of bone. If your pets won't eat the bones then you've overcooked the stock. As I cook my stock in 50 litre stock pots I often cook a veal stock overnight because of the sheer volume of the pot.

One of the reasons why I concentrate on making a good veal stock is that I use it as the basis for my pheasant and game stocks. The veal stock is very much a chameleon and will take on the flavour of the pheasant, venison or kangaroo. These days in the restaurant we are constantly working against the clock to keep up with the stocks. I take the pheasant carcasses from the previous cooking session and take out my frustration with the cleaver, making a great deal of noise as I chop the bones into small pieces! Then I caramelise the vegetables in a very large, flat baking dish in a hot oven, using a little olive oil and making sure the vegetables are well coloured but not burnt. I then add the chopped bones to the residue oil and either put them on the top of the stove or in the oven to brown further, keeping an eagle eye on them. I deglaze the pan with white wine or medium sherry and add a good jellied veal stock. The sauce boils vigorously and amalgamates. Once reduced to the right consistency, I strain it through a conical sieve while still hot, pressing down to extract as much liquid as possible. This gives a wonderful instant sauce. (Stephanie Alexander taught me this method and I utilise it every day in the restaurant.)

THIS IS A VERY inexpensive chicken stock to make as I use old boilers which I buy for about $1.60 each. This stock is a marvellous base for the soups of winter. I roast the chicken bones before simmering, giving the stock a golden colour and if reduced (see the veal stock recipe), it is an easy alternative to the demi-glace. I would also add a pig's trotter to the initial cooking if I set out to do this.

If you prefer a blond stock for the making of white sauces or a vegetable soup, there is no need to roast the bones.

CHICKEN STOCK

1 boiling chicken	*1/2 bay leaf*
1 onion	*sprig thyme*
1 carrot	*sprig parsley*
1 leek	*optional: 2 cloves garlic; 1 tomato,*
100 g mushrooms	*seeded; 100 ml white wine*
1 stick celery	*100 ml oil of preference*

Using poultry scissors, cut the chicken into pieces and roast with oil in the oven until the pieces turn golden brown, adding the onion and carrot to the browning process. Keep turning to avoid burning; this process will take about 20 minutes. Transfer the bones and vegetables to a tall stockpot and deglaze with the wine if you wish to use it. Add the extra vegetables and herbs to the pot and cover with water. Bring to the boil slowly, skimming off the scum, and simmer for 3 to 4 hours. Cool the stock quickly by immersing it in a sink of cold water and strain through muslin. Refrigerate the stock to allow any fat to settle on the surface and then remove the fat.

A STRAIGHT VEGETABLE stock is another inexpensive and very simple stock that is marvellous for adding freshness to your cooking, for lightening sauces or for making vegetable soup. The trick to this stock is to cook it for only about 10 minutes to retain the freshness of the vegetables. I dice the vegetables finely to get the maximum flavour from them in such a short cooking time.

VEGETABLE STOCK

3 onions, finely chopped
3 carrots, finely chopped
2 leeks, washed and finely chopped (using the white and pale green parts)
3 stalks celery, finely chopped
2 ripe tomatoes, seeded and chopped

1/2 fennel bulb (in season), finely chopped
100 g sliced mushrooms (optional)
2 zucchini (in season), finely chopped
1 clove garlic
4 stalks parsley
2 tablespoons butter

Sweat the finely chopped vegetables in butter without browning them. Add the parsley, cover with water and bring to the boil. Season with pepper if desired, but no salt. Simmer for 10 minutes. Strain the stock, pressing through some of the vegetables, if desired. Vary the herbs depending on what you will be using the stock for. Refrigerate or freeze.

F ISH STOCK is always worth the trouble. It is certainly cheap to make and very quick—you only need cook it for 20 minutes. Schnapper heads are always my first choice as the ratio of bone to meat applies very well. I use this stock for fish soups, some oyster dishes or as a base for making crab or yabbie sauces. It is fantastic for a dish such as reducing some white wine, cream and fish stock and then tossing some smoked trout through to make a pasta sauce.

Do not make this stock in an aluminium pot; use enamel or steel so as not to discolour the stock.

For fish heads Madeleine Kamman recommends you 'Cut the pointed underside of the head and around the gills, pull the whole bottom part of the head off and throw it away. Scrape out any trace of internal organs left in the top part of the head, rinse again and put into the pot.'

FISH STOCK

1 kg schnapper heads, cleaned
*   and chopped roughly*
1 large onion, finely chopped
1 leek, washed and finely chopped
1 carrot, finely chopped
1/2 celery stalk, finely chopped
10 parsley stems, chopped

1 sprig thyme
1/2 bay leaf
1/2 cup dry white wine
11/2 to 2 litres water
2 tablespoons butter

Put all the vegetables into a stockpot and sweat in butter for 2 minutes without browning the vegetables. Add the schnapper heads and sweat for 1 more minute. Pour in the white wine and boil vigorously for a few minutes, then add the cold water and herbs. Simmer for about 20 minutes. Strain through a sieve or muslin, pressing down gently on the bones and vegetables. A good fish stock is jellied after refrigeration.

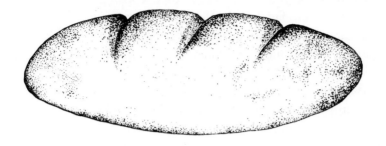

Bread

IONCE READ somewhere that making bread was not cooking at all, just pure primitive pleasure. And it is. There is no better antidote to stress than feeling and kneading bread until it tells you it is ready. The sense of satisfaction gained is way out of proportion to the trouble taken. I can't urge you enough to give it a go! The aroma that pervades the kitchen when the bread comes out of the oven has an incredibly 'safe' smell. You feel sure of warmth and loving whether it be in a restaurant or family home.

Bread is not just an adjunct to a meal, it can be a meal in itself—drizzled with some extra virgin olive oil, with a ripe tomato or a piece of cheese. Don't forget the jug of wine!

Did you know that flour, like wine, improves with age? That is, so long as it is good flour to begin with. Like wine, no amount of cellaring will improve a bad one.

There are other similarities too; the quality of flour changes every year, and millers blend their flours to achieve their desired quality of protein levels. And as with cellar door sales from wineries, there are sales outlets at some flour mills. We buy the flour for the bread at the restaurant this way.

Many of our restaurant customers ask us for our bread recipe which we gladly share. Yet, unless I also give them a kilo of flour from our sack, they are often disappointed with the result. It took me a while to work out that it wasn't their cooking skills which were causing their bread to fail, but the flour they were using.

I often talk about the riches of the Barossa Valley region and the Laucke Flour Mill is one of the many examples. The Mill is 115 years old and has been run in a fairly old-fashioned way by people who have retained the pride and passion for their product.

I was writing a newspaper article about bread and went to talk to Kip Laucke and Colin Cooke. They soon expanded on what I have learnt about bread making over the years and made me realise how important it is to buy the right flour for the job. There are two groups of wheat grown in South Australia, the hard wheat and the Australian Standard White (ASW). The differences between the groups are the strength and quality of protein. Hard wheat makes strong flour and ASW makes softer, blending flour. Protein manifests itself in bread as gluten and some people add straight gluten to ordinary flour, but Kip tells an old miller's saying, 'A good amount of gluten can hide a multitude of faults in bread.'

The gluten is important because it gives the dough elasticity—the ability to rise, stretch and hold. The higher the gluten content, the better the lift.

The most important point to remember when you are wanting to make bread is that you should buy strong flour, not plain flour. Just to confuse you in the supermarket, strong flour can be called bread-making flour, baking flour or baker's flour. Never buy plain flour for bread. Plain flour is a cheaper flour with less gluten and is used in general cooking for making cakes, pastry and scones. Ask your shopkeeper to stock strong flour if they don't already.

The other question you need to ask your shopkeeper is, 'How good is the flour on the shelves?' As with wine, buy flour on quality, not price. Many shopkeepers are unaware of the difference a good flour makes and so this information is not passed on to consumers.

Flour such as that from Laucke Mills may not be available on every supermarket shelf but there are alternatives. The best is to take a day out in the country and buy directly from the mill. Check your Yellow Pages for flour manufacturers and wholesalers. In South Australia Laucke Mills are open in Daveystown, Stockwell, Eudunda and Strathalbyn. You can buy a ten kilogram bag for about $5.20. And as flour improves with age, as long as it is stored correctly, this quantity, which makes about 40 loaves, is a good investment. All Laucke Mills flour is totally natural. It is unbleached and cholesterol free.

There is a mill at Port Adelaide, W. Thomas and Co., that sells at the mill door. Another mill in Adelaide is Allied Flour at Mile End, but their products are only available through wholesalers. Gavin Dunn of Tarlee goes a step further and has organically grown wheat and flour for sale.

One of the most distressing things about obtaining information for my newspaper article was the reluctance of everyone but the Lauckes to answer my simple questions about their product. I heard later that other mills were cross that Laucke's received the exposure they did. This was not just due to the fact that I was known to them but they were happy that information about their product be shared with the public.

This is an incredibly important point—that there is communication between grower or producer, supplier or distributor and the general public. There needs to be more discussion, more information shared and the public needs to ask more questions. Producers need to listen to the end users of their product, and, in many cases become more 'interested' in their own product. Food in Australia can only improve with everyone involved in the food chain communicating with each other.

Check that the flour is not turning rancid, giving off a sour or musty smell, or becoming infested with insects. Store the flour in an airtight ceramic crockpot or you could try to buy a 16 kilogram rubber-sealed drum from a mill. (These are mainly used to send flour to Aboriginal communities in the Northern Territory, but they serve very well in the household pantry, and are inexpensive.)

Here are some simple tips to alleviate the most common bread making problems:

- To make bread by hand give yourself plenty of space on a workbench with everything cleared off before you start, and as for all recipes, have your quantities measured out and standing by. You will need a huge bowl the size of a wash basin, preferably an old ceramic one, although an inexpensive oversized stainless steel bowl from a commercial kitchenware shop will do, but remember a little warmth helps.
- The temperature of the water, next to the quality of the flour, is the most important thing. If the water is too hot, it will kill the yeast, and if too cold, it will not start acting. When a recipe calls for tepid water, this means that your hand should feel comfortable in the water—not

cold and not hot. If you have a thermometer, it should read 34°C. A test worth knowing is to leave your finger in the water for 10 seconds. If it becomes uncomfortably hot, you will need to add a little cold water. Your utensils and ingredients should be blood warm, even the flour.

- Make sure the yeast is fresh. I prefer compressed yeast but Fermipan yeast is easier to handle and more readily available. Make sure you use the correct weight of yeast specified in the recipe. Dry yeast is more concentrated and you would need twice the quantity of compressed yeast.

- Not to make the bread by hand is to deny yourself an addictive pleasure, but if you use a machine, be sure not to overmix. When the mixing is finished the dough should be at about 28°C.

- Bring the bread to the first rise on a bench away from any draughts. Cover it with a tea towel. In winter you could try putting it in tins in the oven with just the pilot light on if it is gas or at about 50°C if electric.

- If you like crusty bread, cut down on the fat content (although this will reduce its keeping qualities) and bake at a lower temperature for longer, say 190°C for 40 minutes instead of the usual 220°C for 30 minutes. You could also try putting a bowl of water in the oven to make steam, but the first method is better.

- Fat gives a softer loaf and helps the bread last longer. Butter is better than oil as oil is a liquid and gives the dough a different structure. The butter should be soft and pliable, not melted.

- Sugar gives a softer texture and adds colour to the crumb. It feeds the yeast, but bread can be made without it.

- Salt is very important because it flavours the bread and controls the yeast activity. Too much salt will actually retard the yeast. Saltless bread is possible but has to be handled quickly as the dough will go mad.

- Freezing bread will dry it out, but if you must do so, take the hot loaves straight from the oven and put them into bags and into the freezer. The condensation seems to make the bread fresher on thawing out. Splash the thawed loaf with a little water and put it in the oven to recrisp. Make sure you have added some fat content to the dough of the bread you freeze.

I have never used natural bread improvers. They are made of ascorbic acid or Vitamin C and modify the gluten so it is more extendible and gives a better crumb and height. The gas given off by the yeast is carbon dioxide—this blows up the gluten and forms bubbles like bubble gum. Using a bread improver allows a better 'bounce back' after retarding the bread in the fridge overnight. This is useful when you want to bake fresh bread in the morning but don't want to wake as early as the bakers.

The last alternative is to buy bread mix from the mill door. To this you need only add water and yeast.

PHEASANT FARM BREAD

1 kg strong flour	2 teaspoons salt
25 g dried yeast or	1 teaspoon sugar
50 g compressed yeast	50 ml olive oil
1 teaspoon freeze-dried tarragon	about 400 ml warm water

If using fresh compressed yeast, mix it with your fingers with a teaspoon of sugar and some warm water. It will liquefy within minutes. Add the salt and tarragon to the flour in the bowl with the olive oil. Make a well in the centre of the flour and pour in the yeast and about three quarters of the measured warm water. Mix with your hand, adding extra water if it is needed to bring the mixture together. The amount of water will differ every day you make the bread, depending on the atmosphere. The trick is to make the dough just moist enough. Tip the mixture on to the bench and knead the dough for 20 minutes until it is shiny. If not enough liquid is added the mixture will be too heavy and it will not expand properly. Cover the bowl with a clean damp cloth and put it in a warm place for the dough to double in size. It will take somewhere near an hour, depending on the weather, but if left to overprove (when the dough stops pushing upwards and starts pushing over the edge of the bowl) the bread will be tough and hardly rise in the baking at all.

If you are not yet ready to handle the bread you can knock it back until you are ready. When you scoop the dough out of the bowl to put it on the bench it will feel incredibly light like a puff ball. With lightly floured hands knead the dough until it is smooth and elastic. Divide the dough into 4 parts and shape into loaves to slip into bread tins which have been sparsely oiled or brushed with melted butter. Leave in the same warm space, away from any draughts, to double again in size. Bake in a hot oven for about 30 minutes. The bread will readily fall out of the tin and feel hollow when tapped from the bottom. Allow to cool on wire racks.

Spring

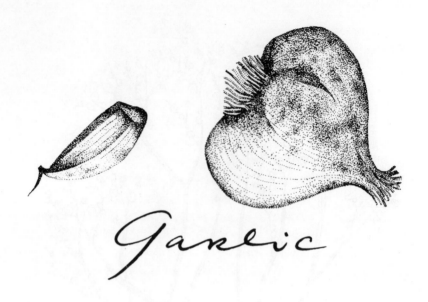

Garlic

T HERE IS A garlic festival at Tours in France on 28 July each
year, held on St Anne's day since 1838. More recently there
has also been a garlic festival held at Gilroy, California,
each August. In her book *Chez Panisse*, Alice Waters talks at
length about the garlic dinner she prepared for their third
garlic festival.

It is amazing to think of a whole menu using garlic.
There were vegetables with garlic, Chinese garlic cakes,
tortellini with garlic, fish with dried chillies and garlic, quail
stuffed with whole garlics baked in grape leaves and a
Moroccan eggplant salad with garlic. Even the dessert was
wine-spiced garlic sherbets. One might think that such a
dessert was a novelty to justify the inclusion of garlic but
Alice Waters' notes on the menu said that, 'The most
memorable aspect of this meal for me was the garlic
sherbets, which were made with red fruits macerated with
red wine and garlic cloves and with white fruits macerated
with white wine and garlic cloves to create a very fruity
beginning flavour to the sherbet with a lovely garlic
aftertaste.'

When you think of the importance of garlic in food, it is no
wonder it is celebrated. It is hard to think of a cuisine that

doesn't embrace garlic. However, it is misunderstood by many.

Raw garlic is very powerful and the finer it is chopped or sliced, the stronger it will be.

Depending on the weather, garlic will take 2 to 3 weeks to dry, spread out on wire netting or a rack. If it looks like raining, the garlic will have to be shifted to a dry shed.

Using a garlic press to crush garlic will make it bitter. Take the clove of garlic—pulled away from the quorm—and press down on it on a chopping board with a large bladed knife. This will pop the skin off, which you can then remove. Add a sprinkle of salt, continue the pressure of the knife, and the garlic will become 'creamed' and ready for use without any trace of bitterness. If you do not want to add salt, use the sharp knife to cut the clove into fine pieces.

Be careful when sautéing garlic as it burns easily and will become bitter.

If you want a subtle, fresh flavour of garlic in a salad, rub the inside of a bowl with a clove of garlic and then discard the garlic.

Raw garlic mixed with lemon zest and parsley is delicious with boiled meats, but my favourite way is baking the whole garlic, whether fresh or dried, and using it many different ways. When garlic is cooked it becomes rich and nutty and marries well with foods as diverse as lamb, kid, beef, quail, chicken, goat's cheese and eggplant. Either rub the quorm with some olive oil and put it in a moderate oven with a little thyme or cover it with oil or stock. The whole baked quorm of garlic can be served or cut in half horizontally or each clove squeezed out on to the plate. Green striped fresh garlic heads just pulled from the ground and roasted whole are incredibly sweet, although fresh jumbo garlic can be very bitter.

A note of caution: When roasting dried garlic, use the fattest head you can find and prick each clove with a skewer to prevent explosions.

Make garlic butter by mixing roasted garlic together with unsalted butter and keep it in the fridge to add richness to a sauce at the last minute.

———

AOLI IS A garlic mayonnaise—a garlic lover's dream. It is a very important dish in Mediterranean cooking and a great accompaniment to something like octopus which has been marinated in olive oil and lemon juice and then thrown on the barbecue.

I had a young man with a Catalan background spend a few weeks in my kitchen and from him I learnt that the original aoli in its purest form contains no eggs and is white and shiny and very strong in garlic flavour. It is also said to be impossible to make a true aoli in a food processor as the oil and garlic become too homogenised. So for a truly authentic aoli take out your mortar and pestle.

AUTHENTIC AOLI

6 cloves garlic   *1 cup virgin olive oil*
1/2 teaspoon salt

The ingredients should be at room temperature. Finely mince the garlic and discard any green pieces. Mash the garlic with the pestle, mixing in the salt until it is a thick paste. Add the olive oil very slowly, a few drops at a time and always stir in the one direction with the pestle. Continue adding the oil slowly until an emulsion forms. Serve immediately.

I am more at home with the way I have always made it—with eggs.

MAGGIE'S AOLI

6 cloves garlic   *2 egg yolks*
1/2 teaspoon salt   *1 cup virgin olive oil*

Mix the garlic and salt as outlined above. When the paste forms add the egg yolks before proceeding with the oil, remembering to begin very slowly.

A PUNGENT AND particularly more-ish way of using garlic is making this paste to serve with a fish soup, stew, braised oxtail, lamb shanks or with a crudité of fresh vegetables.

ROUILLE

1 large, very red capsicum	*a little milk*
4 cloves garlic	*3 egg yolks*
1/2 teaspoon cayenne pepper	*50 ml white wine vinegar*
a few threads saffron (optional)	*200 ml olive oil*
2 slices bread, crusts removed	

Take the top off the capsicum and remove the seeds. Rub with some olive oil and roast in a hot oven until it collapses and seems to be burnt. Take the capsicum from the oven and let it rest for a few minutes before putting it in a plastic bag to sweat. When it is cool enough to handle, peel the skin and remove all traces of black. Soak the bread in a little milk for 10 minutes and squeeze it thoroughly.

If using a food processor, place the capsicum, cayenne, garlic, bread, vinegar, saffron threads and egg yolks in the bowl and purée well. Season. Then pour in the olive oil in a stream as you would for mayonnaise. It can be adjusted by including a chilli with the red capsicum. Rouille is French for rust—this should be the colour of your sauce.

W HEN I WROTE once on garlic in my weekly column I received letters from readers asking what to do about their garlic preserved in olive oil turning blue. I contacted the CSIRO and they told me the following about the dangers of holding garlic or similar products in oil.

The main cause of the problem is the level of acidity. The outer leaves of garlic, and to some extent the bulbs themselves, may contain anthocyanin pigments, which are colourless at the normal pH of garlic but turn blue or even pink under acid conditions. Most garlic cloves do not contain sufficient of this pigment for the discoloration to pose a problem. Test each batch of garlic by adding vinegar to a small sample of garlic and warm it. If it discolours, seek out another supply of garlic.

At the same time the CSIRO made me aware of incidents of botulism in the United States involving garlic in oil products. Oil has no anti-microbial preservative action—its only function in preserving is to prevent oxidation which can lead to discoloration of some foods. By excluding oxygen from the surface of vegetables, one is establishing anaerobic conditions which actually favour the growth of some types of bacteria, one of which is *Clostridium botulinum*, the organism which causes botulism.

It is therefore essential that sufficient acid, usually in the form of vinegar, must be added to the vegetable before oil is poured on so that these bacteria cannot grow. This means that the pH must be reduced below 4.6. Domestic vinegar contains 4 per cent acetic acid. Any mixture should therefore have a vegetable to vinegar ratio by weight not greater than three to one, which would give one per cent acetic acid, ensuring the final pH is below 4.6.

Asparagus

I PULLED ONE of my favourite books, *The Food Lover's Garden* by Angelo Pellegrini, from the shelves and read: '...when I use the word "gardening" my reference is invariably to the cultivation of those plants, such as asparagus, that are used as food; and those, such as rosemary, that are used to make food taste good. In other words, my approach to gardening is fundamentally utilitarian. I cultivate as much of the necessary herbs, vegetables, and fruit as time and place and space will allow, in order to enjoy a fine, even a distinguished, dinner every day.'

What a wonderful philosophy and certainly one I would be following more if I didn't have the huge demands of the normal weekly workload that is necessary to run a restaurant. Even though most of us have work or family commitments that preclude us from living such a rewarding life as to be able to have that fine dinner from the fruits of our own labour in our kitchen garden, we can, with a few well-chosen fruits and vegetables, supply ourselves with the 'special things' that can add that extravagance to our table.

Asparagus comes immediately to mind. You really know spring has arrived when you see asparagus on sale. Although for the first week or two it is fairly pricey, that first taste of spring is worth the expense. Asparagus is not only simple to grow, but simple to cook.

I tend to serve asparagus on its own with just a hollandaise, cooking a bunch in boiling water with a little salt and half a teaspoon of sugar. I use a flat enamel pan (it was actually a griller tray from a very old stove that I bought in a second-hand shop) with about 3 cm water. I begin to make the hollandaise just as I put the water on to boil.

To prepare the asparagus, snap off the end of the stalk and then, using a potato peeler, peel the first 2 cm of the stalk to make sure it is not stringy or woody.

At the restaurant we receive two to three deliveries of asparagus a week. It has been picked 'that morning' and is so crisp that the 'snapping' is a simple procedure. If the asparagus is limp from sitting on the shelf it may be better just to cut off about 3 cm of the stalk. Once you experience the difference of a very fresh product, you will find it difficult to accept any less.

You needn't go to the trouble of hollandaise—just some nut-brown butter, or some olive oil, or olive oil and lemon juice and freshly grated Parmesan is great. Stephanie Alexander's first book, *Stephanie's Menus for Food Lovers*, has a recipe for asparagus served with coddled egg that makes a lovely luncheon dish on its own, particularly when served with the asparagus lying on crisp linen and the egg in an old porcelain coddler.

Asparagus is usually eaten with the fingers, so serve a finger bowl on the table.

If you can buy a blood orange in the markets you could make the Maltaise mayonnaise in Jane Grigson's *Good Things*, which in my opinion is the very best combination with asparagus.

The asparagus I have been describing is that where the whole stalk is green. A highly prized luxury is white asparagus. It is grown in a similar manner to celery, mounded up like a pyramid for the whole of its growing life and the only part to have any colour is the tip that breaks out of the ground. This is certainly something for the home gardener to consider.

Two-year-old asparagus crowns can be bought at nurseries so you don't have to experience the frustration of not having a crop in the first year.

ASPARAGUS AND HOLLANDAISE

Bring some water to the boil in a shallow pan or dish with a little salt and sugar. After snapping and peeling the ends of the asparagus, lay the stalks in the pan and simmer for about 3 minutes if they are thin and around 6 minutes if they are thick. I brush them quickly with a little butter to give them a shine. Serve immediately with hollandaise.

HOLLANDAISE
4 egg yolks   *125 g hot unsalted butter*
juice of 1/4 lemon

Beat the egg yolks and lemon in a food processor and slowly add a stream of hot butter. Adjust the lemon if necessary. Season.

———————

WHILE STAYING with Patricia Wells in Vaison-la-Romaine in Provence we bought a bunch of white asparagus at the wonderful food market there, which has a totally different flavour from the green asparagus we commonly eat. This is how Patricia prepared it:

WHITE ASPARAGUS

Peel the asparagus stems right to the tip. Cook the spears in a steamer for 8 minutes and then throw them into an ice slurry. Sauté the already cooked asparagus in the oil of your choice. Serve with a squeeze of lemon.

———————

THE FOLLOWING is one of Cheong Liew's recipes. Cheong used to run the famous Neddy's restaurant in Adelaide and is now a lecturer at Adelaide's Regency Park College. The salt water duck is served at room temperature with warm asparagus and a Japanese-style mayonnaise as the only accompaniment. Together they make a great meal.

SALT WATER DUCK ACCOMPANIED BY ASPARAGUS

2 ducks, with legs　　　　　　　*coarse salt*
Sichuan peppercorn

Toast the salt with the Sichuan peppercorn, 1 part spice to 5 parts salt.
Use 20 g of this mix for each kilogram of duck. Cure the duck while the
spiced salt is warm and let it stand for at least 3 days.

WHITE MASTER STOCK

500 ml boiling water　　　　　　*3 pieces mandarin or tangerine*
100 g sugar　　　　　　　　　　*peel (the size of a 50 cent coin),*
1 star anise, whole　　　　　　　*dried*
1 cinnamon stick　　　　　　　　*5 g Sichuan pepper*
5 g cumin seeds　　　　　　　　 *5 g licorice root, dried*
10 g ginger, bruised　　　　　　 *2 stalks spring onion*

Combine all ingredients. Bring to the boil and simmer for 30 minutes.
Pass the sauce through a sieve.

Submerge the duck in water for an hour. Blanch the duck in boiling
water and refresh it in iced water. Put the duck in the master stock and
poach it for 20 minutes at 90°C. Cool the duck in the stock overnight.

JAPANESE-STYLE MAYONNAISE FOR ASPARAGUS

2 egg yolks　　　　　　　　　　*50 ml rice vinegar*
100 ml sugar stock (1/2 sugar,　 *500 ml warm olive oil*
* 1/2 water)*　　　　　　　　　　*1/2 tablespoon Keens dry mustard*

Take the powdered mustard and slowly mix in the vinegar, then the sugar
stock. Stir in the egg yolks. Slowly pour warm oil into the mixture and mix
as a mayonnaise. Check the balance and add more vinegar if necessary.

———————

THIS SALT water duck was one of the dishes the members of the
South Australian team of the Seppelts Menu of the Year
Competition Cheong Liew, Urs Inauen, Tom Milligan and myself,
took to New York for a special dinner for the New York media.

After that very exciting occasion Colin and I went on to travel in Europe. We met up with Cheong and his wife Mary in Paris to celebrate Cheong's birthday and dined at Jamin—the hottest 3-star restaurant in Paris, run by chef Joël Robuchon. One of the dishes Cheong ordered on that very memorable night was a pig's head salad. It was a toss-up between Cheong and myself as to who would order it as we both love offal so much, but as the dish seemed to have a Chinese connection, Cheong won. It was a beautifully structured dish and the green salad was a mass of baby green asparagus tips. The asparagus and also the wonderful green beans were no longer than 5 cm long.

The vegetable growers in France seem to have a penchant for baby greens and are able to develop immense flavours in a tiny package— unlike the tiny root vegetables which were so popular here a few years ago where the flavour was lacking while the package was pretty.

artichoke

NOT ENOUGH people are aware of the delights of artichokes. They are wonderful served with the sauces which go well with asparagus—hollandaise, Maltaise mayonnaise and nut-brown butter.

We certainly have the right climate here in South Australia, as evidenced by the large number of wild artichokes that grow as noxious weeds in the countryside and need constant spraying. There are two varieties sold commercially in South Australia. One has a choke that is so insignificant you can eat the whole of it. The later variety is larger, with a hairier choke that requires scraping out before eating.

Like most vegetables, the most important thing is to buy them at their very freshest. If you are lucky you may be able to find a grower, such as ours in Angle Vale, who will cut them for you while you wait. If you require a large amount, for pickling for example, you can let them know your requirements ahead of time. They can be ready for you in wet hessian bags and you can spend the rest of the day pickling—the fresher the better.

Not only are artichokes a great flavour, they are a food to become involved in—with your fingers! The sight of a huge bouquet of artichokes on the table is a delight. They are available from mid-August and are inexpensive. In short, they create such a show on the table that they should be part of everyone's spring diet!

The traditional way to cook artichokes is to trim the first inch or two from the top and rub them with lemon or vinegar to stop discoloration. Peel off the darker outer leaves and then rub the whole artichoke with lemon. Soak them in acidulated water (water with lemon juice added) until you are ready to cook them.

Boil the artichokes in salted water in an enamel pot until tender. Add herbs or lemon slices to the water. They take about 20 minutes to cook, depending on their size. An enamel or stainless steel pot is essential—an aluminium pot will cause severe discoloration.

Artichokes are something of an acquired taste and are not the easiest vegetables to eat. The simplest way is to open the artichoke like a flower and serve it with your chosen sauce. Pick each leaf from the outside, rub it in the sauce or butter and then suck on it, leaving the fibrous remains of the leaf. When you get to the choke you can discard the hairy part. But if they are young and fresh, you can eat the lot. It really is a finger job—be sure to have finger bowls on the table.

I love the artichoke in all its forms, though if treated with disrespect they can taste like old tea leaves. They are delicious when they have been immersed and braised in olive oil at a low temperature. Another alternative is to prepare them, cut them in quarters and sauté them quickly in olive oil or butter before they become oxidised and discoloured.

One of my favourite recipes is Stephanie Alexander's Raw Artichoke Salad, from her book *Stephanie's Feasts and Stories*.

At the end of the season baby artichokes are available. They are the lateral buds pruned from the main plant. These are the ones we preserve for use during summer as the season finishes some time in November. If you are not inspired to pickle your own, you can buy top-quality artichoke hearts in oil from the best delicatessens. They have myriad uses—such as on an antipasto plate with olives, pickled lemons and prosciutto. All of these foods can be sitting in the pantry or refrigerator, perfect for a 'spur of the moment' meal needing virtually no effort at all.

Preserved artichoke hearts can be used as a bed for a dish of grilled chicken livers and can be tossed with a warm salad of quail.

They can be used for an artichoke risotto, or with a brandade (purée of salt cod) or simply just in a salad.

SANTIN FAMILY PRESERVED ARTICHOKES

tiny artichokes   *parsley*
white wine vinegar   *olive oil*
garlic   *lemon*
salt

Take as many tiny artichokes as available and clean them by taking off the outside leaves and cutting off the top third of the globe. Rub the cut surfaces with lemon.

Put them in a stainless steel or enamel pot, cover with vinegar and bring to the boil for about 5 minutes until just tender, being careful not to overcook. Dry carefully with a tea towel. In a large stainless steel bowl mix the chopped parsley, whole garlic cloves, salt and a little olive oil and toss in the cooked artichokes. The amounts will depend on your personal taste and the number of artichokes you have. Put into sterilised jars and cover completely with olive oil. They are best kept refrigerated.

———————

THE FOLLOWING recipe marries both Jerusalem and globe artichokes, an earthy combination.

RAGOUT OF GLOBE AND JERUSALEM ARTICHOKES WITH MUSHROOMS

6 shallots, peeled and sliced   *6 small globe artichokes*
300 g large mushrooms,   *150 g butter*
*   preferably pine or cepes, or*   *1 lemon*
*   large field mushrooms*   *fresh thyme*
300 g shitake mushrooms,   *15 ml balsamic vinegar*
*   sliced thinly*   *salt and pepper*
6 Jerusalem artichokes

Slice the Jerusalem artichokes and hold them in acidulated water.

Remove the outer leaves of the globe artichokes. Reserve 18 good leaves for the garnish. Cook these immediately in salted water with a little lemon juice.

Fry the shallots in a little butter until wilted, and then the mushrooms with the shallots, adding extra butter as required. Season with salt, pepper and thyme. Reserve.

Quarter the artichokes and remove the choke if necessary. Rub with lemon. Toss the globe artichokes in butter until slightly golden. Add the Jerusalem artichokes and sauté until slightly golden. Add the mushroom mixture. Sprinkle with balsamic vinegar and serve.

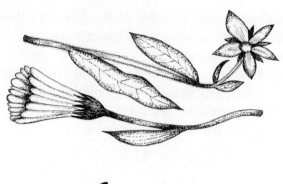

flowers

I REMEMBER CLEARLY a review of my restaurant by John McGrath in *The Adelaide Review* where he slapped me over the knuckles, quite rightly, for the use of agapanthus on an entree. It was one of those things that can happen when you have an enthusiastic apprentice in the wings, but it certainly taught me a lesson and I have made sure that any new member of staff understands the importance of 'edible' flowers only!

Not everyone thinks of using edible flowers. When Patricia Wells was in Australia to judge the Remy/*Gourmet* Best Restaurant Award, in summing up what she saw of Australia's restaurants, one of her small criticisms was the use of inedible flowers.

There are many wonderful flowers to play with, not only to decorate your plate (something we do little of now) but as flavours that are part of a dish in the same way herbs are. Indeed, many flowers are herbs, but the list goes beyond that. I use a book, *Edible Flowers* by Claire Clifton, as a basic source of knowledge.

The first thing to do is to check whether the flower you fancy is edible (if you don't have a reference book, you can always consult the Botanic Gardens advisory service), and then let some of the following ideas help your imagination to run riot!

There are now several specialist green grocers and plant

nurseries selling edible flowers across the country.

I love the peppery flavour of nasturtium flowers when thrown into a salad. Nasturtiums grow like weeds in spring. If you have a dam or swimming pool they can cascade over, you will have the beauty of a Monet landscape reflected in the water as well as an edible feast.

Marigold flowers come to mind, but be sure to plant calendulas if you want to eat them. Marigolds themselves are quite bitter, with the exception of a miniature one available in the USA which has a delightful lemony flavour.

I recently ate a cheese from Gippsland that contained lavender flowers. Although a bit strong for my taste, it was interesting. Lavender ice-cream is delicious. We make a lavender vinegar to use when cooking cabbage. (Partridge and cabbage are one of the classic game combinations.)

I discovered rocket flowers by chance when, as often happens, we didn't have the time to pick the rocket young enough and it went to seed. Now there is a bed of 'overgrown' rocket just outside the restaurant—it is amazing how many people pick the flowers to nibble as they walk past.

Chive flowers are beautiful to look at with their mauve, frilly head and they are great to flavour any savoury dish—throw them into pastas or salads. These are available right through to December.

Jill Stone of Herbivorous in Adelaide has just told me of a plant she is propagating called Tulbaghia. It is a South African plant, also called Society Garlic. It has a green or variegated leaf and its flower has a crunchy, garlicky sensation.

Garlic chive flowers are around in March and make sensational fritters.

Elderflowers can often be found in old-fashioned gardens. We have four elderflower bushes. We cook elderflowers in a light batter and dust them with icing sugar to serve with the first raspberries and vanilla ice-cream. This is also a great way to prepare the flowers of the grapevine. You know they are ready to pick from their heady perfume. Unfortunately Colin gets a bit touchy if I start decimating the grape crop for a dessert!

Elderflowers are used to flavour vinegars and the flowers can be pickled with sugar and vinegar for salads. In England elderflowers were used for making wine and champagne. That alone makes this beautiful bush worth having in the garden.

In the summer basil flowers are used in pickling vinegars. Dill flowers are used for pickling dills and the like.

Zucchini or squash flowers can be stuffed with anchovies, olives or soft cheeses and deep-fried.

A whole world of old-fashioned flowers such as roses, violets and violas are edible. Roses can be transformed into rose petal jam, rose water ice and rose omelette soufflé. Sauce made from rose hips can be teamed with rabbit or used as the base for a soup. Primroses make a delightful tart and violets or carnations make a fragrant liqueur.

———

THE FOLLOWING is a favourite dish that appears on my spring menu as a special when the flowers are in abundance. It was inspired by the *Chez Panisse Pasta Book*.

HERB PASTA WITH SORREL BUTTER AND THYME FLOWERS

PASTA

300 g hard flour	*pinch salt*
5 duck egg yolks	*100 g parsley, no stalks*
dash olive oil	

Blanch the parsley quickly—straight in and out of the boiling water—don't refresh. Purée the parsley in a food processor and add egg yolks immediately to take up the maximum colour from the parsley, then add the dash of oil and the salt. Add the flour. Bring together and knead by hand until shiny. Rest and then roll through the pasta machine to angel hair size.

SORREL BUTTER

250 g low salt butter	*juice of 1 lemon*
30 g parsley	*one bunch flowering thyme*
50 g stripped sorrel leaves	*pepper*

Process the parsley and sorrel leaves together and then add the slightly softened butter and lemon juice. Add pepper if required. Roll into a cylinder and reserve in the refrigerator.

Cook the pasta in salted boiling water. Drain and moisten with slices of sorrel butter. Toss with thyme flowers and serve.

CHIVE FLOWER FRITTERS

24 chive flowers
125 g plain flour
pinch salt
20 g butter
120 ml water

80 ml milk
1/4 teaspoon vinegar
1 large egg white
olive oil for frying

Melt butter and heat with water and milk. Add vinegar and allow to cool. In a bowl add the salt to the flour and combine with the liquid slowly to avoid lumps. Leave the batter to rest for at least 20 minutes.

Heat about 2 cm oil in a heavy-based pan until it is hot enough for a piece of stale bread to turn golden brown. Beat the egg white until stiff and fold into the batter. Dip a few flowers at a time into the batter and drop them in the hot oil. Remove on to absorbent paper while the balance is cooking. Serve quickly.

LEMON VERBENA ICE-CREAM

4 egg yolks
1/2 cup sugar
250 ml milk

250 ml cream
8 good sprigs lemon verbena in
    flower

Finely chop the leaves and stalks of the lemon verbena. Add to the milk and bring to the boil. Mix in the other ingredients and cook in the microwave for 8 minutes on medium. Take out and whisk and then return to the microwave for a further 4 minutes on medium-high. Whisk again and leave to cool. Turn in the ice-cream machine and then add the lemon verbena flowers.

Kids and Goats

ONE OF THE REALLY important foods to go on my spring menu is kid. As with all game, kid (or goat) is very healthy—low in fat and cholesterol. It is simple to prepare and quite delicious. Australian producers market the meat under the name of chevon. Italian butchers call it capretto.

With the exception of the Greek and Italian communities, chevon is new to most people. Those producers keen to provide the public with goat meat are finding it difficult to keep up with the demand and if the public gets behind the meat, as is hoped, they will have to increase their stocks dramatically to ensure its ready availability. As the price of mohair has bottomed out, farming for meat may be the way to go.

Chevon is sweeter than lamb. Its distinctive flavour is considered a delicacy in most Mediterranean countries.

The animal should be hung for a week in a cold store before cutting. It should basically be cut in the same way as lamb. If the animal is very young (3-4 months) the shoulder, braised whole, is my favourite cut. If the animal is older (8-12 months) the shoulder is best boned out and cubed for casseroles or curries, or stuffed and rolled and pot roasted. The loins of the younger animal can also be boned out, stuffed and rolled and baked. With the older animals the loins can also be roasted or diced for curries and casseroles.

The legs of the younger animal are marvellous pot roasted slowly on a bed of fresh vegetables and tomatoes, or wrapped in crepinette (also known as caul fat from the butcher) with some finely chopped mint, olive oil and ground pepper trapped inside the crepinette.

I asked our kid supplier, Rosemary Langley of Elm Tree Farm at Springton, about some of her cooking methods for kid. She finds baking in an oven bag an effective way to handle a leg of kid; she rubs it with olive oil and garlic beforehand. Alternatively she bastes the leg with a mixture of olive oil, red wine, redcurrant jelly and honey before roasting it in a covered baking dish, adding a tiny amount of water in the bottom if it looks like burning.

Rosemary recommends using kid for making lean mince—use it for lasagne or in any way you might use mince. Rosemary gets the butcher in Mount Pleasant in the Adelaide Hills to smoke the meat for her. It can be hot-smoked as for ham or cold-smoked.

The main point to remember when cooking kid, young or not, is that it should be cooked more slowly and at a lower temperature than lamb.

A very special way of using chevon is to roast it on a spit. Rosemary Langley's son-in-law, Bronte Mawson, seems to have perfected the art. He always uses an animal between 8 and 12 months old and says that with salads and accompaniments it will feed 40 to 50 people. He uses a spit oven (which can be bought or hired) rather like a Weber. The advantage is that it has a lid and so, once stuffed, the animal does not need basting. The oven needs preheating for half an hour and then its even, slow heat will cook the kid in two hours.

A MORE ROMANTIC version is the spit rigged over an open fire. This is more difficult to control because one needs to dig a pit and have sufficient coals for a four-hour cooking period. The spit has to be turned and the meat basted during this time. Baste with a mixture of white wine and olive oil—I would add some garlic and rosemary for good measure.

ELM TREE FARM'S SPIT ROAST STUFFING FOR KID

2 loaves stale bread	*150 ml white wine*
1 large onion, chopped	*150 ml home-made plum sauce*
2 rashers bacon, chopped	*2 handfuls fresh parsley and*
2-3 cans pitted Morello cherries,	*marjoram, chopped*
drained and used whole	*1 tablespoon coarse black pepper*
250 g pine nuts	*salt to taste*
250 g almond slivers	

Mix together all the ingredients. The stuffing must be moist but not sloppy. It is helpful to use an apple to stop the stuffing escaping during cooking.

I CAN IMAGINE a baked whole kid served with native currant jelly. I have just tried my first native currants, found in the Williamstown area, and am delighted by their sharp yet sweet flavour. (If they are picked under-ripe the tannin will dominate so they should be avoided.)

I have only ever cooked using the younger animals. I have braised all cuts of kid, browned first with rosemary and then tossed into a pot with tomatoes (frozen from the summer crop at the peak of their flavour) and lots of onions and heads of garlic, turning frequently to make sure the juices don't burn. This takes 2-3 hours, even for such a young animal, because I cook it very slowly using two simmer pads under the pot sitting on the lowest possible flame. In the last half-hour of cooking I throw in some black olives.

Another favourite at the restaurant is to cook a cut of kid with a little vinegar, white wine, lemon, fresh bay leaves and oregano. During the slow cooking the meat creates its own syrupy glaze. Globe artichokes and eggplant are natural accompaniments. The trick is to have no more than 1 cm of liquid in the pan at any one time.

Rub a leg with coriander seed (heat the seeds first in a dry frypan and then pound them in a mortar and pestle to release the flavour), olive oil, salt and pepper. You could substitute the coriander seed with rosemary. Brown the leg in a roasting pan in a little more olive oil and then deglaze with dry sherry. Chop up a base of onions, carrots and celery and place the meat on top with some heads of garlic and a tin of peeled tomatoes.

Cook slowly and add more tomatoes if the liquid has evaporated. Serve with the following sauce: Cook 4 quorms (heads) of garlic in the oven or fire and then squeeze out the garlic. (The flavour of the garlic is wonderfully nutty and buttery, without the pungent taste of raw garlic.) Soak four salted anchovies in milk for an hour and then pound them, before adding to the garlic. Pour any essences of the kid into this mixture, stirring as if it were a mayonnaise.

———

Mardie Palmer of Cafe C at Springton is justly famous for this goat curry.

CAFE C GOAT CURRY

2 kg diced goat
8 tablespoons red curry paste
4 sliced onions
8 red chillies, chopped (optional)
60 g fresh ginger, grated
4 cloves garlic, chopped
4 x 400 g tins coconut milk

8 tablespoons desiccated coconut, toasted
20 kaffir lime leaves (from Asian grocers)
juice 4 limes
1200 ml rain or spring water
peanut oil to sauté

Sauté the onions, chillies, ginger and garlic in peanut oil until onion is transparent—do not brown. Add the curry paste and fry gently for 3 minutes. Add the diced goat and stir until coated by the paste mixture. Add the coconut milk and water, lime leaves and lime juice. Simmer until tender. Add the toasted coconut and cook for about 5 minutes. Adjust seasonings to taste. We substitute light soy sauce for salt in curries.

———

Whilst in Provence with Patricia Wells we visited her local butcher, Monsieur Henny, who delighted in showing us the food he was preparing for an evening party for friends. He took us upstairs by a steep spiral staircase where there were coolrooms and a kitchen with a huge oven which could accommmodate cooking an animal in one piece. That afternoon M. Henny had a baby kid cut into legs, shoulder and rack marinating in a stainless steel oven tray with olive oil, lemon zest, finely sliced lemon pieces, finely chopped garlic and parsley. The head was also cut in half with the brain left in for roasting. M. Henny intended to roast the kid, let it rest in the baking dish and then serve it with just the juices that accumulated around it.

———————

THE FOLLOWING recipe is an old favourite taken from Theodora Fitzgibbon's 1963 book *Game Cooking*.

ROAST SUCKLING KID

1 kid, about 5 kg	*1 teaspoon ginger*
500 g cooking apples	*cloves*
6 cloves garlic	*juice and grated peel of 1 lemon*
60 g butter	*olive oil*
285 ml cider	*salt and pepper*
rashers of streaky bacon	

Squeeze the lemon juice inside the prepared kid and insert the lemon peel as well. Peel and core the apples, wrap them in bacon rashers and stick a clove in each. Stuff the kid with these and use skewers to keep them in. Insert the cloves of garlic into the legs and then rub the entire animal with the ginger, salt and pepper all mixed together. Put into a roasting pan with the butter and some olive oil and roast at a low temperature for 30 minutes per kilo, basting frequently. When it is cooked, remove the kid to a warm dish to rest, pour off the surplus fat and add the cider to the essence. Boil rapidly on top of the stove until reduced by half.

Spring Lamb

ONE OF THE most obvious spring delights is lamb. Prime lamb is up to 8 months old, and may be called lamb for up to one year. Bulk packaged 'lamb' is a very loose term and it can often be much older.

The best lamb I have ever eaten was a Suffolk lamb. A few years ago some enterprising farmers who were breeding Suffolk lambs brought me a carcass to try. It was a taste revelation. I put it on the menu as 'Suffolk lamb' and it was a great hit.

There are two small farms near here that are breeding a Suffolk merino cross and that meat is almost as good. But the Pheasant Farm is a game restaurant and as I cook most of my main courses to order, I have difficulty with cuts of meat that cannot be cooked 'à la minute', and to buy a whole carcass is not practical for me.

I understand that the Corriedale or Corriedale merino cross also has superior texture and an outstanding flavour and is being bred especially for eating.

Most butchers are an incredibly friendly lot and certainly those of the old school know a great deal about their trade and are only too happy to help with advice. So many people buy on price only, not understanding the differences in quality. In these times it is important to receive value for money—and you should try to make an informed choice about the meat you are buying. Larger retailers will package whole sides of lamb, showcasing the leg at the top, and advertise it for $1.99 a kilo. Those in a hurry may think, 'What a bargain—a leg of lamb usually costs at least three times as much.'

It is of course clever marketing because under the leg are the lesser cuts of meat which are more likely to be wasted. These lesser cuts, if cooked correctly, can make good honest meals by pot roasting, say the shoulder (though this would be better if sold in one piece and not as chops), or by making a stew or curry. My main complaint is the insistence of so many people who buy just by cost to use these neck, shoulder or chump chops of inferior meat as barbecue chops. They are served up as leathery offerings and then considered a proper meal! There is no food I dislike more and it would fast make me a vegetarian.

Many farmers prefer the taste of mutton to lamb and hogget. Hogget is older than mutton. I have to say my husband shows his Mallala upbringing in loving a rolled, seasoned lamb flap. His family never bothered with spring lamb!

Let your butcher guide you. Ask about the differences in price, cooking and final taste. A small piece of prime lamb will be at least twice the price but will taste ten times better. If cost is a limiting factor, then just serve a smaller, perfectly-cooked portion as the highlight of the meal instead of the filler.

For those in a hurry, prime lamb will cook very quickly and need little preparation. Lamb loin chops will grill in just 10 minutes. The butcher can cut a leg of lamb into steaks across the leg for grilling or barbecuing. They can also section the leg into the silverside, topside and flank to make small roasts.

The shoulder can be boned out into cubes of meat for a stir-fry or curry. This will need much less cooking than the cheaper cuts that need long, slow cooking in a crockpot.

Don't be worried about the fat on the loin chops or saddle. Cook these cuts with the fat on—the flavour of the lamb is so much better this way; cut it off by all means before eating.

I can understand farmers requiring a deep freeze for holding their meat but I can't help thinking that it might be false economy to buy and freeze these pre-packed, bulk sides of 'lamb'. Do your sums for those cuts of meat which work best for you and your family and be honest about which pieces you waste. See if it isn't worth buying smaller amounts of quality cuts of lamb. I am sure you will be converted once you try it!

Cook lamb quickly at a high temperature and then let it rest. Lamb should be served pink (and by that I don't mean raw). Resist the temptation to overcook it as you will not appreciate the taste sensations I have been talking about. Again, ask your butcher for their cooking tips.

Visitors to Australia can't believe how good and cheap our prime lamb is. What is missing in Australian farming is communication between consumers and producers. As consumers, we have to demand quality and not be swayed by looks or packaging. We have to make an effort to be aware of food in terms of taste and to know how to handle and make the most of our food.

LAMB SHOULDER POT ROASTED WITH GARLIC

1 shoulder lamb
3-4 tablespoons olive oil
1 cup white wine
2 cups chicken stock

4 heads garlic, separated into
cloves but unpeeled
fresh rosemary

In a heavy-bottomed pot on top of the stove, brown the shoulder gently in the olive oil with the rosemary. Season. Pour off any excess oil and deglaze the pan with the white wine. Add the garlic cloves and extra herbs if you wish. Add the stock and bring to the boil. Seal with a lid and cook on a very low flame until the meat is tender, turning occasionally. Be careful that the liquid doesn't evaporate, leaving the meat stuck to the bottom of the pan.

Remove the garlic cloves and cool before squeezing them out of their skins to serve alongside the lamb. Skim the grease from the surface of the cooking liquid and reduce the sauce over a high temperature. Serve with mashed potatoes. Garnish with chopped parsley.

Sas's Leg of Lamb

1 leg lamb   *rosemary*
garlic   *sea salt*
olive oil

Make little pockets over the lamb with a sharp knife and slip slithers of garlic into these cuts. Baste with oil and rub salt into the lamb. Sprinkle generously with rosemary. Bake at a high temperature, turning at least once, halfway through the cooking. Cook for approximately 1 hour for a medium-sized leg. Leave the meat to rest, turned over once again, for at least half an hour before carving. (Every oven is different, so it is difficult to give an exact formula of time to weight to produce pink meat.)

IF YOU GET the chance to try saltbush mutton you'll be in for a treat. It has a superb flavour from the saltbush the lamb feeds on. Saltbush mutton can be bought from butchers in Quorn and further north in South Australia. It should definitely be slow-roasted—the ultimate 'baked dinner' in my opinion.

Also try cooking with the same method as that for a leg of kid (see page 50), pot roasting very slowly with garlic and rosemary and adding just half a cup of stock at a time so that the juices become thick and caramelly.

In childhood books I read of these—
Cherry and quince and walnut trees
And many another old-world tree.
Exotic and far they seemed to be,
For all there was, my dears, for me,
Was just one little quandong tree.

THIS IS THE first stanza of 'The Quandong Tree', a poem by Mary Flyn that appeared in the *Women's Mirror* some forty years ago. I have no doubt that the quandong evokes fond memories for people in the outback—memories of gathering wild quandongs as children, of eating quandong pies at station homesteads, of making necklaces out of the seeds.

The Aborigines treasured the quandong and ate the fruit raw or dried it for later use. It was a valuable source of Vitamin C for them. Jennifer Isaacs, in *Bush Food*, describes how Aborigines burnt the branches of the quandong tree and stood their children in the smoke in order to make them strong for long journeys. A tea was made from quandong leaves and drunk as a purgative, and an infusion made from the roots of the quandong tree was believed to help rheumatism sufferers. The bark was used for tanning leather and the wood was also of value, being closely related to sandalwood.

The quandong tree will survive in the harshest of conditions and will cope with an amazingly high level of salinity in watering.

I have enjoyed using quandongs in cooking for some years, in a dried form supplied by Brian Powell, of Quorn. There has been a lot of interest in small commercial quandong orchards, and they are beginning to appear. Ruth Anderson, of Cooyerdoo Station, was generous with her information compiled for a paper on quandongs given at a seminar. She markets quandong seed kits through Dick Smith's *Australian Geographic*. I also gleaned information from the Eatts family at Kimba, who have planted a small quandong orchard, and Ben McNamara, who has gathered together some 62 growers who have between them planted 20,000 trees that will start to bear fruit in four years. And I spoke with CSIRO researcher Jenny Treeby, who is working full-time on the development of the quandong

There is a lot of interest in propagating quandongs, which have definite potential as a dried fruit and possibly also as a fresh fruit, although the latter will be slower to develop as there are so few source trees of a high enough calibre. Until now, most of the selection work has probably been carried out by Brian Powell, and there is a feeling among the growers and those interested that the CSIRO work, although important, has been too slow. Of the 400 trees in the CSIRO collection, only 12 per cent had an acceptable yield and only 15-20 per cent of this yield had good taste and appearance.

Dissatisfaction aside, this spring the Sunraysia nursery at Gol Gol, NSW, will be selling quandong trees grown from the root-stocks and budwood selected by the CSIRO and Brian Powell.

The availability of these trees will be of great assistance to a budding industry in that it is only by selecting for quality that quandongs will reach their potential. Grading for grub infestation is being carried out now by the growers, but it is grading for flavour and size that will ensure market growth.

Most of the work is being done on the dried fruit, but it is fascinating to hear Ruth Anderson talk of the pleasures of the fresh variety called 'moonshine peach'. It has a taste between peach and rhubarb and a piquancy that makes your mouth pucker. I am excited about trying them in season—September and October. Apparently the fresh fruit tends to blemish, which consumers find difficult to accept: although, intellectually, they prefer pesticide-free fruit, they find it difficult to accept its appearance.

Those wanting to taste quandongs have the following options: The Cleve Field Day is held in August and features seedlings, demonstrations of dehydrating and cooking quandongs, and opportunities to see in action the specially-developed cutting machine. Ben McNamara's property, Shoalmarra Quandong Farm, 5 km from Tumby Bay, is open to the public every Tuesday, with tours at 9.30 am and 2.30 pm. He sells quandong pies and quandong jam, and serves scones, jam and cream. Brian Powell has posted me dried quandongs for years and both Mrs Anderson of Cooyerdoo and Mrs Eatts of Kimba can supply home-manufactured dried quandong slab or 'leather'.

The dried quandong's flavour is quite adaptable in that it can be used for both savoury and sweet dishes. The only time I have tasted a commercially-made quandong pie, in the Flinders Ranges, I felt that too much sugar had been added and this masked the unique flavour. I have been told by many people that it is better to use honey as a sweetener as this is less likely to disguise the original flavour.

In the restaurant, I have successfully teamed quandong with venison and kangaroo, and was delighted with a dessert of quandong bread-and-butter pudding. As well as using quandongs in the pudding itself, I reconstituted some and served them in a caramel, which gave a delightful 'sweet/sour' flavour to the dessert.

————

RUTH ANDERSON SHARED this recipe sent to her by Bernard Oehrli of the Hyatt in Adelaide.

QUANDONG CHUTNEY

30 g dried quandongs   *200 ml vinegar*
400 ml water   *30 g sugar*

Place all ingredients in a saucepan and boil for 10 minutes. Take quandongs out when soft. Reduce liquid to a thick glaze and then return quandongs to pan. Boil for a few minutes. Serve with barbecued kangaroo fillet.

QUANDONG PIE (ANDREW FIELKE'S RECIPE)

shortcrust pastry (see below)   *20 g sugar*
200 g dried quandongs   *35 g arrowroot*
1.2 litres water

Simmer quandongs, water and sugar for 10 minutes. Remove fruit and thicken sauce with arrowroot. Return fruit to sauce and cool. Line pie tin with shortcrust pastry. Fill with mixture and top with pastry lid. Bake at 190°C for 45 minutes.

MAGGIE'S SOUR CREAM PASTRY

250 g flour   *125 ml sour cream*
200 g unsalted butter, very cold

Chop the cold butter and add it to the flour in the bowl of the food precessor. Pulse the butter and flour until the butter resembles chunks the size of olives. Add the sour cream and pulse again until it is 'just' incorporated. The mixture does not need to be smooth and will have 'patches'. Turn onto a well-floured, cool surface and, using a rolling pin, manoeuvre the dough into a rectangle. Cover and leave to rest in the refrigerator for 20 minutes. Roll into the desired shape. Rest again in the fridge. Bake.

THIS RECIPE CAME from Jenny Treeby of CSIRO and is of particular interest to me because it is more of a marmalade than a sweet jam. It is wonderful to see a researcher who looks at the end product—the cooking of the fruit!

QUANDONG JAM

250 g fresh or frozen quandong,   *10 ml water*
cut into small pieces   *240 g sugar*

Boil fruit and water down till pulpy, then add sugar. Simmer for 20 minutes and pack in clean glass jars.

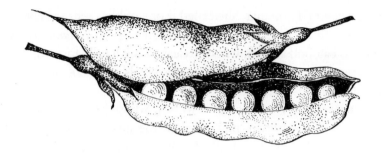

Peas

THE BEST POSSIBLE pea comes direct from the garden in the warmth of the afternoon. The sugar content of the pea picked this way is enough to satisfy the sweetest tooth. I'm sure any mother could persuade a recalcitrant child to eat greens like this! Who needs to cook greens anyway? Raw peas, pods and all, if they are young enough, are a gourmet's delight when eaten straight from the garden.

As peas grow older and larger they convert their sugar into starch and are not nearly as tasty. Few people bother shelling young peas. If you cannot buy young, freshly harvested peas then the inimitable frozen pea will taste better. These peas have truly been snap frozen with all their natural sugar intact, so it is no wonder that fresh peas have been ignored in recent years.

Shelling peas is definitely a job to be shared around the kitchen table. I remember as a child, I put more in my mouth than in the pot! This never seemed to worry my mother—I'm sure she was a lot smarter about these things than me!

I wasn't aware of how many varieties of pea there are. A close friend talked of eating telephone peas from her sister's garden in Tasmania. She called it one of life's sensuous pleasures.

We have all become familiar with the snow pea or *mangetout*, which is picked to eat, pod and all, with the peas inside hardly formed. This is a lovely, crisp pea to eat raw or throw in salads, or to blanch for just a second and serve as a vegetable.

The newest pea is the sugar snap pea, whose name says it all. It is incredibly sweet and crisp, picked when the peas are fully formed but meant to be eaten pod and all. They are more expensive than the traditional pea, but as more people grow them, they should come down in price. They are however a real treat, and worth the price.

Having declared myself over the occasional use of frozen peas, I know a lovely woman who runs a marvellous delicatessen in the city markets who confessed to me that she uses dried packet peas for her risotto (see page 220). A packet of Surprise peas thrown in at the beginning (when sweating the onions and rice in olive oil) has them beautifully reconstituted by the end of the cooking period and that lovely pea flavour thoroughly absorbed by the rice.

Convenience foods are not necessarily bad but nothing can compare with fresh produce in the most perfect conditions.

My favourite way of serving fresh peas (those that make it to the pot!) is to simmer them in a good stock until half done and then to finish cooking them in a little butter, salt and pepper. Throw in some prosciutto—the fatty parts particularly—just before finishing.

A new chef in my kitchen comes from the north of England and to him peas are mushy and accompany fish and chips—all home-made of course. For this dish dried peas are soaked in bicarbonate of soda for 4 days. The peas are washed and then simmered in fresh water for 6 to 8 hours. When cooked (mushy), add black pepper, butter and nutmeg.

SWEETBREADS WITH GREEN PEA PURÉE, SHALLOTS AND PROSCIUTTO
(SERVES 4)

1 kg fresh peas in pod
10 shallots, 4 sliced finely
  and 6 whole
butter

juice of 1 lemon
1 bay leaf
100 g prosciutto, cut into
  pieces 4 x 2 cm

1 kg sweetbreads, thymus gland	*salt and pepper*
if possible, oval shape	*sugar*

Soak the sweetbreads, replacing the water several times until no signs if blood remain. Place the sweetbreads in a pan with cold water, lemon juice and the bay leaf. Bring very slowly to a simmer and remove the sweetbreads as they become opaque (about 3 minutes). Drain well and place on a flat dish with a similar dish on top with weights on top of that. Press for 4 hours in the fridge. Peel the sweetbreads of skin and gristle, keeping their shape intact.

Sweat the chopped shallots in butter. Pod the peas. Blanch the peas twice in boiling water, with a little sugar and salt. Sweat the whole shallots in oil, beginning with cold oil in a cold pan so they don't burn. Cook them until they are a gentle, golden brown and cooked all the way through. Purée the cut shallots and peas whilst still warm, adding a little of the pea water. Season. If you wish the purée to be very smooth, you may wish to blanch them for a third time.

Slice the sweetbreads to desired size and pan fry them with the prosciutto pieces until golden brown. Add caramelised shallots. Serve on a base of green pea purée.

THE POSTHUMOUS publication *The Best of Jane Grigson* has a great recipe for a chilled soufflé of snow peas which I could imagine serving with some prosciutto, crusty bread and a glass of white wine for lunch.

Eggs

EGGS ARE A simple food but full of soul. We have one goose who makes a nest every year in the same spot on a little strip of earth in front of the restaurant (in view of table three). At around lunch time every day she lays her egg. I swear she does it because she likes the attention of the customers who are obviously enchanted by her. She has never been successful with her 'sitting', as she likes to put on a show by going for a swim in the middle of lunch, leaving the nest for a lot longer than a good mum ought. She sits there for the whole of spring in the vain hope that she will hatch. Usually the smell of a rotten egg will remind us that it is time to take over from nature and chase her away.

When talking of eggs, most people think of chooks' eggs, but at the Pheasant Farm we use the eggs of quail, bantams, pheasants, ducks and geese.

We sometimes have scrambled duck eggs which we serve with smoked salmon or salmon caviar—elevating eggs to the luxury class. Using duck or pheasant eggs for this dish is like injecting a creamy mayonnaise into it. This may not be everyone's cup of tea but I love it!

Cooking scrambled eggs is an art form. Use half a tablespoon of butter and one tablespoon of cream to each egg. Use only a little salt. Beat eggs well, add cream and butter in small lumps. Cook over a very low heat, stirring until the egg begins to form a custard. When the eggs are two-thirds cooked, take the pan off and allow the mixture to set away from the stove.

Eggs are certainly one of the more versatile foods we have. They stand marvellously on their own (think of a soft-boiled egg standing in an egg cup with soldiers of toast or fresh brown bread to dunk), and they can be cooked in a variety of ways (soft-boiled, hard-boiled, poached or fried). Eggs combine well with other ingredients, either using the richness of the egg yolk with olive oil or butter to make mayonnaise, aoli (see page 32), hollandaise or béarnaise; or whole eggs in custards, quiches, soufflés or cakes.

Then there is the question of leftover egg whites that every restaurant faces. How many meringues can you make? We put egg whites into dated and numbered containers in the fridge hoping for an excuse to use them. I wonder if the Brownies or Scouts, instead of having a 'bottle-round', could collect egg whites and make confectionery to sell.

Eggs are easier to beat in a copper bowl with a whisk than taking out the electric mixer and then having to wash it all up afterwards. You are less likely to overbeat the eggs this way, and the copper bowl gives the whites a creamier, yellowish foam. The same eggs beaten in a mixer or stainless steel bowl will be snowy white and drier.

A meringue can be both over- and under-beaten. Soft meringues should be baked at 180-190°C for 15 minutes. This crisps the surface and leaves the interior moist and chewy. Hard meringues are baked at 100°C for up to two hours, or left in the oven overnight after being put into a hot oven, turned off just as you put them in. If they leak syrup or collapse it is because they are undercooked. If they have beads of syrup on the surface, they have been cooked at too high a temperature.

And it is not just egg whites that are whipped. Whipped yolks are added to various breads and cakes to contribute to the yolky flavour or to help reinforce a foam. Zabaglione is a warm, frothy, rich mixture of yolks, sugar and Marsala wine.

Tips for hard-boiled eggs would have saved me hours of anguish in the first few years of our business when I sat in the evening and peeled bucket after bucket of quail eggs. My daughters Saskia and Eliette were only 4 and 2 years old when we began quail production, a year before we started the farm shop.

I used to sit with the buckets between my legs and the girls either side of me. We had a book propped on a chair and I would read to them, my hands in the bucket as they turned the pages. They used to love to eat the yolks as I tore the egg white. They don't often eat eggs now! I don't know how I managed this for so many evenings for so many years. After 4 years we contracted the job out and life started to improve.

The most important tip is that all eggs should not be too fresh for boiling. Preferably they should be one week old. For pickling, boil quail eggs for 6 minutes—you need to use a paddle to move the eggs around in the water so that at their 'setting point' the yolks will be in the centre of the egg. Quail egg skins are much tougher than chook eggs. They are difficult to peel and if the yolk is too close to one end of the egg, the skin will be torn and the egg useless. The moment the eggs come out of the boiling water they should be thrown into an ice slurry to cool, and be kept in this until you are ready to peel them. To peel, pick up the egg and crush the pointier end against the table so that the whole shell crazes in your hand. The skin will slip off in one.

Soaking the eggs overnight in straight vinegar dissolves the outer membrane of the eggshell and makes it very easy to peel. This is only useful if you are going to pickle the eggs rather then having them fresh, as the vinegar flavour is so strong. It is also expensive and plays havoc with your hands.

PICKLED QUAIL EGGS

36 quail eggs,
   at least one week old
375 ml white wine vinegar
50 g sugar

1 level teaspoon whole
   peppercorns
1 level teaspoon whole allspice
1 bay leaf

Place the quail eggs in a saucepan and cover with cold water. Stir them gently with a wooden spoon until they come to the boil. Boil the eggs for 5–6 minutes and tip them straight into an ice slurry to cool. Boil the other ingredients together and then pour them over the peeled eggs which have been placed in a jar.

FRESHLY BOILED quail eggs (boiled for only 2 to 3 minutes), cut in half lengthways and topped with caviar, make wonderful hors d'oeuvres.

I have often wondered why quail or chook eggs sometimes have a greenish-grey discoloration on the surface of the yolk. It happens most with less than fresh eggs (of course I noticed it with the quail eggs because I was using them not so fresh for ease of peeling). I recently discovered, while reading Harold McGee's book *On Food and Cooking*, that the colour is caused by a harmless compound of iron and sulphur—ferrous sulphide—which is formed only when the egg is heated. Minimising the amount of hydrogen sulphide that reaches the yolk will reduce the discoloration: cook the eggs only as long as necessary to set the yolk and then plunge the eggs immediately into cold water and peel them promptly.

THE FOLLOWING dish is nearly always on my menu and is a firm favourite of many of my regular customers.

DUCK EGG PASTA WITH SMOKED KANGAROO, SUN-DRIED TOMATOES AND PINE NUTS

PASTA
500 g hard flour
4-5 duck eggs, depending on their size

Make a well in the centre of the flour on the bench. Whisk the eggs together and pour into the well. Incorporate them into the flour. Add an extra yolk if needed. Knead the pasta dough until it forms a shiny ball ad is firm to the touch. Cover the dough with plastic wrap and rest it in the refrigerator for 30 minutes.

Before beginning to roll the pasta, bring a pot of salted water to the boil.

Roll the pasta through a hand pasta machine to desired thickness and cut into fettuccine strips.

Cook the pasta until the water comes vigorously back to the boil, strain into a colander, but do not refresh. Lay the pasta out on a large tray and moisten it with olive oil.

Cool the pasta in the fridge for about 10 minutes. Otherwise toss it frequently to help it cool.

For detailed pasta making see Marcella Hazan's *Classic Italian Cookbook*.

SAUCE

100 g sun-dried tomatoes, cut into strips	*200 g toasted pine nuts*
	olive oil
400 g smoked kangaroo fillet, or prosciutto ham, sliced very thin	*Parmesan cheese, freshly grated*

Warm the sun-dried tomatoes and pine nuts gently in olive oil. Be careful not to crisp or burn the tomatoes or nuts. Combine these with the kangaroo or ham and then pile the mixture on top of the servings of hot pasta. Scatter on liberal amounts of Parmesan.

O NE OF THE recipes I am asked for most often is that of our Crème Caramel—eggs are the most important ingredient.

CRÈME CARAMEL

CARAMEL
1/2 cup sugar
1/2 cup water

Use a heavy-bottomed pan to dissolve the sugar and water over a low to medium heat. Leave it until the mixture turns a very deep golden colour (one step before burning) and pour into four individual dishes. Turn the dishes around so the caramel coats the sides.

CUSTARD

1 1/2 cups milk	*4 eggs*
3/4 cup cream	*1 vanilla bean*
1/4 cup sugar, less one tablespoon	

Beat the eggs and sugar lightly together and cover with a cartouche (a piece of plastic wrap or greaseproof paper placed on the surface to save it 'burning' until it is needed).

Combine the milk and cream in a saucepan with the vanilla bean and bring to scalding point. Cool slightly. Gradually pour this over the egg mixture, stirring carefully. Then strain the mixture into another bowl to remove any tiny traces of egg. Carefully pour the custard into the dishes, over the caramel.

Put the dishes into a bain-marie (a baking dish with hot water reaching halfway up the sides of the dishes) and bake in a moderate oven for 25 minutes or until set.

Remove the dishes from the water, cool, then refrigerate. Turn out to serve.

I find these are best made the day beforehand. I often make one large crème caramel in a cake tin and then turn it out and slice it into wedges.

———————

WITH A BIT OF luck with the seasons you can use the last of the goose eggs to team with the first of the mulberries.

GOOSE EGG CUSTARD TO SERVE WITH MULBERRIES

2 goose eggs   *2 tablespoons castor sugar*
250 ml fresh cream   *1/2 vanilla bean*
250 ml milk   *freshly grated nutmeg to taste*

Heat milk and cream in a pot with the halved vanilla bean. Beat eggs and sugar in a bowl and then pour over the milk and cream. Strain into a baking dish lightly greased with butter. Preheat the oven to about 120°C and place the baking dish in a bain-marie with the water reaching two thirds up the sides of the dish. Bake for 1 to 1¹/2 hours. Remove from the oven and allow to cool in the bain-marie. Serve at room temperature or refrigerate to become more solid. Garnish with nutmeg.

Strawberries

PERFUMING MY OFFICE is a 5 kilo tray of the most beautiful large strawberries you can imagine. These fragrant strawberries came from Bill Gray of Rainbow Valley Producers at Springton. I buy them when they are perfect; they have been left on the vine to ripen (just like tomatoes should be) and picked in the early morning. I prefer not to refrigerate them so that the flavour is not masked by chilling and other 'fridge smells'.

When they are in this perfect condition there is nothing better than a big plateful with fresh cream—the definitive no-nonsense dessert. Another simple treat is to serve them unhulled on a dish with brown sugar and crème fraiche.

If you think big is beautiful when buying strawberries, let me tell you that the best strawberries in the world are the wild strawberries of Europe. There are the alpine strawberries and beach strawberries (actually found by the seashore in parts of Europe). And there is the French passion for their *fraises de bois* (wood strawberries). After 200 years of development of strawberry varieties it is still this wild one that is supreme in both taste and smell. They are very small and picked very ripe. Plants of these alpine strawberries are available in Australia, in particular in South Australia and Victoria, but they have not been viable for the fresh food market because the consumer demand is for big, colourful fruit that will last.

Strawberries can be used for so many desserts—strawberry shortcake, strawberry bread, strawberry tart, and as a filling for sponges. They can be used as a syrup, in a liqueur, as a sauce or a coulis and to make jam or jellies. Strawberries can be teamed with other flavours such as rhubarb, oranges and raspberries.

Strawberry plants look so pretty in a garden, especially when planted along a path. I love to pick a warm, ripe strawberry after I've driven home at night. The only trouble is that everyone in the family does the same thing and we have to buy them from Bill if they are to constitute a whole dessert!

Strawberries do ripen very quickly. Our biggest pest is the millipede, which burrows into the warm berries. It is not pleasant to find these in your fruit.

It is interesting that strawberry varieties are known by their European names—such as the June Bearer, which crops during spring, and the Ever Bearer, which crops during spring and autumn. Bill is also working with a very old European breed called the Red Gauntlet, which is a big, firm, juicy, sweet, pink fruit.

Bill's association with strawberries goes back to his childhood in England. He grew up on an 8000 ha estate which had a lot of shooting land. He and his friends were employed to beat the grasses in the shooting season. They would watch the grouse fly away from where they had been feeding—on wild strawberries. Bill and his friends would feast on the berries the birds had left behind.

A few years ago a colleague, Di Holuigue, gave me a fascinating little book called *The Compleat Strawberry*, by Stafford Whitaker. It gives the history of the strawberry and talks about how expensive a treat they were in days gone by. It also details their nutritional aspects. Although these figures will vary from species to species, generally they consist of 89.5% water, 5.8% sugar, 2.463% cellulose and seeds and then small amounts of soluble salts, protein, oily matter, lime and iron salts.

Fruit sugar is more easily assimilated by diabetics than any other type of sugar. The salts have a laxative effect and the fibre is good for a sluggish bowel. As well as Vitamins A and B1, they contain a large amount of Vitamin C.

A N INTERESTING ACCOMPANIMENT to strawberries is balsamic vinegar. This is particularly useful when the strawberries are less than perfectly ripe.

STRAWBERRIES IN BALSAMIC VINEGAR

To a 250 g punnet strawberries, add 1 to 2 tablespoons balsamic vinegar to suit individual taste (balsamic vinegar ranges in quality and age; it can be 1 or 100 years old, the latter being incredibly syrupy and intense with variations in between).

A ND WHILE talking about interesting combinations, I remember some 12 years ago having a dish prepared for me by Ingo Schwarze, senior lecturer of the advanced certificate of Pâtisserie at Regency Park College. Ingo is known in the trade as a very talented teacher and pâtissière and was happy to share the following recipe. As I am not so fond of very sweet sweets my memory of this dish is that it was sensational.

STRAWBERRIES WITH BLACK PEPPER

2 x 250 g punnets fresh	*256 ml fresh lemon juice*
strawberries	*30 ml kirsch, and a further 70 ml*
70 g brown sugar	*kirsch*
25 g butter	*1 tablespoon finely grated orange rind*
160 ml fresh orange juice	*pepper*

Melt sugar in a pan, add butter and then lemon and orange juice. Cook until syrupy and add 30 ml kirsch and orange rind. Reserve and keep hot. Prepare the strawberries by hulling or cutting them and using a pepper mill, give them about 10 turns of the mill and place in a dish. (I prefer not to have a fine mill for this.) In a separate pan warm slightly the 70 ml kirsch and ignite. Pour over the fruit and then pour the hot sauce on top. Serve with vanilla ice cream.

STRAWBERRY COULIS

250 g strawberries
20 g castor sugar

Purée together until liquid. The amount of the sugar should reflect the ripeness of the strawberries. If the berries are unripe and woody, place them in the blender and pour a little hot stock syrup (a syrup of equal amounts of sugar and water) over them. Leave for a few seconds and then purée.

———

WE BOUGHT A food dehydrator for our daughter Sassie who was interested in pursuing her own food production business. Her first effort was dehydrated strawberries and this marvellous recipe for dried strawberry brioche resulted from our wondering what on earth we were going to use them for.

DRIED STRAWBERRY BRIOCHE

3 tablespoons luke-warm water   *1 teaspoon salt*
7 g dried yeast   *3 large eggs, beaten*
* (or 15 g fresh yeast)*   *185 g unsalted butter*
3 teaspoons sugar   *1 cup dried strawberries,*
220 g flour   * reconstituted in orange liqueur*

GLAZE
1 egg, beaten with a little of the
liquid from the strawberries

Pour the warm water into a small bowl and add the yeast and one teaspoon of the sugar. Set the bowl aside until the yeast dissolves.

Put the flour, remaining 2 teaspoons sugar and the salt into a bowl and add the yeast mixture and the eggs. Mix by hand, squeezing and pulling the dough upwards, until it becomes elastic. This should take about 20 minutes.

Divide the butter into 6 even pieces and again using your hand, incorporate the butter piece by piece. Each new piece should be added only when the last has been absorbed. The dough will be sticky but should retain its elasticity.

Put the dough into a clean bowl, cover with a towel, and set aside in an area free of draughts to triple its bulk. The dough does not need to be in a warm area in order to rise; if the butter starts to melt and the dough looks oily, place it in the refrigerator from time to time. It will take about 4 hours to rise.

Turn the dough on to a lightly floured board and shape it into a rectangle. Drain the excess liquid from the strawberries and place them on the dough. Fold the dough into three, as if you were making puff pastry, press out again, and again fold it into three. Put the dough back into the bowl, cover, and leave it for about 1¹/2 hours, until the bulk has doubled.

Shape the dough into a round and place it on a plate in the refrigerator for 30 minutes. This is to make the dough firm enough to shape.

Grease a loaf tin, shape the dough into a sausage and place it in the tin. Set it aside for the dough to double in bulk.

Preheat the oven to 240°C. Just before baking, brush the top of the loaf with the glaze. Bake for 15 minutes, reduce the temperature to 200°C and bake for another 30 minutes. Cool on a wire rack.

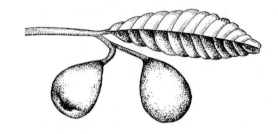

L
OQUATS CAN, in the right circumstances, be a very welcome fruit. They are not much known or revered but it is their timing that, to me, makes them special. They are, along with strawberries, the first hint that summer is to come. Oranges are past their peak, apples and pears are only from the cold store and apart from the imported exotics, the loquat it is until the first flush of raspberries starts to appear. The fruit has a distinctive flavour and is beautifully juicy.

The loquat is actually native to China and South Japan and I think it has a 'Japanese' look to it. The fruit is orange, oval, shiny and firm. There has not been much done to improve the genes of loquats in Australia and as far as I know they are only grown commercially in Japan and the Mediterranean, where they grow to be easily 5 cm long by 4 cm across. The Japanese have worked at improving the size of the fruit as the seeds of the loquat take up a large part of the fruit. I love the shiny, slippery feel of the seeds in my hand!

The South Australian climate, being Mediterranean, certainly allows loquats to flourish and many an old-fashioned garden has a huge specimen. The fruit marks easily yet the tree will respond to good care. What a delight it is to come across this evergreen tree with wonderful large leaves and boughs, laden with fruit, in a well-watered garden. My grandfather's garden in Sydney had a huge tree and as children we used to love lying in its shade and eating the ripe fruit that had fallen to the ground.

I have just planted three loquat trees as a screen to shield us from the road on our home property of nine hectares and two dams. We have far more fruit trees than we could ever utilise if we didn't have the restaurant, but it is a joy to plant and make the most of these 'food-bearing' trees. When we enclose the orchard into a walled garden we plan to have 'weeder' geese to control the weeds. I have a vision of the geese feeding from the ripe loquats that fall to the ground. I'm sure they will make especially good eating!

Unfortunately loquats are very susceptible to birds as they can't be picked until they are very ripe and the birds often get there first.

———

L oquats make a superior jelly for using with fruit flans or tarts in the summer. The flavour of the loquat blends beautifully with the fruit rather than overpowering it. You could make a pastry base, then a crème pâtissière filling topped with fresh apricots that have been poached in a syrup, with loquat jelly glazed over the fruit for a marvellous finish. Most recipes will call for apricot jam for this but I find the loquat jelly more subtle. The best recipe I know is Helen's Loquat Jelly from Stephanie Alexander's book *Stephanie's Menus for Food Lovers*.

HELEN'S LOQUAT JELLY

Pick available amount of fruit—ripe but not over-ripe, and absolutely dry. Put the fruit in a saucepan and barely cover with water. Boil until the fruit is soft, approximately 15-20 minutes, and then strain it through a fine strainer, pressing very hard on the fruit pulp to extract the maximum juice. Discard the solids.

Measure out one 1 cup sugar for each cup of juice and combine in an enamelled cast iron or stainless steel pan. Boil together, skimming until it jells, using the usual test of a teaspoonful dropped into a saucer. Cool it and then push your finger or a spoon through the jelly. It should wrinkle and leave a clear path where the spoon or finger has been.

———

Apricot Tart with Crème Pâtissière and Helen's Loquat Jelly

Make a quantity of Sour Cream Pastry (see page 60) and bake it in your favourite pastry dish.

Apricots

25 fresh apricots	*2 cups water*
1 cup sugar	*lemon juice*

Halve the apricots and poach them in the water and sugar with a little lemon juice.

Crème Pâtissière

6 egg yolks	*500 ml milk*
70 g sugar	*1 vanilla bean*
30 g flour	

Split the vanilla bean lengthways. Bring the milk to the boil and allow the vanilla to infuse in it for 10 minutes. Whisk the egg yolks with the sugar until pale and the mixture forms a light ribbon. Sift in the flour and whisk again. Strain the heated milk into the egg mixture, stirring constantly so no lumps form. Cook over a gentle yet direct heat, whisking constantly. Allow it to come to the boil for a good 2 minutes to allow the flour to cook out. Add a tiny bit of butter at the last minute if you wish. Transfer the crème to a bowl to cool and place a piece of plastic wrap on the surface of the custard to prevent a skin forming.

Loquat Glaze

Heat 2 tablespoons Helen's Loquat Jelly with a squeeze of lemon juice and a little water to thin it.

Assemble the dessert by filling the pastry case with the crème pâtissière and covering this generously with poached apricot halves. Brush the hot loquat glaze over the apricots.

COOKED IN A light sugar syrup with the addition of lemon to highlight their flavour, loquats make a lovely poached fruit to serve cold with fresh cream. To cook them, I quarter the fruit and remove those wonderful stones first. If you wish to peel them, do so after the fruit has cooked.

At the restaurant we poach loquats (using strips of lemon peel or juice) and then make a caramel syrup by boiling equal quantities of sugar and water until almost burnt—rich in colour but not too sweet. The loquats are then put into the caramel syrup and served together with Olive Oil and Sauternes Cake. This is a cake from Alice Waters' first book *Chez Panisse*. It is a cake I keep on using as a dessert in one guise or another—so moist it is almost a pudding with a lovely lemony flavour.

Cumquats

T HE CUMQUAT IS A very special fruit to those who know and love its many uses in cooking and ornamental beauty. There is nothing like the simple beauty of a cumquat tree in a large, terracotta pot in a north-facing courtyard.

Cumquats don't appear to be grown commercially today, probably for the same reasons as the quandong. Which do you develop first—a market or an orchard? They were grown commercially in South Australia many years ago but found not to be profitable. I understand that it was actually the calamondin that was grown, which looks like a cumquat but is more like a sour orange. It has a very strong flavour and is used in some Scottish marmalades. Both calamondins and cumquats are an acquired taste and not profitable if grown only for jam-making.

Commercial purposes aside, Ian Tolley, the well-known Renmark nurseryman, says the important factors in growing cumquat trees, either in the ground or in pots, are reasonable drainage and consistent watering.

In his many years working with citrus fruit, the problem he has most often been asked about is splitting fruit. The fruit splits when trees are allowed to dry out, then overwatered, and then allowed to dry out again. The cumquat is grafted to a dwarfing rootstock to control its size to half an orange tree in an effort to improve the quality of the fruit. As a small tree it is often grown in pots and the problem of drying out becomes particularly relevant. All citrus trees do better with good drainage, although there are special rootstocks available for marginal drainage situations. The best way of watering is with a conventional dripper system, for 1-2 hours a day from late spring to early autumn.

Fertilising is important and two reasonable applications per year are recommended. It is better to use slow-release blood-and-bone, or Complete D, rather than inorganic fertilisers. It isn't necessary to put it through a dripper system, which is expensive and difficult. Simply spread it around the tree, scratch it in, and water with a sprinkling hose.

Ian describes the cumquat as a 'precocious bearer' because it yields fruit in the second or third year, and a reasonable crop in six to eight years.

———

O NE OF THE reasons that the cumquat wasn't commercially successful in the past was that the market saw it as suitable only for jam or glacé material, and the glacé manufacturers weren't interested because cumquats have too many seeds. Work to reduce the number of seeds in cumquats and other citrus fruit is slowly progressing. This is happening mainly through growers noticing trees that produce fruit particularly free of seeds and letting nurseries grow stock from them. Talking with Ian about one of my favourite topics—cooks getting together with growers—I became quite excited about the possibilities until he told me that the development of seed-free cumquats would mean reduced crop and fruit sizes. Sometimes it makes more sense to quit while you're ahead!

Although the commercial glacé manufacturers traditionally have not been interested in the cumquat, over the past year I have persuaded Ian's wife, Noel Tolley, that there is a market for her home-made glacé cumquats. I am delighted with her product and have featured it in my dessert menus for some months with great success. Noel is now selling it through Turner's Country Store, a delightfully-restored butcher's shop at 50 Murray Street, Angaston, which sells home-made produce. She says that she is quietly extending her cumquat orchard to meet the demand.

There are two varieties of cumquat—the Marumi (Meiwa), with a sweet rind, or the Nagami. I prefer the Marumi glacéed for desserts, but the Nagami, treated with less sugar, is a wonderful accompaniment for game. Noel recently sent me some cumquat slices dried, using no sugar at all, in a dehydrator rather than in the sun. I found the flavour wonderful for stocks with poultry or venison. It is truly exciting to see products of such quality.

Marmalade and glacé are not the only uses for cumquats. Try pricking ripe cumquats once or twice with a needle, placing them in a sterile glass jar, adding a little sugar if you have a sweet tooth, and then covering them with brandy. Leave them for a year—if you are strong enough.

I enjoy peeling cumquats and poaching them whole in a sugar syrup to team with a very rich dessert, particularly one made of chocolate. Cumquat marries with chocolate even better than orange does. I also find that the glaze from glacéed cumquats makes a wonderful basting liquid for the slow cooking of ducks. The Marumi is delicious eaten fresh, straight from the tree.

I was interested to learn that in the Philippines there are few lemons available and the people actually prefer to use sliced green cumquats in drinks. The greener and more bitter the fruit, the more they enjoy it. They squeeze ripe cumquats for juice in the same way as we squeeze oranges, and use the juice of green cumquats on noodles in an Asian dish, where we would use lemon. They also combine soy sauce with cumquat juice (in roughly equal quantities, to get that balance of salt and sour) to use with fried fish or chicken. And they do not limit the cumquat to enjoyment of food, using the luke-warm juice of grilled cumquats as a remedy for an itchy throat after continued coughing.

―――――

IN THE FOLLOWING recipe I use the liquor from Noel's glacéed fruit to make what was originally an Almond and Honey Tart, and then serve the glacéed fruit as an accompaniment with some whipped cream.

ALMOND AND CUMQUAT TART
(SERVES 8)

pâté brisée or short pastry
sufficient for 22 cm flan tin
with high sides (see Sour Cream
Pastry, page 60)
6 cups ground almonds (oven-
roasted first to release flavour)
1 1/2 cups cumquat glaze (available
from Turner's Country Store,
Angaston) or honey

1 teaspoon cinnamon
1 tablespoon grated cumquat zest
1/2 cup brandy
1/2 cup unsalted butter, softened

Roll pastry into a circle to cover the flan tin, and refrigerate until required. Mix the almonds with the cinnamon and cumquat zest. Stir in the brandy, cumquat glaze and butter. Pat almond mixture into the tart shell and dot with butter. Bake in oven at 175°C until crust is golden (approximately 30 minutes). Leave to cool at room temperature.

GLAZE
175 g bitter chocolate
1/4 cup heavy cream
1 1/2 tablespoons cumquat glaze
or honey

1 tablespoon brandy
1/4 cup unsalted butter
1 tablespoon water

To make glaze, combine chocolate, cream, water and cumquat glaze in the top of a double boiler until chocolate has melted. Remove from heat and stir in brandy and butter. Smooth glaze over tart with spatula. Do not refrigerate.

Serve with mascarpone (an Italian cream cheese which is free of rennet and preservatives, and keeps for about a week) with a little cumquat zest and a dash of juice stirred through carefully. Be careful not to make the mascarpone too runny.

Summer

Beans

THE BEGINNING of summer is heralded by the best stringless beans available. Look for specimens that are round, about 10 cm long and bright green. All you need to do is cook them in boiling salted water for a few minutes and then toss them in butter and herbs.

Butter beans are their own taste sensation—a very distinctive flavour. They are a buttery colour and are best when not too long.

Colder climates may be more successful at growing snake beans than we are in South Australia. They tend to be more coarse in Adelaide than in Melbourne, but are still very interesting. They can be found in good greengrocers and in the Asian supermarkets. Dark green in colour, they 'snake' over the plate and I love the look of astonishment on people's faces when I serve them.

Flat beans are my beans of the moment—perfectly flat and bright green—I prefer them to any stringless beans I have bought from a greengrocer. If cooked for just a few minutes in boiling salted water and then tossed in butter, they are crisp and juicy.

Scarlet runners are another great bean but I have never seen them available commercially.

GREEN BEAN SALAD

280 g green beans, cooked al dente   100 ml walnut oil
200 g prosciutto, thinly sliced   40 ml sherry vinegar
100 g artichoke hearts, sliced   salt and pepper
80 g walnuts, roasted and peeled   60 g Parmigiano Reggiano, shaved

Make a vinaigrette with the walnut oil, sherry vinegar, salt and pepper. Toss all the ingredients together and serve.

B ROAD BEANS engender passion in some people. There are those who hate them and those who love them. My children hate them—they must have had a deprived childhood!

I had two very special 'maiden aunts' who shared house. Auntie Reta did the cooking, usually a roast, and Auntie Glad was a 'school marm' in the traditional sense. Auntie Glad knew herself to be a good headmistress but a particularly bad cook, so she learnt, practised and delivered two main courses served with vegetables, and two desserts. The desserts were Spanish cream or a very sherried trifle. Neither of the main 'repertoire' dishes were ones that I enjoyed but I did understand the love that went into their preparation and the saving grace was that she used vegetables in season from their back garden.

Auntie Glad's favourites and mine were the broad bean and the choko, but the broad beans were never peeled. Only in the last 10 years have I discovered that 'in the very best places' they peeled the skin from the broad beans after having podded them. The sheer colour is probably worth this peeling but the flavour is different and as so many food memories are evocative, I'll stick to them unskinned.

I have on the menu at the moment a very simple country dish of unpeeled broad beans. The last layer remains so that their colour is a dullish green and contrasts with another more elegant dish of squab with beans where we take the beans to their final green stage—but to me they don't taste as good!

Broad beans must be eaten young and as freshly picked as possible to save the sugar from turning to starch and causing the skins to toughen. If, after podding, the skin is quite white, it will be a sure sign that the bean is old. The pods should be bright green, crisp to the touch and without blemishes. It is best to buy them under 10 cm long. If you grow them yourself, try cooking the smallest ones pod and all and toss them with butter and fresh herbs. The small ones are also perfect when eaten raw.

Fresh, tender broad beans team well with other spring delights such as artichokes, asparagus and fresh peas. Try braising them in a little olive oil and water. Start with the artichokes, then the asparagus and broad beans. Lastly you could add freshly shelled peas. Adjust with a little vinegar and serve warm as a complete dish.

BROAD BEANS WITH PASTA AND PROSCIUTTO

2 kg fresh young broad beans
1/2 cup water
1/2 cup olive oil
1/2 cup freshly chopped mint leaves
150 g prosciutto, cut into strips

250 g fresh pasta sheets (I use
hand-made fine ravioli dough cut
into 6 x 4 cm sheets)
1 cup toasted breadcrumbs
1 tablespoon red wine vinegar
salt and pepper

Bring a large saucepan of salted water to the boil in readiness for the pasta. Shell the beans and simmer them in water and oil with a pinch of salt until just cooked (about 7 to 10 minutes). While this is simmering, cook the pasta sheets and drain them (do not refresh, this removes the flavour). Put the sheets out on to a plate or dish and spread them with a little olive oil. Put the pasta in the fridge for 10 minutes to stop it cooking any further.

While the beans are still warm, stir in the breadcrumbs, mint, freshly ground black pepper and vinegar. Add the prosciutto. Adjust with more oil if necessary. Remove the pasta from the fridge, toss with the bean mixture and serve at once at room temperature.

B ROAD BEANS ARE also called fava beans and are available dried. They feature in Italian cookery, especially in soups and casseroles. A purée of fava beans has been a staple in Sicilian cookery for centuries—true 'cucina povera', the traditional cooking of the peasants that is today having a resurgence amongst the more affluent.

STEVE'S BEANS

80 g fava or haricot beans
10 Roma tomatoes or 6
  medium to large tomatoes
100 g stale bread from a crusty
  french stick, cut into slices,
  brushed with olive oil and
  crisped in the oven

1 small bunch basil
1 large red onion, peeled
  and sliced thinly
30 ml red wine vinegar
80 ml olive oil to finish
salt and pepper to taste

Cut the Roma tomatoes into quarters or larger ones into eighths. Allow the crisped bread to cool. Break up the basil leaves and toss them with the cut tomatoes. Season with salt and pepper. Add sliced red onion, beans and bread. Add vinegar and olive oil. Check for seasoning. You could finish this off with some thinly sliced pancetta rounds crisped in the oven and tossed on at the last minute.

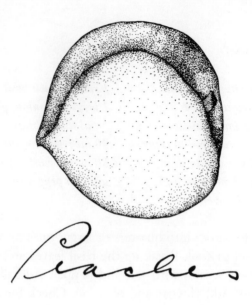

Peaches

THERE IS NOTHING to compare with the perfume and blush of a freshly picked peach! The full potential of white peaches can only really be appreciated if you buy direct from an orchardist who has picked the peach ripe off the tree that day.

The opening quote by James de Coquet in the Peach and Nectarine chapter of *Jane Grigson's Fruit Book* tells us that there are definitely peaches and peaches:

'Renoir used to say to young artists longing to paint—like him—the pinkish-brown tones of an opulent breast: "First paint apples and peaches in a fruit bowl." My greengrocer sold me worthy models for painting. Their curves were perfect and graceful. Their grooves were in exactly the right place. Their gradations of colour were an art school exercise, and as for the velvety down of their skin…"It's the left cheek of my girl", as the Japanese poet has written.'

Peaches bring to mind an abundance of fruit that leads to swapping with friends—when the whole tree ripens at once the spoils must be shared!

Should one eat the skin or not? I asked a few cooks with whom I was sharing a lunch and they were adamant that eating them skins and all is the go. Colin said that the very idea made the hairs on his arms stand on end! It is difficult to eat a peach delicately. I love the juice running down your arm in the effort to savour every mouthful. It is a truly sensuous fruit.

There have been some examples of peaches on the supermarket shelves that I almost have to pick up and smell to make sure they are what they are purporting to be! Seek out those shopkeepers who take extra care and who know the meaning of tree-ripened fruit.

Both in Europe and Japan, many of the fruits we so value are packaged in such a way that they have the same significance as buying a piece of jewellery as a gift. I'm sure we take our natural bounty for granted—our fruit is so inexpensive. But we must be sure that growers receive the return they need to make a good living and be ready to pay for extra quality from those orchardists and shops who take the trouble to present the perfect product.

I had heard for years of a wonderful drink called a 'Bellini', made from white peaches, made famous by Harry's Bar in Venice. My first attempt gave me a drink of such a disappointing grey colour that it made me wonder what people talked about. Then I read the beautiful book *The Harry's Bar Cookbook* by Arrigo Cipriani, the son of the founder of Harry's Bar, and found the reason for my disappointment. Arrigo tells us of the tediousness of making the white peach juice for Bellinis and says that in the 'good old days' they had a man who did nothing all day but cut up and pit small white peaches and squeeze them with his hands to extract the juice. The juice and pulp were then forced through a chinois (a fine, cone-shaped sieve) to form the rose-coloured elixir that is mixed with champagne to make Bellinis. In my first trial I puréed the pulp of the peach in a machine to extract the juice, and this is what made the juice go brown. In France you can now buy frozen white peach juice to make things easier.

HERE IS THE recipe for the Bellini from Harry's Bar. Use white peaches only, and if you do not have a food mill or meat grinder, use your hands.

BELLINI

Use a food mill or meat grinder to make the pulp and then force it through a fine sieve. If the peach purée is very tart, sweeten it with just a little sugar syrup (see below). Refrigerate the purée until it is very cold. Mix it with very cold, dry Prosecco (Italian version of champagne) in the proportion of 1 part peach purée to 3 parts wine or, for each drink, 30 ml (1 ounce) peach purée and 100 ml (3 ounces) wine. Pour the mixture into well-chilled glasses.

SYRUP

1³/4 cups sugar (390 g)
1³/4 cups water (425 ml)

Combine the sugar and water in a medium saucepan over low heat, stirring occasionally, until the sugar is completely dissolved. Increase the heat, bring the mixture to a boil, and boil for 2 or 3 minutes. Remove from the heat and let it cool. Cover the syrup and chill it until it is cold.

———————

The following recipe for baked peaches is a simple Italian-style dessert. We prepare a large tray of this for luncheon service as a summer dessert. To our delight, we found out that if you run out unexpectedly (as we did one day when a particularly frightening food critic visited the restaurant), you can flash the peaches in the microwave for about 3 minutes and the result is perfection!

BAKED PEACHES STUFFED WITH ALMONDS

6 ripe yellow peaches
3/4 cup toasted whole almonds
6 Amaretti biscuits
100 g castor sugar

1 teaspoon crystallised ginger,
finely chopped
200 g unsalted butter
1 cup sauternes

Halve the peaches and remove the pits. Combine the biscuits, almonds and sugar until crumbled. Slightly soften the butter and add it to the crumbs together with the ginger to make a paste. Place the peach halves in a baking dish and mound the mixture around them. Place 1/4 cup sauternes in the bottom of the dish. Bake in a moderate oven for about 15 minutes, basting with the rest of the wine. Slip the peach skins off if you wish and serve with cream or almond ice-cream.

Lemons

T HE VERY CONVENIENCE of having a supply of lemons on a tree is absolutely wonderful—just to be able to walk into the garden when you need a squeeze of lemon for some fresh fish or to make a mayonnaise at the last moment or if, like me, you have a squirt of lemon in very strong black coffee in the morning. To say nothing of the natural beauty of the tree laden with fruit and flowers. And don't forget the gin and tonic on a summer afternoon!

Lemons are as indispensable to my cooking as garlic is. I use lemon zest in my game pies; lemon juice squeezed into the cavity of all the game I cook; lemon juice to curdle the milk for banana cake; lemons in jam to increase the pectin; lemon juice in mayonnaise, hollandaise and vinaigrettes; lemon with seafood; lemon juice added to a pan of frying mushrooms; lemon juice added to water to stop oxidising of vegetables; lemon juice to add balance and zip to a sauce; lemons squeezed on pancakes sprinkled with sugar and then rolled up tight; lemons in home-made lemonade; lemons for squeezing over grilled offal; lemons for adding to jugs of rainwater on the table; lemons for cleaning your hands after peeling beetroot; lemons for a burnt butter sauce with capers and parsley to go with brains; and lemons for lemon curd or lemon meringue pie.

Lemons are not at their peak until late spring or early summer. If you have a lemon crop in your back yard and would like to have lemons the year round, then you must thin the crop of growing lemons heavily. Take up to half the lemons off now and in 6 months' time you will be picking mature lemons alongside baby lemons forming and there will be flowers on the tree to keep the cycle going.

Lance Minge is my local nurseryman and he has loads of citrus experience. He is adamant that the Lisbon lemon is the only one to have in the home garden. If you thin the crop as outlined above, this lemon will perform for your household for the whole year.

Lemons don't like clay, nor do they like wet feet. The tree needs consistent watering through the hot summer months and shouldn't be overfed. Overfeeding will give very large fruit and will make the skins too thick. If you have the wrong kind of soil you can plant a lemon tree in a 1¹/2 metre square patch of sandy loam built up about 30cm high with railway sleepers. Mr Minge recommends planting in the hottest spot you have in your garden, against the northern side of a fence or shed. Do this for all citrus trees and ensure that you keep the ground moist.

There are two other lemons freely available. The Meyer, a cross between the orange and lemon, more orange in colour than the lemon and not nearly as sour, is a bushy tree and does well in pots. The Eureka is a more upright tree like the Lisbon, growing up to 5 m tall. Its fruit is deliciously sour! It is used particularly for commercial juicing as it has a large fruit and is easy to pick with a thicker skin and barely any thorns.

The thick skin of the Lisbon occurs only when the tree is young and growing vigorously. As the tree gets older, the skins become thinner.

A handy tip for extracting more juice from a lemon or lime is to pour boiling water over the skin 5 minutes before squeezing it. If you have a microwave, put the fruit in on medium for 1 minute and leave to cool a little before squeezing. This is a particularly handy tip for limes when you require enough juice for a refreshing summer juice of lemon, lime and bitters or, after a hard day at the hot stoves, something more exotic such as a daiquiri or a margarita.

Never waste the skin (or zest) of a lemon. Jane Grigson, in her *Fruit Book*, describes cutting the skin from the fruit and hanging it to dry in a warm place—by an open window if sunny. Put 80 g of the leathery skin into a jar with 500 g sugar to make aromatic lemon-flavoured sugar. Jane Grigson's recipe for Candied Grapefruit and Citrus Peel is a classic.

PRESERVED LEMONS

Make the lemons as juicy as possible by warming them in the microwave. Then quarter them from the top to within 1 cm of the bottom. Sprinkle salt on the flesh and then push the lemon back into shape. Place 1 tablespoon salt on the bottom of the jar and pack in the lemons, pressing them down as much as possible to release the lemon juice. Squeeze more juice into the jar so that the lemons are covered.

Shake the jar each day to distribute the salt and juice. Rinse the lemons before using them.

Most people use only the rind—the pulp will be very salty and sour. After opening, pour a layer of olive oil over the lemons.

PICKLED LIMES OR LEMONS

This recipe is inspired by Claudia Roden's version. Make it with whichever fruit is cheapest and most plentiful.

Scrub and slice the fruit. Put a single layer in a colander or a pierced strainer, or on a tilted plate. Sprinkle generously with salt. Leave to drain for at least 24 hours until they are soft, limp and have lost their bitterness. Put the slices in layers in a glass jar, sprinkling each layer with a little paprika. Pour on some ground nut oil or sunflower oil (olive oil will be too strong). Close the jar and leave for at least three weeks. Serve the rind with rice and meat or fish dishes, or as a pickle with cold meat or fish.

SPINACH WITH LEMON

1 bunch spinach (210 g after *freshly ground black pepper*
cleaning and trimming) *Maldon sea salt*
2 cloves garlic, bruised *juice of 1 lemon*
4 dessertspoons virgin olive oil

Break up the spinach leaves. Toss quickly in the olive oil with the bruised garlic cloves until just limp. Season with salt and pepper and the lemon juice. Remove from the heat and toss until well incorporated. The spinach should be only just cooked and have kept its colour. Good with any grills, chicken and of course fish.

LEMON TART

This is my version of Tony Bilson's Lemon Tart.

1 short crust tart base, baked
blind (see Sour Cream
Pastry, page 60)
150 g sugar

100 ml lemon juice
grated zest of one lemon
8 egg yolks
600 ml cream or crème fraîche

Beat the sugar, egg yolks, lemon juice and zest together until smooth (you could use 9 eggs if you require a firmer sit to the dessert). Incorporate the cream.

Check the tart case to make sure there are no cracks. These can be repaired with a little raw dough. Place the tart case, still in its baking dish, on the central oven shelf (pre-heated to 180°C) and fill the case with the cream mixture, taking care not to overfill the case. Bake until the custard has just set, about 25 minutes. Serve lukewarm, dusted with icing sugar. The texture should be that of a light brie (depending on how many eggs are used).

LEMON ICE-CREAM

5 egg yolks
1 1/2 cups sugar
250 ml milk

250 ml cream
juice and zest of 3 lemons

Heat the milk with the lemon zest and juice. Bring to the boil. Make custard with the egg yolks, sugar and cream. Add the milk to the custard. Cool and turn in ice-cream machine.

L IMES ARE AN offshoot of the lemon and have a very special flavour of their own. They fruit at the same time as lemons and are well worth a position in the garden or a tub although they do not do as well in Mediterranean climates as lemons. To be very successful, limes need to grow in tropical conditions. Limes are aromatic and have a strange coconut smell about them. They are interchangeable with lemon for most uses, bringing an extra tang to a dish as they are stronger than lemons.

Mrs Beeton's Cookbook has a recipe for half lemon and half lime cordial where the juice and zest are reduced on the stove with sugar to taste and then kept cold in the fridge with a jug of iced water.

For those of us who love lime cordial but don't have the time to make it, there is the truly South Australian institution of Bickford's Lime Cordial, widely available in Australia. Bickford's have been producing this top class product since 1874. The base of lime concentrate actually has to come from the West Indies because no one in Australia can supply them with adequate quantities of lime. The cordial is a brown colour because when transported from the West Indies 100 years ago the limes oxidised en route and the public have been familiar with this colour cordial since the beginning. Bickfords' managing director suggests that to change the colour now would be like making Coca-Cola clear! He also says that should there be sufficient limes available in Australia, they would be happy to use the local product.

I READ A LOVELY Japanese folk saying in Cherry Ripe's column in the *Australian*, quoted from Max Lake's *Scents and Sensuality*, 'To find and enjoy a new flavour adds seventy-five days to your life.'

Cherry was discussing the fervour with which the Japanese embrace new food flavours from other countries, in particular McDonalds and Coca-Cola. It is possible to break away from 'junk' foods yet find variety in new foods that can be prepared so easily they can almost be called 'convenience foods'. Variety is not only important to the diet, it's fun as well!

Quail has become standard fare in restaurants over the last few years and is well worth considering for variety in cooking at home. It is tasty, healthy and relatively inexpensive, and can be prepared and cooked in less than fifteen minutes (if you choose not to marinate it). It can be barbecued, pan fried, pot roasted or oven baked and is equally tasty served cold at picnics, warm in salads or hot for dinner. What more could you want?

There is a world of difference between a perfectly-cooked quail and one that has been abused by overcooking. The best tip I can give you is to prepare quail by cutting them along the spine and squashing them flat with the palm of your hand ('butterflying') for easier cooking. (This will not apply, of course, if you wish to stuff and bake them.)

Make sure to tuck their wings behind them so the breast can cook evenly. In readiness for cooking you can coat them lightly with olive oil, some freshly-ground black pepper and fresh herbs, or make a marinade. The restaurant kitchen's favourite marinade is made of fresh ginger, sliced garlic and equal quantities of honey and soy sauce. The quail is marinated overnight, skin side down, and brushed with the mixture while cooking.

If you prefer something simpler, try some honey and lemon juice, or just olive oil, lemon juice and thyme. Be careful with the lemon, though, as the juice will actually begin 'cooking' the meat before any contact with the stove. I use the lemon juice options for only about 20 minutes maximum. These ideas could also be used for chicken legs, breasts or wings.

An important trick of the trade when barbecuing these small birds (particularly those which have had honey in the marinade) is to turn them at no more than two-minute intervals. It may seem a bit of trouble but such small details make the difference between good and average cooking. If you don't turn them, you will end up with a burnt offering.

As they are such small birds, quail will dry out rapidly if overcooked, so, if barbecuing, allow about 8 minutes for cooking and then pull to the side to rest for 5 minutes before serving. The quail should still be a little pink on the breast (I don't mean raw) and will be juicy and delicious. If overcooked, they will be like cardboard.

When buying several quail, you will find at least some variance in their sizes: the plumper ones will need an extra minute or two of cooking time. This is another of those small details that make cooking more difficult, but also more rewarding when you get it right.

If you wish to pan fry your quail on the stove, allow closer to 12 minutes. The trick here is to choose a pan large enough so that you do indeed fry gently (instead of poach) your food. For example, for two quail that have been butterflied you will need a pan measuring about 22 cm, with about 2-3 teaspoons of butter or olive oil. I prefer to use butter, making sure it turns golden brown before I put the quail in, skin side down. I then season with a sprinkle of salt and pepper and wait until the skin is a light golden brown all over before turning.

The important thing is to adjust the flame so the butter doesn't burn. If you can keep the butter that lovely golden brown then you know the quail is cooking gently enough. Add a touch of oil if you are worried about giving it your undivided attention so that the butter doesn't burn.

It is also important not to sear the quail as, not only will it look unattractive, it will toughen it. This is a simple principle of cooking I see most often abused.

Because you start with quite a high temperature to get the butter golden and need to turn it down to save the quail from burning, it's difficult to move far from the stove. If you prefer, you can just brown the birds on both sides and then place the pan in a hot oven to finish off. If you choose this method, cook the quail for about 4 to 6 minutes in the oven and leave it to rest for another 5 minutes on a plate on top of the stove. As everyone's oven is different, it is only practice that will teach you the right cooking time.

If you wish to serve one quail per person for a meal, you would probably need either to stuff each one or serve it with polenta—both are fabulous options. When we first opened the farm shop I used to make a simple stuffing of rice, lots of diced onion softened in butter, orange rind, currants, almond slices and a little thyme. It was tasty and filling and still stands up as a dish I would cook today. I would also glaze the outside of the bird with a little orange juice and olive oil to caramelise the skin as it baked. The stuffed birds require about 10 minutes in the oven. Test for cooking by gently prising one leg away—if it resists being pulled, it is not ready.

My favourite way of eating quail is at autumn picnics and barbecues, when I stuff them with figs, and wrap them in either bacon or a thin slice of pork fat, fastened with a toothpick. These must not be prepared in advance, however, because if the fig is left in the quail for any period before cooking it has a most unusual effect on the uncooked meat and turns it mushy.

⸻

I PARTICULARLY LIKE a bowl of soft polenta served in a large dish, topped with pan fried quail with all their juices, and perhaps some caramelised onions. A great winter's meal!

POLENTA TO TEAM WITH QUAIL

2 cups polenta
32/3 cups good jellied chicken stock
100 g Parmesan, grated

2 teaspoons salt
1 dessertspoon butter (optional)

Heat half the stock until simmering. Mix the other half of the stock with the polenta while it is still cold, to make a paste. Add the hot stock, stirring constantly to avoid lumping. Season. Stir continuously over a low flame until you see the polenta coming away from the sides of the saucepan (about 20 minutes). Add the Parmesan and the butter if desired. Serve.

THERE IS A very good recipe for grilled quail in *Mediterranean Cooking* by Paula Wolfert which embodies the simplicity of cooking quail. It calls for leaving the quail in a marinade of olive oil, dried oregano, crumbled bay leaves, salt and pepper for a few hours before grilling them on a barbecue and serving with lemon wedges.

Here is a recipe for something more formal.

TART OF QUAIL BREAST WITH SAGE, BACON AND GRAPES

PASTRY
250 g flour   *125 g sour cream*
200 g butter

Combine the flour, butter and cream by pulsing in the food processor. Rest for 20 minutes and then roll into desired tart shapes. I use a brioche mould for this tart. Bake the tart bases.

FILLING
6 quails   *200 ml verjuice (see page 161)*
8 sage leaves   *1 litre golden chicken stock*
200 g seedless grapes, taken off   *butter*
* the stem*   *2 onions*
3 slices sugar-cured bacon (my   *1 carrot*
* favourite is from Schulz's*   *2 sticks celery*
* of Angaston)*   *salt and pepper*

Seal the quail with the sage leaves in a large frypan, taking care to keep the butter nut-brown. Season with salt and pepper. Reserve the sage leaves, making sure they are crispy but not burnt. Place the quail in the oven at 220°C for 4 to 5 minutes. Remove from the oven, turn over and rest for at least 10 minutes. While the quail are resting, brown the stock vegetables in the oven, allowing them to caramelise but not burn.

Gently pull the legs away from the frame and carve the breasts off the bone.

Taking the pan the quails were browned in, discard any excess butter and deglaze the pan with verjuice. Reduce.

Add the browned stock vegetables and the litre of chicken stock and boil the sauce until it reaches a thick syrupy consistency. Strain.

Cut the bacon slices in half and cook. Warm the pastry cases in the oven. Also warm the quail, bacon and sage. To assemble, pile the quail, bacon and sage into the cases. Bring the sauce back to the boil and throw in the grapes for about 30 seconds. Using a slotted spoon, place most of the grapes on top of the tarts, letting the balance cascade with the sauce.

Salad

THE LETTUCE HAS advanced so far from the humble iceberg that we all know, and some love. We can now choose from mignonette (both red and green), butter lettuce, regency, cos (red and green), oakleaf (red and green) and elkhorn. These are all soft lettuces—they don't form a heart the same way as the iceberg, though cos does form an inner heart of a kind and it is the brilliant 'apple green' inner leaves that I use.

Not only can you buy all these lettuces from good greengrocers, you can also grow many of them successfully in even the smallest plot at home—and then just pick the fresh leaves as you need them. Mignonette, cos and butter lettuce seeds should be available from your local nursery. If you are having trouble locating any particular varieties you could request a catalogue from the New Gippsland Seed Farm, PO Box 1, Silvan, Victoria, 3795.

Rocket is a peppery herb—known as arugula in Italian cooking and roquette in French. It is a green I hate to be without—it has such a distinctive flavour. Not everyone shares my feelings; a few weeks ago a customer complained about the plate of weeds I served. As we use rocket when it is very young, we often serve it well washed with roots and all. Pile it in a plate with freshly shaved Parmigiano Reggiano and slivers of fresh pear. You could also thrown in olives, sun-dried tomatoes and roasted almond slivers.

Lamb's lettuce is also known as corn salad or mache. A lovely salad our South Australian team served in the Seppelt's Menu of the Year competition was just 4 or 5 tiny lamb's lettuce leaves per person, served on an individual plate with roasted pine nuts, small garlic croutons and a delicate dressing. Now that's what I call a salad!

Don't forget the various varieties of cress when making salads or sandwiches. Watch out for land cress, curled cress, mustard cress and English cress (milder than the others).

Snow pea sprouts have a lovely sweet flavour with a crunch and I love to use them in any tossed or warm salad. A warm salad of quail with, say, bacon, garlic croutons and snow pea sprouts tossed with some other bitter greens can make a very delicious and pretty luncheon dish.

There is a green called mizuna and one called tat soy that has an oriental feel. Tat soy teams perfectly with squid and mizuna, and combined with any other greens, will accompany goat's cheese or roasted capsicum.

Many greengrocers now have a mesclun mix for sale. You can make your own mix by buying a variety of lettuces, choosing for colour and flavour, and then adding whatever you like from the herb range. For example, take some rocket, mizuna, snow pea sprouts, cress and lamb's lettuce and toss them together.

Another group of salad plants with a stronger flavour are those such as radicchio, witlof or chickory. Both witlof and chickory are wonderful braised or baked as well as used in salads. One really needs an illustrated atlas of greens, there are so many, and certainly witlof, chickory and endive are often confused.

Sorrel looks a little like baby spinach leaves. It has a strong piquant flavour and I like to use the baby leaves in a salad. You can use sorrel for sauces, mayonnaises or compound butters as it has an unmistakable flavour.

Mustards are lovely to throw in a salad too. Don't forget nasturtium leaves and flowers, with their peppery flavour. It is interesting to observe the difference in taste between the normal orange nasturtium and the pale lemony one.

The important tool for salads is the salad spinner. Having washed the leaves and dried them in a spinner, store them in an everfresh bag in the fridge until required.

The options for salad dressings are as varied as the possibilities for the salad itself. As a rule of thumb, I use a ration of 4 parts oil to 1 part acidulant. That could be red wine vinegar, balsamic vinegar, verjuice, sherry, champagne, cider vinegar or lime juice. Or a combination of vinegar with grapefruit or orange juice. The other components of a salad dressing can be fresh herbs, garlic, pepper, mustard or mustard seeds, cream and sugar.

I always crush garlic with the wide blade of a knife and never use a garlic press. A stone mortar and pestle is best for pounding mustard seeds or similar.

A salad should have colour, flavour and crunch—use any combination of foods that appeal to you but remember not to dress the salad until the last minute. A wonderfully fresh salad will make a difference to any meal.

CAESAR SALAD

2 to 3 medium-sized heads cos lettuce (about 6 leaves per person, use only the brilliant green inner leaves)
2 eggs
150 ml olive oil, plus extra for frying
juice of one lemon

salt and pepper to taste
1 teaspoon finely chopped garlic
bread for croutons cut 1 1/2 cm thick
—use about 6 to 8 croutons per person
8 to 12 anchovy fillets
200 g Parmigiano Reggiano, shaved

Wash and spin dry the lettuces. Chill. Trim the crusts from the bread and cut into squares. Cover a heavy-based pan with 1 cm olive oil and bring to a high heat. Brown the croutons on all sides, adding more oil if necessary. Take the pan from the heat and add the garlic. Remove the croutons with a slotted spoon and drain on absorbent paper.

In a separate saucepan, bring water to the boil and plunge the eggs in for one minute only. Remove and leave to rest. Beat together the olive oil, lemon juice, salt and pepper. Break in the very soft eggs and whisk until creamy. Toss the lettuce leaves with the dressing, until thoroughly coated. Sprinkle with Parmesan and scatter anchovies and warm croutons over the top. Serve.

Tomatoes

THE TOMATO IS surely the essence of summer and is the simplest food to make into a tasty snack, a light lunch or a substantial dinner with the smallest amount of effort and fuss.

A piece of rye toast spread with unsalted butter and thick slices of very ripe tomatoes topped with a little ground pepper is something I love. Until I came to live in South Australia tomato on toast meant cooked tomatoes that made the toast sloppy, and it was one of the few food horrors of my childhood.

Tomatoes for lunch might mean toast again but this time slices of thick, crusty white or rye bread, toasted until light brown on both sides, and rubbed on one side with a clove of garlic. Then take a very ripe tomato, cut it in half and rub it over the garlic toast, squeezing until the juice soaks through the toast. Sprinkle with a little olive oil, salt and pepper.

The most important point about tomatoes is that they must be very ripe. Tomatoes that have ripened on the vine will be the sweetest but even if you buy them partially ripe, leave them on the kitchen table or window sill to colour to a deep red before refrigerating them. If possible, organise your shopping so that you have only enough tomatoes ripe at one time that you don't have to put them in the fridge. Like strawberries and many other foods, their flavour is dulled by refrigeration.

Many recipes call for peeled, seeded and chopped tomatoes. This is very simple to do. Bring a large pan of water to the boil. With a small, sharp knife cut out the core of the tomato, and then using the point of the knife make a small cross at the bottom of the tomato. Immerse it in the boiling water on a large slotted spoon and hold it there for about 12 seconds until the skin starts to peel away from the cross. Lift the tomato out and let it cool a little before peeling. If you wish to seed the tomato, cut the peeled tomato in half crosswise and squeeze, then use your knife to scrape away the remaining seeds. Chop as required.

I buy my tomatoes from Bill Gray of Springton who runs Rainbow Valley Producers. As well as his wonderful strawberries, he grows perfect tomatoes which he picks ripe for selling commercially. I try to spread the word to find as many outlets for him as possible. Sometimes Bill is left with hundreds of kilos of ripe tomatoes which the general trade would call over-ripe. Knowing of my passion for them and my horror of waste of such quality, Bill will give them to me to pulp for the winter. Luckily he is a man who loves his food and has a particular passion for guinea fowl so I have the chance to repay him from time to time. I, however, have been the winner many times over as his enthusiasm for his product and anything new to experiment with is such a delight. He looks a little like a leprechaun and will just appear at my kitchen door saying, 'Maggie, I think these are just your type of thing, come and have a taste.'

———

THIS SOUP WAS inspired by Richard Olney's Grape Harvester's Soup from his book *Simple French Food*. I first made it to feed my staff when we closed up shop to hand pick the semillon in our vineyard. I wanted something tasty, filling and easy to transport, a meal in itself. I used about double the tomatoes and a lot less water than the original recipe and I love it so much that it always goes back on the menu during vintage.

Tomato Soup for Vintage

1 kg onions, thinly sliced (I use
 brown onions)
4 tablespoons olive oil
salt
4 cloves garlic, peeled and finely
 chopped

6 medium tomatoes, very ripe yet
 firm
1/2 teaspoon sugar
125 ml dry white wine
1 litre boiling water
slices of stale bread

Using a large, heavy pan, cook the onions gently in the oil, stirring with a wooden spoon until they are uniformly light golden and very soft. Add the salt and the garlic. Cut out the core of the tomatoes—for this rustic soup I do not peel or seed them. Cut each tomato in half and then into quarters or eighths. Add the tomatoes to the pan and the sugar to sweeten if you wish. (The sugar merely enhances the flavour of the tomato and gives a boost if they are not in perfect condition.)

Cook for 10 minutes and then add the wine and water. (For an over-the-top soup you could leave out the water altogether! This is also wonderful as a topping for a hot or cold pasta dish.) Simmer covered for 45 minutes before serving. Spread a little olive oil over each slice of stale bread and place a slice on each serving bowl. Pour the soup over the bread.

Fresh tomato sauce or concasse is a simple sauce to make as an accompaniment to a dish or to heighten the flavour of a slow-cooking pot roast. Add fresh herbs such as basil, chervil or fresh thyme flowers to suit. Thyme flowers, chopped and added to the tomato for a rabbit pot roast, would be wonderful—with some chopped olives thrown in too.

Tomato Concasse

750 g ripe tomatoes, peeled, seeded
 and coarsely chopped
25 g butter
5 tablespoons olive oil
3 golden shallots, finely chopped
2 cloves garlic, peeled

3 sprigs thyme
4 sprigs Italian parsley
1/2 tablespoon sugar
coarse salt and freshly ground black
 pepper

Use a big pan or saucepan with a large surface area. Gently bring the butter and oil to a moderate heat and cook the shallots carefully until they soften (do not allow them to burn). Add the tomatoes and then the garlic and herbs (unchopped) together with the salt, pepper and sugar. Bring to the boil, stirring thoroughly with a wooden spoon, allowing the liquid to evaporate. (If the tomatoes lack colour you could add 2 teaspoons of tomato purée.)

When the sauce has reduced remove the herbs and garlic cloves. Purée in a food processor. The tomato seeds contain a bitter oil and if any seeds have remained the processing will increase their bitterness. Most Italian grocers can sell you a special tomato food mill to simplify this process. This sauce can be kept in the fridge for days or frozen until needed. It is wonderful with pasta.

TOMATO YABBIE JELLY

600 g firm, ripe tomatoes
1 large clove garlic
1/2 dessertspoon brown sugar
3 gelatine leaves
6 basil leaves

freshly ground black pepper and salt
12 large yabbies to cook in a
large pot of boiling water with
1 tablespoon salt and
1 tablespoon dill seed

Roughly chop the tomatoes and put them in a large enamel saucepan to boil with the garlic. Use the brown sugar only if required to enhance the flavour of the tomatoes. Cook the tomatoes down to a pulp and strain all the juice, rejecting the skins and seeds.

Cook the yabbies by bringing the water, salt and dill to the boil vigorously, throwing the yabbies in and allowing the water to come back to the boil. Boil for 3 minutes (for large yabbies). Take the yabbies out and set them aside (do not refresh). Peel when cool.

Soak the gelatine sheets in water and add to tomato juice with the torn basil leaves. Season. Take glass jelly moulds or similar and set a little tomato jelly in the bottom. Place the peeled yabbies on top of the first layer of set jelly and cover with the balance of the tomato. Set in the refrigerator and serve with a little virgin olive oil, crushed black pepper and perhaps a wedge of lemon. Eat with crusty bread.

A CLOSE FRIEND from Tasmania kindly passed on two of her family recipes for tomato sauce and chutney. The sauce was always poured into 'three empty gin bottles'. I have played with the balance of quantities in the chutney recipe and added the onions.

LITTLE BLANCHE'S TOMATO SAUCE

5 kg tomatoes, ripened on the vine
1 kg onions, peeled and
 roughly chopped
1.2 litres rain water
1.8 litres vinegar
25 g garlic cloves

10 g cayenne pepper
50 g whole black peppercorns
30 g whole cloves
100 g salt
30 g ground allspice
1.25 kg brown sugar

Mince together all the ingredients (an old hand mincer is perfect for this) and cook in a stainless steel or enamel pot for 4 hours, stirring constantly. Strain through a fine colander and bottle.

LITTLE BLANCHE'S RIPE TOMATO CHUTNEY

750 g raisins
1.5 kg granny smith apples
4.5 kg tomatoes, ripened on the vine
2 kg brown onions, peeled
 and finely chopped
125 g salt

2 kg sugar
800 ml vinegar
125 g garlic cloves
60 g grated green ginger
1 ripe chilli

Peel and core the apples and chop them roughly. Cut the tomatoes into eighths and cook with the apples and onions. Add all other ingredients and boil gently for 2 to 3 hours. Reduce any excess liquid at a high temperature. Bottle.

Christmas

THERE ARE SO many options for Christmas lunch but, for me, the best is a lunch of simplicity and style with people you care about. I feel strongly about family traditions and somehow, in my family, all our traditions come back to food. The difficulty arises in a partnership when you suddenly find you have two differing sets of traditions.

There are two options! One is to compromise to keep the extended family together; the other is for each family, at some stage, to begin their own set of traditions. When children are young, nothing is more fun than the gathering together of all the cousins and sharing the fun of presents under the tree. As the children grow up, they start to want their 'special friends' to join them on Christmas Day. So, either the family group becomes larger (as long as each contributing family can find common ground to enjoy the day) or an alternative day is found for the extended family get-together and new traditions develop that will probably stay in place for the next generation. Whatever path is chosen, the most important thing, as far as food is concerned, is the sharing of good food.

As a child in Sydney, our Christmas lunch was casual but wonderful. Both my mum and dad were great cooks but very little work was done on Christmas Day. We shared the day with relatives and friends and the common theme was always a large table laden with food. Sometimes this would be inside, sometimes in the garden, several times, actually on the beach.

When I was very young, the pride of the table would be a roast chook. It's hard to remember just what a luxury that was, though I do remember the kerfuffle when dad killed it in the back yard, which my brothers delighted in—but mum and I always had the job of plucking and cleaning it. A pretty typical household of the time!

Our food became more lavish as the years progressed and goose became the star of the table. For me it has been so ever since—Christmas without goose just doesn't seem right. There was sometimes duck or chook as well, depending on how many people there were to feed. We often began with fresh Hawkesbury River oysters, and I do remember having wine with the meal (but never champagne, as we might today). There would be lots of salads on the table—simple things like fresh tomatoes and beetroots cooked and sliced into vinegar with onion, and lovely fresh potato salad. I think the mayonnaise was made with condensed milk and vinegar then, but I remember it tasting wonderful. The only thing we would actually cook on the day were the potatoes—even the goose would be cooked on Christmas Eve and left in the food safe.

We would also have a ham or a hand of pork, and a wonderful brawn my parents made that filled the crispers of our old fridge.

———

BRAWN

1 pig's head, cut into 4 (the tongue was not present in the one I bought)
4 sheep's tongues, brined
2 brined pig's trotters (they are not salty enough if not brined)
1 knuckle veal
3 tablespoons white wine vinegar
3 onions

2 carrots
3 leeks
5 sprigs parsley, plus extra
2 fresh bay leaves
2 sprigs thyme
10 crushed juniper berries
10 allspice berries
1 cup white wine
juice of a lemon, and zest of lemon or orange

Remove the brain from the pig's head—otherwise it will limit the life of the finished brawn. Wash all the pieces of meat and vegetables well. Put the meat into a large stockpot. Add the chopped vegetables, herbs and berries. Just cover with water and simmer very, very slowly until the meat falls off the bone. This takes about 5 hours with a simmer pad under the pot to slow the cooking. Brawn, like stock, can be cooked too much so that all the goodness is cooked out of it. Skim occasionally as it cooks and, when finished, allow to cool in the pot and remove any fat residue. The cooking liquid will be jellied when it is cold, so pick through the meat while still warm, trimming off any skin, bone or gristle, and put it in a bowl. I prefer to leave some meat whole, or in large chunks, such as the tongues and cheeks. There should be a mixture of sizes and textures in the finished product.

Bring the stock to the boil and strain immediately. Take two cups of strained stock and the wine and boil it, reducing it by half. Taste and add salt if required and pepper, and lemon juice if you think it needs it.

Add the meat pieces to the reduced stock and wine and simmer for just a few minutes. Check the seasoning. Remember that you will eat it cold, so it will need to be more highly seasoned than usual. Add lemon or orange zest to taste and freshly chopped parsley. Pour into a glass bowl and leave it to set. Serve cold with crusty bread and homemade pickles.

The one constant of my family's tradition was my Aunty Reta's Christmas pudding. I remember, as a child, the thrill of finding threepence in it—I know this practice is discouraged now but it isn't the same without it. My aunt is now eighty years old and still contributes the pudding wherever she spends Christmas. It remains the best pudding I have ever tasted—so moist and luscious, with both fruit and rum. I must admit we never had room for it at lunch and would always walk or sleep in the afternoon and have the pudding at night. Although my aunt gave me her recipe three years ago I have yet to make it as, in my mind, it is her province.

Since my parents died, it has possibly become even more important to me to keep their traditions going for my children to enjoy. This is a simple sort of lunch for Christmas Day, which we eat either sitting under the pear tree at the bottom of the garden or in the cool of the evening on the beach at Colin's family's holiday shack.

Yabbies with a walnut dressing

Roast goose with stuffing of apples, onions and sage, served with a warm salad of waxy potatoes, prosciutto and bitter greens

---

Traditional Christmas pudding

YABBIES WITH WALNUT DRESSING

Yabbies are best cooked in boiling salted water with fresh dill and caraway seeds. Bring the water to the boil and throw in the yabbies. Boil them rapidly for 3 minutes. Drain and allow to cool. Peel and toss with sauce.

WALNUT SAUCE
150 g walnuts	*60 ml lemon juice*
1 slice white bread	*salt and pepper to taste*
2 tablespoons milk	*70 ml walnut oil*
2 cloves garlic	

Roast the walnuts in the oven and, while still warm, rub skins off in a tea towel. Using a mortar and pestle or food processor, grind walnuts to a fine paste. Remove crusts from bread and soak in the milk, squeezing out as much liquid as possible by hand. Peel garlic cloves and crush with a little salt under the wide blade of a cooking knife. Mix with the soaked bread and lemon juice to a smooth paste. Add walnuts and continue mixing in the food processor, adding the walnut oil slowly as if making a mayonnaise. Season with salt and pepper if necessary. Serve, chilled, with yabbies.

ROAST GOOSE WITH APPLE, ONION AND SAGE STUFFING

3¹/₂ to 4 kg goose

STUFFING

8 onions, finely chopped
30 sage leaves
1 cup chopped pale green celery
leaves
250 g dried apples, minced

2 cups walnuts, chopped after
roasting and rubbing off skins
5 cups stale grated breadcrumbs
salt, pepper and nutmeg to taste
2/3 cup butter

Sauté chopped onion in butter and, when almost cooked, add celery leaves. Take half a cup of this onion and celery and mix it with one third of the apple mince and half the sage. Ease as much of this mixture as you can between the skin and flesh to prevent the bird from drying out. Put any that is left into the stuffing for the cavity.

To the rest of the onion and celery, add breadcrumbs, walnuts and apple and season. Moisten mixture with a little dry sherry if needed. Stuff bird and secure cavity. Either sew it up or use a whole apple to stop the stuffing protruding. When I use an apple I find a metal skewer sufficient to keep the stuffing from falling out.

Place stuffed goose in a large baking tray and coat with a little olive oil and verjuice (or lemon juice) to create a caramelisation of the skin. If you wish, pour a little stock or water in the bottom of the baking dish and cook in the oven at 175°C for approximately one and a half hours. Let it rest upside down for at least 30 minutes before carving (I am talking of a goose which is about 10-12 weeks old). When cooked, the legs must easily come away from the bone.

For such a casual meal, I would serve with an apple aoli rather than a sauce. An alternative would be a jar of quality cranberry jelly.

APPLE AOLI

4 egg yolks
2 cloves garlic
juice of one lemon

2 cups olive oil
grated flesh of 1 granny smith,
soaked immediately with the
lemon juice

Process the yolks with the garlic, grated apple and lemon juice. Add half the oil in a thin stream and then more rapidly. Season.

AUNT RETA'S CHRISTMAS PUDDING
(SERVES 12 TO 16)

500 g currants	*380 g dark brown sugar*
400 g sultanas	*8 eggs*
200 g muscatels	*1 tablespoon mixed nutmeg and*
200 g mixed peel	*cinnamon*
200 g glacé cherries	*675 g self-raising flour*
1 1/2 cups overproof rum	*pinch salt*
380 g butter	

Mix the fruit and soak overnight in rum. Cream butter and sugar then mix in eggs, one at a time. Stir in the fruit, rum and spices. Sift in flour with a large pinch of salt and mix well. Dust a square of washed calico (approximately 45 cm square) with flour. Spoon pudding mixture into the centre of the cloth, pull the corners and edges to the centre and tie well to secure.

Fill a large pan with water and boil. Immerse pudding, bring water back to the boil and let it bubble quietly for 6 hours. Keep pudding immersed. When cooked, hang in a well-ventilated place to dry until required. Boil pudding again in a large pot of water for an hour. Unwrap and serve.

Gooseberries

GOOSEBERRIES ARE BECOMING more readily available and the sharp green gooseberry we know is worth remembering for refreshing summer desserts and for accompanying game.

So far I have not seen the white, yellow and red varieties which are sweeter than the green and can be eaten like strawberries. These are popular in England and Scotland. As with all foods, as soon as an interest is created, some enterprising gardener will seek out the plants and attempt to find and supply a market. Let's hope this soon happens with these sweet gooseberries.

The hairy outer skin can be off-putting if the fruit is not ripe. Gooseberries are a naturally tart fruit but picked at the right stage are beautiful eaten raw from the garden—firm and green and yet lush! There are many seeds and the fruit is juicy and sharp. They are the perfect fruit for people like myself who have a taste for the sour. Gooseberries are wonderful for using in cakes and puddings and also with goose, pheasant or duck where the sharp flavour cuts into the richness of the meat.

Gooseberries have a lyrical connection with elder-flowers. Gooseberry and Elderflower Jelly, from *Jane Grigson's Fruit Book*, inspired our own version which follows her procedure exactly except that we halve the amount of sugar. The elderflower gives a vanilla quality to the jelly and when some of the tiny, lacy flowers are scattered on top of the almost-set jelly, it shimmers as it quivers!

Gooseberry Sauce for Game

250 g punnet gooseberries   *30 g sugar*
90 g butter   *200 ml chicken or game stock*

Wash the fruit well and then top and tail each berry. Melt the butter and sugar and add the gooseberries. Simmer for about 3 minutes. Add stock and reduce a little. If you wish to serve the gooseberries in the sauce, remove them with a slotted spoon after a few minutes' reduction to keep them whole. If you desire a purée, reduce them further. The seeds are very soft and it is optional whether you pass the purée through a sieve or not.

Preserves

I HAD AN ENORMOUS amount of satisfaction recently seeing a marked increase in the 'Preserves' section of the Angaston Show and watching the theatrical Mrs Stiller, who had the task of judging the many entries. This satisfaction came from our sponsorship (with a modest sum, in business terms) of that part of our local show that seemed to be dying. The delight versus the financial outlay made it the most pleasurable donation we have ever made, and I would encourage others to get involved. For instance, it would be good to see flour manufacturers sponsor the cake section and an appropriate organisation sponsor the home-made butter (there was even a goat butter there). Perhaps the show committee could add an 'Unusual Vegetables' category to their vegetable section, to encourage growers of salsify and scorzonera and other exotics that tend not to be grown commercially.

Certainly we restaurateurs would benefit from this, but the flow-on would be to the general public. It really is important that these crafts are not lost to the younger generation, particularly in the Barossa, where the life of self-sufficiency and barter was well-established in the early days of settlement.

I live my life in such a rush that I can seldom take the time to enjoy such occasions, but it was a privilege to see the final stages of setting up the hall and the judging, and brought to mind the resourcefulness of Barossa Valley people. The base of our food source is in the hands of such country people, so we should encourage them and make it worth their while.

If you are looking for a reason for a family day in the country that won't cost you a fortune, there is also the Tanunda show in March. It is always a delight to see the display set up each year by the Lone Pine Agricultural Bureau, and to see what small communities can achieve. As well as the agricultural emphasis, there are the very important dog and horse shows. There are no expensive show bags and lots of things for the children to do. Country shows such as this are held throughout the year in different districts all over Australia. People like Mrs Stiller and her husband travel the circuit and obviously enjoy immensely the life they have created. I only hope that she is training a successor!

One of the attractions of the Tanunda Show is the Dill Pickle Championship, which is taken extremely seriously by both locals and judges. Having spent three years as Associate Judge and then a year as 'Chief Dill', I can assure you that the white coats and spittoons are there for very practical reasons. Not every dill pickle is worthy of eating, particularly at 9 am on a Sunday morning! This is, however, another example of an important tradition being kept alive by sponsorship. The judges of this competition have been drawn from most of the top wine people of the Valley, with Peter Lehmann, the man who started the ball rolling, as Chief Judge.

I haven't been able to get a recipe direct from one of the winners of this competition as there is many a small business on the side at stake for the 'right' recipe. However, I found one in a wonderful book of Barossa recipes, *The Barossa Cookery Book*, put out by the Tanunda Soldiers' Memorial Hall Committee in 1917. In its original form, this book had 500 recipes, and four or five years later it had 1000. It hasn't been altered in any way since that publication and has sold well over 180,000 copies. This goes to show that a lot of people are interested in preserving, bottling and home cooking, and certainly in these times of recession there are many financial reasons for the interest, coupled with a great sense of satisfaction in your own achievement.

CUCUMBERS PICKLED WITH VINE LEAVES
originally submitted by Mrs C. Kraft, Vine Vale, 1917

One cup salt, scalded with boiling water and cooled. 2 cups water and a little dill, enough water to fill the tin. Use a benzine tin. Cover bottom of tin with vine leaves, then a layer of cucumbers and dill, another layer of leaves, and so on to the top. Last layer, vine leaves. Use young cucumbers. Cover with plate and weight for 2 weeks. Leave another week before using. Add more water if some should evaporate.

A S WELL AS the traditional German way of handling dill pickles, there is the French cornichon, which is actually a baby dill about 5 cm long, pickled in a straight vinegar solution. These baby dill are very crisp and it would be interesting to use them in the more traditional Barossa way to see if the crispness is related to size or method.

PICKLED CORNICHONS

2 kg baby dills	*8 bay leaves*
8 cups vinegar	*1 tablespoon allspice berries*
1¹/4 cups coarse sea salt	

Rub the dills with a damp teatowel and leave them with the salt in a bowl overnight. The salt will draw out the moisture. Rinse the dills, drain them in a colander and dry with a teatowel. Place them in sterilised jars with the bay leaves and allspice. Cover with vinegar and seal. Keep for 6 to 8 weeks before eating.

U NFORTUNATELY I WAS unable to contact Mrs Roesler of Angaston, who was the outright winner of the preserve section at the Angaston Show, but the second and third place-getters, Mrs Hein of Tanunda and Mrs Loffler of Angaston, were happy to share favourite recipes. Here is Mrs Hein's recipe.

QUINCE JAM

1 kg under-ripe quinces	*1/2 cup sugar*
1.5 litres (6 cups) water	*2 kg (approx.) sugar extra*

Rub and clean quinces well with a rough towel. Cut bumps off one end so they will sit in pan. Place whole quinces in pan with water and half a cup of sugar. Put lid on and boil gently for one and a half to two hours until quinces are light pink.

Carefully lift out quinces on to plate (an egg slice is good for this) and discard core. Chop rest of quince roughly and return to juice. Measure pulp and allow one cup of sugar to one cup of pulp. Heat slowly, stirring, until sugar is dissolved, then boil rapidly for 20-30 minutes or until jam gels when tested.

THIS RECIPE from Mrs Loffler can be made at any time of the year and served with cold meats and cheese or used for sandwiches.

MUSTARD CABBAGE PICKLES

1/2 small cabbage (approx. 1 kg)	*1 tablespoon prepared mustard*
3 onions (approx. 500 g)	*1 teaspoon turmeric*
2 green capsicums	*1 teaspoon ground ginger*
2 red capsicums	*1/4 cup flour*
1/4 cup salt	*1/2 cup water*
2 cups Seppelt's white vinegar	*1 tablespoon mustard seeds (yellow)*
1 cup brown sugar, lightly packed	*1 tablespoon celery seeds*
2 cups white sugar	

Having discarded old leaves and core, shred the cabbage, then combine in a bowl with the peeled and sliced onions and chopped peppers (seeded and cored). Sprinkle salt over and let stand overnight, covered, to draw out the moisture.

Next morning, cover with water, stir well to disperse salt and drain in colander. While this is draining, in a large saucepan combine the vinegar and the brown and white sugars. Stir over heat till sugar dissolves, then bring to the boil and add vegetables. Reduce heat and simmer for 5 minutes. Cooking time may be different depending on the type of cabbage (e.g. less if it is a soft leaf cabbage).

Mix the mustard, turmeric, ginger and flour to a smooth paste with the water. Stir into the vegetable mixture and continue stirring until mixture boils and thickens. Reduce the heat and simmer for 10 minutes (subject to conditions and preferences). Add celery and mustard seeds. Pour into hot jars and cool before sealing.

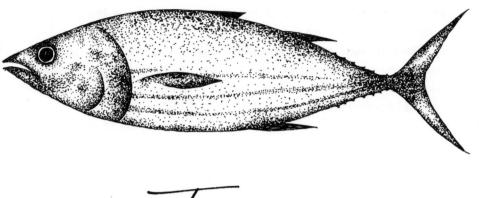

T
HE BLUE FIN TUNA is a cold water fish and is caught from the southern part of Western Australia through to Tasmania. The local blue fin is available from January until some time in March. The season's end date depends entirely on quotas: once they are filled, the season ends. Most of the fish available in Adelaide comes from Port Lincoln and is caught by pole boats, although there are some cray fishermen who line-fish in their off-season. The sashimi market in Japan demands long-line fishing, but most of the top-quality tuna pole caught from Port Lincoln also goes to Japan.

The Japanese revere the tuna, prizing the fatty belly part most of all, and will therefore pay top dollar for it. Until 1990 it was often difficult to get South Australian tuna in Adelaide. Even now, sometimes tuna orders have to be filled from the eastern states. After pressure from restaurateurs, blue fin tuna has become much easier to get.

The process of tuna fishing is fascinating. First, the fishermen go out two to three nights in advance to catch sardines, which are kept alive in tanks on the boats. (The sardines out of Port Lincoln are apparently very sweet, but there is no local commercial fishery for them.) Spotter planes are then sent out to locate schools of tuna. The planes radio the boats, directing them to the schools, which are marked by 'fast boats' for the following pole boats. The schools are then encircled with nets and the tuna excited by the live sardines. A line is run with large, bare hooks which shine through the water like the sardines, and the tuna take the unbaited hooks. These days the boats are big business and carry automatic poling machines.

The main requirement for quality fish is that they are killed immediately and humanely to avoid suffering and to maintain quality. The treatment given to the fish after catching is what dictates the price, and this processing depends on the boat's facilities. Some boats are sophisticated enough to have a freeze-chill operation on board; tuna caught by these boats is shipped straight to Japan. The yellow fin fished off Cairns is killed and gutted on board and put in a brine to chill so as to avoid deterioration.

Tuna is such an important industry that a trial tuna farm has been set up at Port Lincoln in a tripartite agreement between the Japanese Overseas Fishery Co-operation Foundation, the Australian Tuna Boat Owners' Association and the South Australian Government. *Australian Fisheries* of July 1991 reports that, 'The aim of the project is to catch and fatten the blue tuna to a weight of around 30 kg in less than 12 months, making it a better quality product to pitch at Japan's lucrative sashimi market, and at significantly higher prices of more than $35 per kilo.' Hopefully this venture will succeed, but not at the expense of the local market being able to get the fish when in season.

Tuna can differ in the way it is caught and killed, and in the care that is taken to maintain the quality, whether the local blue fin or the highly-prized yellow fin from the Australian east coast. Local tuna is sometimes available for as little as $5.50 per kilo in the markets, but this, because of the way it has been treated, will be no better than canning quality. Premium quality quarter fillets, which are all meat, will sell for as much as $20.50 per kilo for blue fin and $23.00 per kilo for yellow fin. The two qualities are so different it is difficult to believe they are the same fish.

I asked Kim Rogers of International Oysters in Adelaide whether he preferred blue or yellow fin. He was adamant that blue fin was his favourite, provided it had been killed and cared for correctly. He said that his preference could be due to the fact that the fish is local and available to eat within 24 hours of being caught. He also said that blue fin has a higher fat content as well as a higher blood meat content; this makes it vital for the fish to be bled in the correct method. Kim added that his

Japanese customers in Adelaide prefer blue fin to yellow fin, despite the yellow fin having a better colour (less opaque, more translucent). The yellow fin available in South Australia is likely to be 48 to 72 hours old.

Tuna fish are transported to Japan in large cardboard 'coffins' which can hold somewhere around 120 kg of fish and need to be moved by forklift. These plastic lined boxes stop the fish from sliding about and bruising. Each fish is individually wrapped in plastic. Smaller 'coffins' are used in the local market for ease of handling.

Tuna is a very versatile fish and is easy to prepare. It can be tricky to cook because it is very quick to dry out; to avoid this, sear it quickly on both sides and let it rest. Tuna should be served rare, ranging from pink to almost totally raw depending on the quality of the fish and your personal taste. Never cook it till it's 'done' right through.

THE BEST TUNA DISH I have had was at the Hyatt's Fleurieu restaurant: a tuna steak with a red wine sauce. The tuna steak was about 6 cm thick, just seared on each side, rested and served. As I cut into it the meat was as red as the red wine sauce but not cold as you would expect something almost raw to be. It was a true taste sensation!

Many people are nervous of serving anything rare. The following recipe is delicious, and because the tuna is thinly sliced and raw it cooks enough from the warmth of the pasta.

TUNA PASTA

300 g angel hair pasta
200 g piece raw tuna, thinly sliced
1 tablespoon Eolian capers
juice from one lemon
2 tablespoons finely-chopped
  continental parsley

1 red onion, finely sliced
100 ml extra virgin olive oil
salt and pepper

Cook the pasta. Drain and moisten with olive oil. Sweat the red onion in olive oil and add lemon juice (it will turn very pink), capers, salt and pepper. Check the vinaigrette for balance and toss the raw tuna and parsley through. Serve immediately with warm angel hair pasta.

T una, like salmon and ocean trout, is also a fabulous fish for sugar curing. It is great for the barbecue as it really suits the charcoal flavour and can be finished off simply with a compound butter of lemon or dill. Even though it seems expensive you don't need to buy a large quantity of it and there is no waste.

CURED TUNA

1 kg tuna	*fresh dill*
500 g sugar	*1 cup Pernod or dry vermouth*
500 g salt	

Mix the sugar and salt together, then add a good handful of fresh dill, chopped, and the Pernod. Cover the fillet well with the mixture and lay it on a china or plastic dish. Cover and weigh down (you could use empty tins). Refrigerate for 12-24 hours, turning occasionally, until cured as required. To serve, carefully wipe off all of the sugar and salt mixture, and slice thinly. The cured tuna, covered well, keeps for up to 2 weeks in the fridge and is a lovely appetiser served with cucumber and horseradish cream.

SALAD NIÇOISE

500 g fresh tuna, cut into 2¹/2 cm steaks	*4 small waxy potatoes*
	fresh herbs—chives, basil, etc.
12 quail eggs	*heart of iceberg lettuce or lettuce of your choice*
125 g cherry tomatoes	
125 g yellow plum tomatoes	*olive oil*
120 g thin green beans	*2 cloves garlic, finely sliced*
8 preserved baby artichokes	*2 tablespoons lemon juice*
1 tablespoon Eolian capers, soaked in water and drained	*¹/2 teaspoon Dijon mustard*
	salt and pepper
120 g small olives (our local wild olives are perfect)	

Sear the tuna in a very hot pan for about one minute on each side. Cover with olive oil and the garlic. Leave to marinate at room temperature for 2 hours. Wash, dry and chill the lettuce. Boil the potatoes and set aside. Boil the quail eggs for 1 to 2 minutes until just soft.

Top and tail the beans and plunge them in boiling water for about 2 minutes. Drain and refresh.

Cut the tomatoes and artichokes in half. Chop the herbs. Cut the potatoes in half. Peel the quail eggs and cut in half.

Make the vinaigrette using about 8 tablespoons oil from the marinade, lemon juice, Dijon mustard, salt, pepper and herbs.

Distribute the lettuce between the serving plates. Break tuna into small pieces and pile in the centre of the lettuce. Arrange the other ingredients and pour the vinaigrette over.

Apricots

I T TAKES A LONG while for me to get tired of just eating and serving apricots fresh or stewing them simply in a light sugar syrup to have with fresh cream or ice-cream. Once again, as with all fruit, the very best way to buy is ripe, straight from the tree, but to do this you need to have a network of family and friends with backyard trees or make a pilgrimage to a country orchard. If you buy them direct from the shops, look for apricots firm but strong in colour. The richer the colour, the sweeter the apricot.

The issue of fruit being picked when it is green instead of ripe is a difficult one. There is something wrong when growers pick entirely green a crop that is meant to be left to ripen on the tree. It may be up to 6 weeks before the fruit reaches the customer.

Many people would rethink the value of an apricot if they tasted those in perfect condition. Flavour and perfume should be paramount in our decisions about which food to buy, not cosmetics. The spots on backyard apricots, so unacceptable in commercial situations, do not spoil anything but the appearance of the fruit.

This is why organic growing is such a vexed issue—the customer has been taught to demand purity and is unhappy to accept imperfections. Nature just isn't like that!

As in all things, there needs to be some balance. In this last very wet season, many of our local orchardists say that they would have lost their trees if they hadn't sprayed to combat the diseases brought on by uncharacteristic flooding. More discussion is needed to ensure that the growers can deliver a superior and flavoursome product to a public that understands seasonality.

Once you tire of the fruit on its own, there are the obvious tarts, upside down cakes, jam, sorbets and ice-creams, to name a few. In Middle Eastern cookery, apricots are often teamed with lamb. I love the marriage of apricots and almonds.

APRICOT AND ALMOND CRUMBLE

30 large, ripe apricots
sugar

60 g almond flakes, lightly roasted

CRUMBLE
125 g flour
100 g sugar

100 g ground almonds
175 g butter

Cut the apricots in half and remove the stones. Arrange them in a shallow glass or enamel baking dish. Sprinkle with sugar. Mix the dry ingredients together and rub in the butter. Spread over the fruit and sprinkle with almond flakes. Bake for about 30 minutes at 200°C. Be careful not to burn the almond flakes. Cover with foil or lower the temperature if necessary. Serve warm with cream or ice-cream.

THIS A FAVOURITE dish from Jenny Ferguson's book *Cooking for You and Me*. Jenny ran a wonderful restaurant in Sydney called You and Me and when she finally closed her doors she wrote this book as a record of her time at the stoves.

UPSIDE DOWN APRICOT TARTS
(SERVES 2)

6 ripe apricots, halved
(3 per person)
puff pastry leftovers
250 ml water

125 g castor sugar
50 g unsalted butter
a little extra sugar for sprinkling
2 x 14 cm pie tins

Roll out your pastry very thinly and cut out 2 circles that are just a bit wider than the tops of your pie tins. Chill these while you prepare the apricots.

Put the sugar and water in a fry pan and cook to a light golden caramel. Add the butter. Let this mixture bubble for a couple of minutes without stirring, then add the apricots, cooking them for 3 minutes on each side.

Put the apricots rounded side down in the bottom of the tins and cover with the caramel butter. Do not fill quite to the top.

Now drape your pastry circles over the top of each of the tins and sprinkle with some of the extra sugar. Put the pie tins on a tray to catch any of the caramel which may spill over, and bake at 190°C until the pastry is crisp. This will take about 20 minutes.

To serve

Trim off the excess pastry edges and tip upside down (so that the pastry is now underneath) on to serving plates. Serve with thick fresh cream or crème anglaise.

These tarts are extremely versatile. They can be made smaller or larger, as you please. Plums can be substituted for the apricots, or in winter try rounds of granny smith apples.

HILDA LAURENCIS has been a very important person to our business and family and has worked for us since we began 14 years ago. She has done everything from dishwashing and food preparation to looking after my house. It was Hilda who first made pate with me using small household food processors—we burnt out many a motor together. Five years ago Hilda retired but soon found herself bored. So she still comes in one morning a week to make pate. And in all this time she has kept my store cupboard full of jams. Just as we finish one, another appears. When our daughters were still at home the 'topping up' was more frequent; the undisputed family favourite was Hilda's Apricot Jam.

Hilda's Apricot Jam

5 kg apricots   *5 cups water*
3 kg sugar

Cut the apricots into quarters. Cook the apricots in water until 'all mashed up' (approximately 20 minutes). Add the sugar and cook for another half-hour. Bottle in sterilised jars.

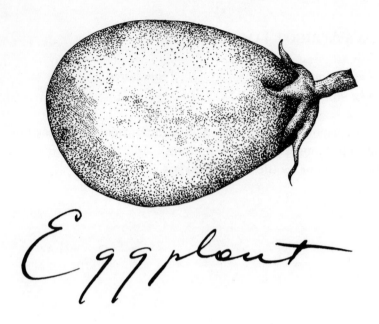

Eggplant

WHAT TO CALL IT: aubergine or eggplant? I have always known it as aubergine but most people seem to call it eggplant. It apparently reached the French and English language from the Catalan word *Alberginia*. But whatever you choose to call it, the important thing for us is that this vegetable has such a special flavour and is so readily available.

The plants are bush-like and reach about a metre high. They need lots of warm weather to mature and will bear fruit prolifically.

The fruiting plant is a beautiful sight—the fruit large, oval and a glossy dark purple. If space is critical in your garden, I wouldn't hesitate to plant them in a general garden bed—but then I love the haphazard mixture of flowers, herbs and vegetables jumbled together.

The eggplant is a very important vegetable in Mediterranean cuisine and tends to be available here almost year round now because of the variance of climate in Australia.

Eggplant would be my family's favourite vegetable and can be prepared in so many ways, as an accompaniment to a dish, as a pickle or paste or as a complete meal in itself.

How to choose your fruit: There is a tremendous variety of shapes and sizes but the best are those that are fully-coloured, very glossy, with smooth, unblemished skins. The medium or small ones make the best eating as their seeds are less evident. The very large fruit with large seeds can be bitter. Do not buy dimpled or brown spotted fruit as these are signs of age and bruising.

To salt or not to salt? To skin or not to skin? Many people both salt and skin the eggplant automatically. I don't bother if the eggplant is in perfect condition and in its natural season. If you are not sure, do a simple test. Heat some oil in a deep fry pan and cut two slices off the eggplant to try. Sometimes the skin is bitter—the second slice in will tell you if it is the skin or the flesh. If it is the skin, peel the eggplant, and if the flesh, salt it.

To salt the eggplant, cut it the way you wish to use it and then sprinkle the exposed flesh with a little salt and leave it in a colander for 20 minutes to drain. The salt will leach out the bitter juices and give a mild, sweeter taste. Rinse off the salt and pat the fruit dry with paper towels before proceeding to cook.

You could deep-fry or sauté the slices in olive oil. The best deep-fryer is a small electric household one controlled by a thermostat. A deep-sided heavy pan or saucepan will work very well, but handle it with care and make sure the pan is only half full of oil. To test if the oil is hot enough, put a small piece of bread crust in the oil and if it shivers around the crust, it is just about there. It needs to be hot enough for the oil to foam when you put the eggplant in but not so hot that the oil is smoking. Do not fry too much at a time as the temperature will drop too quickly and the eggplant will be saturated instead of crisp. Lift out when golden brown and place on crumpled kitchen paper towels.

You could also shallow fry eggplant slices in olive oil. If you find olive oil too pungent or expensive, then a vegetable oil will be fine.

To avoid extra oil being absorbed, you can brush small eggplants with a little oil so any burning is minimised and then dry-bake them until they collapse in an oven dish just big enough to fit them. Serve as a vegetable with lamb chops. Whole small eggplants are also successful on the barbecue, but remember to turn them frequently and to brush them with oil occasionally.

To prepare an eggplant as a meal in itself, cut a larger eggplant in half, spoon out the flesh and then refill each half with a mixture of breadcrumbs, egg, tomato, grated cheese, fresh herbs and chopped eggplant flesh. This can be stewed, baked or barbecued and served with a salad or fresh tomato sauce for dinner.

Eggplant marries wonderfully with anchovies, pesto (paste of basil, pinenuts and Parmesan), goat's cheese, garlic, tomatoes and oregano. To serve as a vegetable, it goes very well with lamb, kid, quail or chicken.

―――――

BAKED EGGPLANT

4 small young eggplant	*salt and pepper to taste*
2 cloves garlic, finely chopped	*1/2 cup fresh tomato purée*
1 teaspoon dried oregano, or	*3 tablespoons olive oil*
1 tablespoon fresh oregano	

Cut the eggplant in half lengthways. Salt it if you prefer. Brush the bottom of a baking dish with olive oil and scatter with garlic. The dish should be just large enough to place the eggplant pieces side by side. Spread the tomato sauce evenly over each half, sprinkle with oregano and drizzle with the oil. Bake until tender. Serve hot.

―――――

A DISH SIMILAR TO this was my first introduction to eggplant about eleven years ago, cooked by a marvellous Frenchwoman, Kiki, who helped me for a short time in the kitchen. You can use sour cream instead of yoghurt.

FRIED EGGPLANT WITH GARLIC, PARSLEY AND YOGHURT

3 medium eggplant	*3 cloves garlic, finely chopped*
1 tablespoon salt	*1 cup yoghurt, or sour cream*
1/4 cup olive oil	*pepper*
2 tablespoons freshly chopped	
parsley	

Peel the eggplant and cut into about 1 x 2 cm pieces. Sprinkle with salt and leave to drain in a colander for 20 minutes. Wash the eggplant pieces and pat them dry. Heat the oil in a fry pan and fry a little at a time until golden brown. Put on paper towels to drain. Combine the garlic, parsley and freshly ground black pepper and scatter over the cooked eggplant. Toss with the sour cream and yoghurt or serve the eggplant with the dressing on the side.

———————

RABBIT SCALOPPINI WITH EGGPLANT
(SERVES 4)

6 double fillets rabbit	*olive oil for frying*
3 medium eggplant	*8 anchovy fillets, soaked in milk*
1 garlic clove, chopped	*for 20 minutes*
1 tablespoon flatleaf parsley leaves	*3 large green olives, sliced*
picked from the stem but left	*flour for coating*
whole	*cracked black pepper*
2 tablespoons red wine vinegar	*salt*
3 tablespoons extra virgin olive oil	

Trim the fillets from the rabbit saddle and, using a sharp knife, remove the sinew as if it were a beef fillet. Wrap each fillet in plastic wrap and 'bash' it into a scaloppini shape (an even, flattened fillet).

Season the flour with salt and pepper. Cut the eggplant into 1 cm slices, discarding the outside pieces. Salt the slices if necessary—if it is the natural season and the fruit is not too large, you shouldn't need to. In a heavy-based pan heat some olive oil until very hot and fry the eggplant slices until brown on both sides. Place on absorbent paper.

Vinaigrette: In a pan, gently warm the garlic in the extra virgin olive oil and then add the red wine vinegar, anchovies, olives and parsley. Keep just warm.

Bring a little butter to nut-brown stage in a heavy pan and take off the heat for a second while you toss the rabbit fillets in the seasoned flour. Put the pan back on the heat for a moment and then seal each fillet for about 30 seconds on each side. Remove the fillets and rest.

Warm the eggplant slices on a tray in the oven and then interleave the rabbit with the eggplant, using 3 pieces of eggplant to 3 scaloppini of rabbit. Serve with the warm vinaigrette or anchovy mayonnaise.

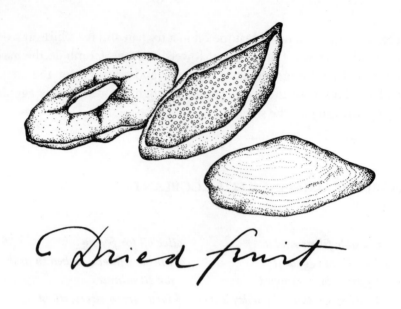

Dried fruit

W ITH THE THOUGHT of late summer I imagine drying stone fruits—I can smell them as I write.

During the months of the year when fresh fruit is not abundant, dried fruits make delicious desserts. And of course dried fruit is essential to those traditional Christmas dried fruit cooks!

If you have excess fruit—and the time—it can be fun to dry your own. In the Barossa the first stone fruits to ripen are the stunning white peaches, although I find it hard to contemplate any being left over for drying! Apricots are for me the most successful fruit for drying. In South Australia they are ready around Christmas day. If it is a cool year picking can sometimes be delayed until just after Christmas, and if it is warm, many a Barossa family has spent their Christmas Day picking the delicate apricots for market or drying.

All fruit to be dried—nectarines, peaches, plums, cherries, grapes, figs, pears, apples, bananas and of course tomatoes—should be ripe without being spoiled. For apricots, nectarines and peaches, halve them and remove the stones. Dry small figs whole and the larger purple figs in halves. Pears are usually peeled, halved and have the main core scooped out with a potato baller. Pull out the thready part. All cut fruit should first be dried cut side up and the pieces should not touch each other. As the pieces of fruit dry, you can rearrange them on the trays. I dry my fruit in the sun in apricot drying racks, which are wooden boxes with slatted bottoms.

Decide whether you want to be totally organic and have a more individual flavour or whether you want your fruit to look like dried fruit. All stone fruits can be dried naturally as halves without any dipping. The fruit finishes darker in colour and can take longer to dry but I prefer the individual flavour.

Commercially-dried fruit achieves its colour from having sodium metabisulphate sprinkled over it or being dipped in it. This is sulphur in manageable form. It has been used since Roman times (the Romans burned brimstone to derive their sulphur) and has long been considered nature's sanitiser. Sulphur is also present in most of the wine we drink.

You can also dry fruit in the oven or in a dehydrator. A plate-warming oven is perfect, particularly in a fuel or fire-oiled stove such as many country people still have in their kitchens. If you use a gas or electric oven you will need to keep the door open as even the lowest temperature will be too hot! If using this method it is important to keep the temperature steady between 50° and 60°C. The appearance of the fruit will be your guide as to when it is ready; the soft fruits will yield no juice when cut. Cool the fruit thoroughly before packing away. Do not store it in plastic—glass is best, and you may want to add some silica gel crystals to absorb the moisture.

Bring the trays inside if rain is expected—there is nothing worse than seeing your whole crop mildewed after all your work, particularly if it is almost ready! Commercial growers say that in the hot months their trays of fruit can take up to 10 points of rain before they will spoil, but later in the season dewy nights are a problem when they are drying pears.

Look carefully at labels when you are buying dried fruits—be sure to support our local industry and buy Australian whenever you can. Don't just buy on price if you can help it.

To reconstitute dried fruit, pour on boiling water until the fruit is just covered. If the fruit absorbs all the boiling water, add a little more. Then cook the fruit in its soaking water.

T HIS RECIPE uses dried apricots, however it can be made using fresh
apricots, peaches, small figs, cherries or glacé fruit. I serve these
mustard fruits with pates, terrines, rillettes or cold meats, especially legs
of sugar-cured ham or baked hands of pork.

MUSTARD FRUITS

500 g sugar	*50 g Keens dried mustard*
250 ml water	*2 sticks cinnamon*
1 kg dried apricots	*5 cloves*
150 ml white wine vinegar	

Combine 400 g of the sugar with the water and cook over a medium
heat until the sugar has completely dissolved. Add the cinnamon sticks
and cloves. Add the fruit and cook over a low heat until the fruit is soft.
This will take about 10 minutes for dried fruit and only about 2 or 3
minutes for fresh fruit.

Remove the fruit from the heat and put it in a bowl.

Combine the remaining sugar with the vinegar and cook for 10
minutes to make a thick syrup. Allow to cool a little, stir in the mustard
and leave to stand for about an hour. Add the mustard syrup to the fruit,
mix well and pour into jars. The pickle will be ready the next day but
will improve with maturity.

———

F IGS ARE A SPECIAL passion of mine and it is a shame that commercial
quantities of Australian figs are not available. If you have your own
dried figs or commercial figs you are happy with, you may enjoy the
following ideas. Figs marry particularly well with lamb or kid, squab or
quail. Try stuffing squab or quail with dried figs sliced and tossed with
prosciutto, lots of sweated onions and rosemary. You will find this very
different to using fresh figs for the same recipe. For people like me who
aren't fond of sweet things, try squeezing lemon juice liberally into the
mixture or add lemon zest. I have also made a dried fig 'tapenade', that
is, reconstituted dried fig added to a mixture of olives, capers, anchovies
and olive oil (see page 153). This goes very well with something as
simple as lamb chops.

An Italian speciality is to stuff dried figs with a toasted almond and some candied orange peel. Bake the figs and then roll them in melted chocolate when cool.

———

M Y FRIEND CHEONG LIEW of Regency Park College used to serve a wonderful sweetmeat in the days he ran his famous Neddy's restaurant in Adelaide. It was a Portuguese speciality where he stuffed a fig with a mixture of ground almonds and grated chocolate. He then poached the fig in chocolate and port. He says he used to have them sitting in a glass jar of port and chocolate to serve after coffee. They make a stunning dessert.

CHEONG'S FIGS

250 g dried figs
120 g almonds, roasted and
 ground
120 g chocolate, grated, plus
 120 g for poaching

1/2 bottle port (I often use white
 port or 12-year-old St. Hallet's
 Pedro Ximenes)

Mix the almonds and grated chocolate together. Loosen each fig at the bottom and create a hole. Stuff with the almond and chocolate mixture. Place the figs in a heavy saucepan and half cover with port. Let them simmer, but do not boil, for 10 minutes. Add extra grated chocolate to taste and simmer for another 5 minutes. Take the figs out and put them in a jar. Reduce the poaching liquid until it is a glaze and pour into the jar.

———

BAROSSA DRIED FRUIT COMPOTES

1 kg mixed dried Barossa fruit
 (prunes, nectarines, apricots,
 peaches and apples)
1 cup water
1 cup sugar

50 ml runny cream
750 ml Amontillado sherry
King Island double cream, for
 serving

Soak the fruit in the sherry for 24 hours. Line individual moulds with foil. Make caramel by boiling the sugar and the water carefully until almost at a burnt stage. Pour a tablespoon of caramel into each mould to coat the bottom. Then half fill each mould with fruit. Pour on some more syrup and then another layer of fruit almost to the top. Finish with a final layer of syrup.

Cover with foil and bake in a water bath in a moderate oven until set. Let the compotes cool a little, then turn them out on to plates and serve with the cream.

DRIED TOMATOES are the most popular form of dried fruit at the moment. It is possible to use any vine-ripened tomato for drying but the Roma variety contains less moisture and makes the best-looking dried specimen.

Due to their popularity in both Europe and Australia, not all tomatoes have been dried in the sun. I have heard stories of hectares of tomatoes drying in racks in disused aircraft hangars, which have the correct ventilation but not a lot of sunlight! When you think of the logistics of drying and the vagaries of the weather this method makes commercial sense. In the parts of Australia enjoying a Mediterranean climate one therefore has the opportunity to achieve sundried tomatoes as good as or better than you would buy anywhere in the world. Maximise the potential by using the best tomatoes, the best salt and the best oil for storage.

The more you dry the tomatoes the darker they will become. I like them not to be 'overdry' and still have their bright tomato colour. To dry the tomatoes, cut them lengthways, place on wooden racks and sprinkle sparingly with Maldon sea salt. Eliminate the salt entirely if you wish. As a rough guide, three days of drying in perfect warm conditions is enough for me!

You can of course dry the tomatoes in the oven as discussed above or you can buy an electric food hydrator, specially for the drying of fruit and herbs.

Pack the dried tomatoes in the best olive oil you can afford. The fruity oils available from McLaren Vale and Angle Vale are perfect. You could also add fresh oregano or thyme. I don't use basil as I find that it makes the tomatoes bitter.

There is an informative book called *Cooking With Sun Dried Tomatoes* by Lois Dribin, Denise Marins and Susan Ivnkovich which should satisfy the curiosity of anyone at a loss for how to use sundried tomatoes! One of my very favourite books, *Honey From a Weed* by Patience Gray, explains the drying of whole stalks or tiny bushes of tomatoes.

———————

The following tips on drying are taken from the Department of Agriculture's informative fact sheets pertaining to drying fruit. They give exact amounts for the dipping solutions and also confirm that natural drying is possible.

Figs
Not all varieties of figs are suitable for drying. Smyrna, Brown Turkey and sugar figs are fine. The fruit has to be fully mature as immature fruits are slower drying and hard and woody when dry. You can tell mature fruit on the tree by the stems starting to shrivel.

After picking, wash the fruit and then dip it in boiling brine solution (15 g salt:1 litre of water) for 30 to 60 seconds.

Alternatively figs could be sulphured for 10 to 15 hours in the following dipping solution. This lightens the colour of the figs but is not essential.

DIPPING SOLUTION:
100 g sodium or potassium   *500 g sugar*
  metabisulphate   *5 litres water*

For drying, spread the figs on to wooden or wire netting trays with the eye of the fig uppermost (do not use plastic or steel trays). This prevents any loss of juice if the figs are prone to bleeding during drying. Figs can be fully sundried in 6 to 10 days, especially if they are turned over several times. Shade drying can be used and will result in a lighter coloured fig. This takes 20 to 30 days to complete. The fruit is dry enough when it is still pliable but does not exude juice when worked between the fingers and the thumb.

Prunes
All varieties of prune plums can be dried and some ordinary varieties of plum. Once again, use only matured fruit as immature fruit dries

without flavour and is more likely to spoil. Often the fruit is actually allowed to fall to the ground as a sign of full maturity, then picked up and processed. To speed drying, the skins of the prunes have to be 'checked' (very finely cracked). This is done by caustic dipping the fruit until checking is visible. The dipping time will depend on the fruit variety and the temperature of the dip, hence fruit should be examined regularly during dipping to determine correct stage or removal. Excessive cracking of skins should be avoided as this will produce sticky fruit that is difficult to handle after dipping.

CAUSTIC DIP:
5 litres water to 50 g caustic potash or caustic soda

Caution: Caustic potash and caustic soda are corrosive and extreme care should be exercised in handling either powder or the made-up dip. Severe burns can result from contact with the skin so be sure to wear rubber gloves. Use only plastic or enamel containers for the dip solution.

After dipping, allow the fruit to drain and then spread it on to wooden or wire netting trays, not plastic or steel. If the weather is hot with bright sunshine, stack the trays of fruit until wilting occurs. This prevents the loss of juice from the prunes by 'boiling'. In cooler weather or after wilting, the drying can be done in direct sunlight. When the prunes are dry enough to handle, compact them on to fewer trays and turn or stir them regularly for more even drying.

Do not allow the prunes to get too dry. They are dry enough for sweating when the flesh is tough but pliable and does not exude juice when squeezed. To sweat the prunes, store them in a covered wooden box for 4 to 6 weeks with regular mixing for redistribution.

Sulphuring of apricots, peaches and nectarines
Select fruit from the tree that is fully mature but not soft and over-ripe, wash it, halve cleanly with a knife and remove stones. Sulphuring is most easily done by placing the fruit in the solution described below for the prescribed time. Dipping is easier than the old method of burning sulphur in a sulphur box. The fruit has to be kept submerged—a weight on a dinner plate in a 10 litre plastic bucket works well.

DIPPING SOLUTION:
10 litres water
200 g sodium or potassium metabisulphate
1.5 kg sugar

DIPPING TIMES:
apricots 12 to 15 hours
peaches 20 to 24 hours
nectarines 15 to 20 hours

This dip will sulphur 20 kg fruit before replenishment when a further 150 g metabisulphate is needed.

After dipping, rinse the fruit in clean water, lay it on drying trays or wooden planks and place in the sun to dry. The cups of the fruit should face upwards. Do not use plastic or metal trays as fruit on these does not dry on the underside and mould can develop during drying. Apricots are best dried to completion in the sun but peaches and nectarines should be removed from the sun after 2 days to prevent the flesh from bleaching. Complete drying by stacking the trays and leaving them so any breeze will blow over the fruit. When dry, remove the fruit from the trays and store in tightly sealed plastic containers.

Drying time is very dependent on the weather conditions during drying but approximate times are:

apricots 5 to 8 days
peaches 20 to 30 days
nectarines 10 to 20 days

Fruit is dry enough for storage when it cannot be easily bent in half and is hard and difficult to eat. Should dried fruit moth get into the dried fruit during storage, a few drops of ethyl format per kilo of dried fruit, placed in the sealed container with the fruit, will eliminate it.

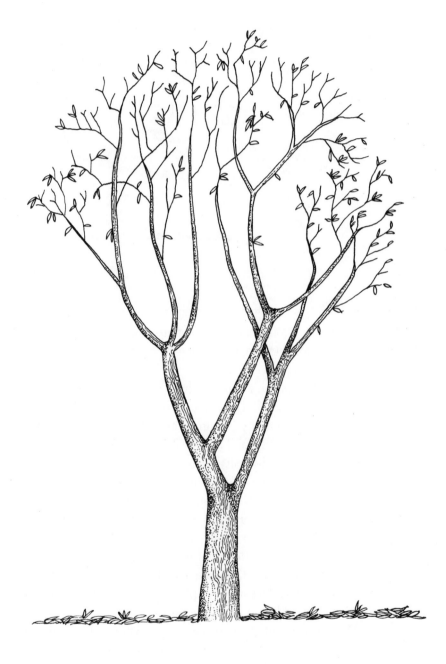

Autumn

Quinces

PEOPLE HAVE ALWAYS been passionate about quinces. I enjoyed reading about them in *Jane Grigson's Fruit Book*: 'Quinces were the golden apple of the Hesperides, the golden apples that prevented Atlanta winning the race. And quince was the golden apple that Paris awarded to Aphrodite. The fruit of love, marriage, fertility.' Quinces are a native of Persia.

They inspire me so! Their look as a fruit, the beauty of the blossom and the diversity of uses of this often ignored fruit seem to me to be the essence of the 'country'.

I am a little prone to romantic illusions and imagined our pheasants wandering around a quince orchard. Colin advised me that the pheasants would peck the fruit as it ripened, so there had to be a little adjustment to my dream. We chose another site to plant the orchard. By October 1992 the land was deep-ripped ready for planting and all the spacings worked out. And then came the rains.

We were flooded for three weeks. When the land finally dried out and the working bee to plant the orchard was organised, we were told by the local nurseryman who was growing the trees for us that he had overcommitted himself and in fact could not supply us with any of the 200 trees we had ordered.

The thing about dreams is that you have to learn to be philosophical when they are delayed in coming true! Everything is in place for the planting this year, floods aside. Bad businessmen can be circumvented but not so the floods. Even though the 12-month delay is distressing, quinces are quick to grow and will actually bear fruit in their first year.

My vision of serving quince wine as an aperitif in the restaurant will, I hope, soon be realised.

I find it easy to see how the cooking of quinces can put fire in a person's breast. Not to mention a gardener—quinces are a pretty fruit with a wonderful blossom and scent. They are perfect espaliered against a garden wall if space is minimal. The two varieties which are readily available are the pineapple quince (which has a large yellow fruit with a pineappley scent and is an early ripener) and the Smyrna (which is the most popular variety, being a prolific bearer, late maturer and having fruit of a very high quality). There are also the wild or seedling quinces which you will find in river beds in the country. These quinces are very small and are probably more like the apple quince you will read about in English books.

The diversity of this fruit is enormous. What other fruit can be used so successfully at any stage of the meal? In Middle Eastern cookery quince is teamed with kid or lamb where its astringency is a perfect balance to the richness of the meat.

LAMB NECK WITH QUINCES

1/2 knob ginger	*1 teaspoon cumin powder*
2 cloves garlic	*1 tablespoon sherry vinegar*
1 teaspoon crushed	*1 lamb neck*
coriander seeds	*20 ml oil*
8 chopped brown onions	*1 litre sugar syrup*
1/2 bunch coriander, chopped	*50 ml lemon juice*
1/2 teaspoon turmeric	*2 peeled quinces*
	veal stock

Heat the oil in a heavy pan and toss in the roughly chopped ginger, garlic and onions. Sweat until golden. Add the lamb neck and brown evenly. Slice one of the quinces roughly and add to the onions. Deglaze with the sherry vinegar and add the spices. Pour in enough stock to half cover the lamb neck. Cook for approximately 3¹/₂ hours on a moderate to low heat until the lamb is very tender.

Place the other quince in the sugar syrup and lemon juice and simmer until it reduces and thickens and the quince begins to turn a deep red colour—this will take about 1¹/₂ hours.

Just before serving the neck place the quince in the cooking liquid and heat up together. At this stage add more lemon juice to balance. Reduce the cooking liquid and pour over the lamb and quince—it should glisten invitingly. Cover with the chopped coriander and serve.

I LOVE FLO BEER'S pickled quinces which have graced the Pheasant Farm tables for years. This is a wonderful pickle for terrines and also for serving with pickled pork. It also makes a delicious glaze for kangaroo and venison.

FLO BEER'S PICKLED QUINCES

quinces	*whole cloves*
white wine vinegar	*peppercorns*
sugar	*cayenne pepper*

Peel the quinces and cut into quarters. Put them immediately into a sink full of water to which lemon juice has been added, to prevent discoloration.

Place the quinces in a preserving pan and almost cover with vinegar. To each 600 ml vinegar used add 2 cups sugar, 1 teaspoon cloves and 1 teaspoon peppercorns. Add a little cayenne to taste, if you like it.

Boil the quinces for about 25 minutes until they are soft and have turned light pink. (The quince goes a lot darker in the jar with age.) Cool, place in bottles and cover with the vinegar. Leave for several weeks before opening.

D ESSERT IS MY LEAST favourite part of the meal but this dish, taught to me by Hazel Mader of the Barossa, is one of such simplicity that in autumn it is my first choice. The effect of the long cooking means that the quince changes from bright yellow to a deep ruby red. The quince remains whole and is so well cooked that you can even eat the core! These baked quinces can be cooked and frozen, in their juices, to bring out in the middle of winter. If you are lucky enough to have picked the quinces yourself and left the stem on with a few leaves still attached, there is nothing more to do than to place them on plates in their own majesty.

POT ROASTED QUINCES

6 whole quinces, picked with
stem and leaf if possible
6 cups water

4 cups sugar
juice 3 lemons

Rub the down off the quinces and wash them. Pack them tightly in a heavy-based pan with the water and sugar. Boil at a reasonably high temperature until a jelly starts to form and then turn the temperature to a simmer for up to five hours. (I often use a simmer pad to control the temperature.) The quinces should be turned at least four times during the cooking process so that the deep ruby colour goes right through to the core. Add lemon juice at the last stage of the cooking to take away the excessive sweetness.

Serve the quince whole with a little of the jelly and fresh cream or crème anglaise (see page 154).

THIS QUINCE PASTE is made just like a jam. You will need to wear a fair amount of armour to stop yourself from being burnt. The end result is worth the effort—every time you serve a beautifully ripe and creamy brie, this paste will be testimony to how clever you are.

QUINCE PASTE

2 kg quinces
400 ml water, enough
to cover the quinces

sugar to equal the weight of
the purée when cooked

Wash and quarter the quinces. Keep the cores to one side, wrap them in some muslin and cook them with the quinces. Cover the quinces with the water and bring to the boil, simmering until they are tender enough to purée easily. Drain the quinces, discard the cores, and purée the fruit, then weigh the purée. Place the purée and the equal amount of sugar in a very heavy pot with high sides. Stir over a low heat until the mixture thickens. At this stage it is advisable to wrap a teatowel around your arm to protect it and to use as long a wooden spoon as possible. The mixture will explode and pop and turn a dark red, and only by constant stirring will you prevent it from burning. Cook until you can hardly push the spoon through the paste. Remove the paste to baking trays lined with greaseproof paper and spread it out to 12 mm thick. When it cools wet your hands and flatten the surface as if you were shaping polenta. Place the trays in an oven on the lowest possible setting (in a gas oven the pilot light would be sufficient) and allow to dry overnight. When it can be cut into squares with a hot knife, it is ready to be cooled and stored. Pack the quince paste between layers of greaseproof paper and store in an airtight container.

———

To STORE FRAGRANT quinces, rub the down off some quinces carefully and place them in a wide necked jar. Pour honey over them. This form of storage gives a wonderful liquid with the taste of honey and quince. The same can be done with brandy to give a quince liqueur. We have a friend who has left his beehives on our land and this is a favourite way to use the honey he kindly leaves with us.

Pick the last fruit off the tree and when you can neither cook nor give away any more of this fragrant fruit put them in a basket in the mustiest part of your house—a cellar, store cupboard, or a room with no ventilation—and the perfume of the quince will transform it.

FIGS HAVE LONG BEEN used in Greek, Italian, Turkish and Moroccan foods. As South Australia has such a 'Mediterranean' climate it is not unusual to find wonderful old fig trees in back gardens. If you have a tree you will know how fleeting figs are. It's a race to see who gets them first, you or the birds! Particularly vulnerable are the large black figs, which I prefer to eat for their moistness, flavour, size and deep red colour. These are grown commercially and are very expensive because they perish so quickly after picking. I have planted my own orchard of ten of these beautiful black fig trees and once they start to bear I will have to net them to preserve the crop from the birds.

I have always fantasised about keeping geese in commercial quantities and letting them graze in the fig orchard. Can't you imagine how those livers would taste?

The sugar fig is the green one, which I can find a million and one uses for. I remember the delight of visiting Belinda Hannaford on Kangaroo Island and seeing her fig tree half the size of a city block. The tree is so old and gnarled that she has been able to make steps in the branches so you can actually walk through the tree and sit under the canopy for lunch on a summer's day. There is space for at least twenty people. One just reaches for a fresh fig to accompany the cheese platter!

It's a toss-up as to which is my favourite jam—burnt fig or bitter marmalade (the one with the whisky). For the five or so years my mother lived with us here in the Barossa, she made jars and jars of fig jam each year. I know she didn't mean to burn it but to this day fig jam doesn't taste the same unless the bottom of the pot has caught! This doesn't suit everyone's taste but it stops it being oversweet. This is an example of the sentimental factor that plays such a large part in the food we love.

Cut fresh figs in half and wrap them with wonderful fresh prosciutto. Just a paper-thin slice wrapped around the cut fig makes an immediate antipasto to mix with other summer treats.

Try serving fresh figs with a plate of ripe and creamy Gippsland blue cheese instead of dessert.

If you have a preserving kit, bottle figs without any added sugar when they are quite firm. Keep them for serving with home-made vanilla ice-cream in the winter months or to have with your morning cereal.

For a simple dessert, take whole figs that are very ripe and wash carefully. While wet, dip into dark brown sugar and place tightly packed in an oven dish. Bake for about 10 minutes in a very high oven, being careful they don't burn. When they are cooked, the sugar turns into caramel in the bottom of the dish. Cool and serve with a big pot of mascarpone cheese (whip it with a little castor sugar if you wish—say 50 g to 250 g of mascarpone). Make sure you serve the juices too.

To make fig ice-cream, simply purée some ripe figs and add a little lemon juice or even some finely-sliced glacé ginger. Stir into some home-made vanilla ice-cream and freeze. Serve with almond biscuits.

Don't forget the leaves of the fig: they can be used in so many ways to serve food. I found this wonderfully evocative quote in *Honey from a Weed* by Patience Gray: 'I recall only the "fig bread" served as a dessert in the shape of a little domed loaf unwrapped from its fig leaves, made of pressed dried figs flavoured with aniseed and bay leaves.'

Dried figs are an important part of culinary life and can be called upon in many a cooking emergency. Try stuffing them with roasted almonds and baking them in the oven for a sweetmeat to finish dinner.

Then there are those wonderful dried figs of Cheong Liew's, poached in port and chocolate (see page 139). Great to finish off a meal.

Because figs have a natural affinity with lamb, try using a shoulder of lamb, boned and stuffed with fresh figs, garlic and lemon zest. Pot roast very slowly in some olive oil, adding a little seasoning. Moisten with stock if lamb is sticking or the figs are causing it to burn. The meat will give off a syrupy glaze that should be served with the lamb, with some boiled potatoes and a green salad.

———

MAKE A FIG TAPENADE by adding finely-diced dried fig to a basic olive tapenade. It keeps in a refrigerator covered with olive oil and can be pulled out to make barbecued lamb chops into something a little more special.

DRIED FIG TAPENADE

3/4 cup reconstituted dried figs
1 cup kalamata olives, pitted
10 anchovy fillets
2 tablespoons capers

4-5 tablespoons lemon juice
3 sprigs rosemary
1 cup oil
salt and pepper

Fry the rosemary sprigs in a little of the oil. Remove the rosemary and set it aside. Cool the rosemary-infused oil and then add it to the balance of the oil. Top and tail the dried figs and cut into small pieces. Process the figs, olives, fried rosemary, capers and anchovies to a purée. Season with lemon juice, salt and pepper. Pour in the olive oil slowly as if making a mayonnaise. Serve with barbecued quail.

———

A BOTTLE OF PICKLED FIGS in the pantry can be used to complement poultry for a last-minute meal, and is especially good with duck or quail. Roast or pan fry the poultry with fresh rosemary and deglaze the pan with a little of the pickling liquid. Add a little chicken stock to the sauce and then toss in some sliced pickled figs, rosemary and slices of lemon.

PICKLED FIGS, FARM FOLLIES STYLE

BRINE
225 g salt
2 litres water

PICKLING

3 kg figs	*2 kg sugar*
1 tablespoon mixed spice	*2 cloves per fig*
1 litre vinegar	

Soak the figs in the brine for 12 hours. Boil the spice, vinegar and 1.5 kg sugar for 15 minutes. Cook the fruit slowly in this syrup for 1 hour. Allow to stand overnight.

The next day, bring the figs to the boil, drain them and place in jars. Add the extra 500 g sugar to the syrup and boil for 30 minutes. Cover the figs with the syrup and seal the jars.

FIGS IN PUFF PASTRY WITH CRÈME ANGLAISE

YOU CAN MAKE a fantastic dessert with puff pastry. Roll out the pastry and rest it in the refrigerator for half an hour before cutting it to your desired shape and brushing it with egg wash. Make sure you don't brush the egg right to the edges as this will inhibit the rising of the layers. Cook in a very hot oven until golden brown and cooked through. Cut the piece in half and pull out any stodgy or uncooked bits of pastry if it is undercooked.

Then make a simple crème anglaise (see below). Cut the figs into thick slices and fry them quickly in a little butter. Don't put too many in the pan at a time—this may cause them to sweat instead of caramelise. Add a squeeze of lemon juice.

Assemble by placing the base of the pastry on a serving plate, pile up with figs and put the top of the pastry on, sprinkling with a little icing sugar if you wish. Pour the custard around the pastry and serve. (If you pour custard on the plate first and then place pastry on top your pastry will get soggy.)

CRÈME ANGLAISE

500 ml milk	*8 egg yolks*
500 ml rich cream	*120 g sugar*
1 vanilla pod, cut in half and the	
seeds scraped into the mixture	

Bring the milk and cream to the boil with the vanilla pod and seeds and leave to infuse. Whisk the egg yolks and sugar until thick and light in colour. Carefully stir the heated milk mixture into the eggs. Return the crème to the pan and heat gently, stirring gently and constantly with a wooden spoon until the mixture begins to thicken. Take the mixture off the heat from time to time if it looks like getting too hot. Have an ice bath standing by in case you take it too far and you need to place the saucepan in it to cool it down. It should be thick enough to draw your finger across the wooden spoon and see the trail. Remove the vanilla pod.

FIG AND WALNUT TART

ONE OF MY most often asked-for desserts, which is almost embarrassingly simple, is a fig and walnut tart. It's really just a meringue made with dark brown sugar—to each 4 egg whites, you need 120 g dark brown sugar—and 1 cup each of roughly-chopped walnuts and finely-cut, reconstituted dried figs (unless you have the shiny Californian ones). To reconstitute the figs, place them in a strainer and steam over a pot of boiling water for 5 minutes. The secret to the walnuts is to roast them in the oven and rub the skins off with a clean, dry tea towel. Make the meringue by beating the egg whites with the brown sugar, adding a pinch of salt and some vanilla essence and, when stiff, folding in the walnuts and figs. Be sure not to overbeat the egg whites as they will dry out.

Line a spring-form pan with greaseproof paper, pour in mixture, and bake in a moderate oven for 30-40 minutes. I serve this with crème fraîche or sour cream and, as it is so rich, I prefer it in a thin slice with coffee rather than a normal dessert serve.

Grapes

I N FEBRUARY the Barossa Valley vintage is in full swing. In the 20
years I have lived here there has been a gradual eroding of the
harvesting traditions and there are now fewer hand-picking gangs.
For economic reasons machine picking has become a fact of life
and with it some of the colour of the valley has gone. The women
of the Barossa were the core of the picking gangs, helped by
hundreds of itinerant workers who would descend on the Valley
looking for work. They were often young people on working
holidays and over the years we had lawyers, teachers, nurses and
chefs picking for us.

The traditional grape pickers' party at the end of the vintage
was often a very spirited affair. After all the hard work of picking
there was an atmosphere of camaraderie and satisfaction in the air
at seeing the crop in.

The vine was one of the earliest cultivated plants and its main
purpose has always been for the making of wine. A large market
has also developed for table grapes, particularly in Europe where
the grape is so revered that the best grapes from Belgium are
wrapped in tissue by the bunch and tied with ribbon or presented
in small wooden boxes. Large black grapes served with a soft brie
is a pretty good combination—especially when teamed with thinly
sliced walnut bread.

To supplement the winter diet, grapes were dried—sultanas, currants and raisins. Our local Gawler Park Fruits have a wonderful product in their dried muscatels; the whole bunch is dried and sold on the stem. These are my favourites—served with cheese—though I do leave them until the fresh grapes or figs are finished.

Many recipes for grapes in desserts or sauces will call for skinning and deseeding. I have to admit that I don't go to the trouble of skinning them. Once you remove the skin you lose the difference in colour between the black and the white grape, as there is little difference in their flavour. It is also difficult to justify the time. Personally I like the skins left on most fruit and vegetables and usually only remove them if absolutely necessary.

I don't mind the seeds too much either. For the restaurant I buy non-seeded grapes as a matter of course, but for a grape bread we made last year using a traditional Italian recipe, we used our Cabernet grapes to replace the Sangiovese ones they would traditionally use in Tuscany, seeds and all.

There is an interesting idea of Carol Field's in her book *Celebrating Italy*, where she adds walnuts to this traditional bread so that the nutty crunch disguises the seeds of the grapes. This is my version.

TUSCAN GRAPE HARVEST SWEET BREAD

SPONGE

12 g fresh yeast or	*1 cup warm milk*
6 g dried yeast	*2 eggs*
30 g sugar	*250 g unbleached all purpose flour*

Stir the yeast and sugar into the milk and let stand for about 10 minutes until frothy. Whisk in the eggs, then stir in the flour a little at a time. Cover tightly with plastic and let stand until bubbly, for about 30-45 minutes. If you use dry yeast, add it to the flour with the sugar and then proceed.

DOUGH

250 g bleached all purpose flour	*100 g unsalted butter,*
30 g sugar	*at room temperature*
1 teaspoon sea salt	

Stir the flour, sugar and salt into the sponge. Add the butter a little at a time and then knead on a lightly floured bench for 6 to 7 minutes. The dough is like brioche—soft, quite sticky and shiny.

TOPPING

5 cups red grapes	*40 g dark brown sugar*
2 cups walnuts, roasted, rubbed	
of their skins and kept whole	

Turn the dough out on to a lightly oiled baking pan. I like to use walnut oil for this and have a bit extra on my fingertips to stretch the dough towards the edges as if making foccaccia. Toss the grapes and walnuts generously over the dough. Cover with a towel and let it rise until double in height again.

Heat the oven to 220°C and bake for 15 minutes. Turn the oven down to 200°C and sprinkle the brown sugar on. Bake another 15 to 20 minutes, being careful the sugar doesn't burn.

———

THE CSIRO ARE at work improving seedless grape varieties. Much hope is held for the Maroo which is suitable for consumption as a fresh table grape or a large black raisin. The berries are naturally large and seedless with a pleasant sweet taste and when dried, produce an excellent, attractive large seedless raisin with a characteristic nutty flavour.

When you tire of just eating bunches of grapes, there are many other ways to use them. I love a green salad with grapes tossed through, with a dressing of walnut oil and a little red wine vinegar (keeping it in the family). I love the explosion of grape juice when I come across them in the salad leaves, particularly if they are icy cold.

Pickled grapes are the perfect accompaniment to pates and terrines, and also with tongue (either smoked or in brine). To pickle the grapes, place them in sterilised jars (I even like to leave the grapes on the bunches if possible) and pour in a spiced vinegar which has been brought to the boil—you can make your own spiced vinegar or use Seppelts Spiced Vinegar. Leave the grapes in the bottle for 6 weeks to mature and they will last for up to 12 months. I prefer a large black grape for this, such as Black Prince.

Grapes team well with offal such as duck livers or hearts, or even sweetbreads, where the freshness of the grapes cuts into the richness of the offal. Just cook the livers, hearts or sweetbreads as normal and, 30 seconds before serving, throw into the pan a handful of grapes picked from the stem. If you want to go to a little more trouble, you could present the grapes in a little pastry tart.

Grapes make very good sauces for chicken, pigeon, quail, pheasant or guinea fowl. Once again the trick is to toss the grapes into the sauce in the last 30 seconds or so.

Try grapes in a stuffing. Add them to the traditional breadcrumbs with onions, fresh tarragon and an egg to bind. Deglaze the chicken with some verjuice (see below).

———————

WE MAKE A cold soup of grapes, almonds and garlic, adapted from the Time Life *Fruit Book*. The combination is brilliant and it makes a refreshing dish for a luncheon. The soup is made a little like a mayonnaise, and if it is too thick, iced water is stirred in just before serving. It should be just like gazpacho. The grapes are added at the last moment and it is best to do this at the table as they sink to the bottom very quickly. The sight of bobbing grapes is worth it!

GARLIC SOUP WITH GRAPES

*250 g crumbs from a french
  loaf, soaked in cold milk
  for 20 minutes
150 g almonds, roasted for
  flavour—I use skins and all
125 ml olive oil
200 g sultana grapes—
  I prefer them green; if they
  have turned yellow, they will
  be overripe for this dish*

*2 large garlic cloves
2 tablespoons white wine vinegar
iced water or ice blocks
  made of verjuice*

Squeeze the milk lightly out of the bread and put the bread in the blender with the garlic, almonds and vinegar. Add the oil slowly until well blended. Add salt if required. Refrigerate. Just before serving, pour

in iced water or ice blocks to suit taste and consistency. Add the grapes
to the soup immediately prior to serving.

VERJUICE

If you have a grapevine in your back garden, you can enjoy verjuice (the
juice of green grapes picked when they are very tart), an ingredient that
dates back to the Middle Ages. Verjuice is available commercially—the
grapes are crushed and the juice is then stabilised and bottled. Verjuice
is an ingredient common to the grape producing areas of Europe. There
are many variations, with sherry vinegar or distilled spirit such as grappa,
vodka or brandy being added to the straight green grape juice. This
addition of alcohol serves to stabilise the juice and to preserve it. (A
bottle of green grape juice without such a stabiliser would be
dangerously explosive.) Verjuice improves with age.

I love the freshness and sharpness verjuice brings to a dish, whether it
is a butter sauce to serve with seafood or to deglaze a dish for poultry. In
the autumn there is hardly a dish in the restaurant where it doesn't
feature in some guise or another—it can be used anywhere a light
vinegar is called for—although it is not as strong as vinegar and will give
a piquancy to the dish with the subtle flavour of grape in the
background. It is wonderful in a salad dressing, particularly if you mix it
with walnut oil. Toss some fresh whole grapes into the salad as well.

If your grapes are sweet enough to eat without puckering your
mouth, they have gone too far and you will have to wait for green grapes
next year. Pick the tart green grapes and freeze them until you need the
juice.

Purée the grapes in a blender and then take the resulting juice. It is
almost clear with a tinge of green. You may want to reduce it to
strengthen the flavour, depending on how you intend to use it.

———————

THE FOLLOWING RECIPE is another created by Urs Inauen, Tom
Milligan, Cheong Liew and myself for the Seppelts Menu of the
Year competition. It is a dish of razorfish, which is a wonderful local
mollusc not well known except among fishermen. I often serve this dish
substituting scallops for the razorfish.

Seared Razorfish on Fine Spinach with Verjuice Butter Sauce

(SERVES 8)

SAUCE

juice of 1 lemon
4 shallots, sliced
250 ml verjuice

250 g unsalted butter, cubed
salt, black pepper

Reduce the shallots and verjuice with salt until syrupy. Gradually whisk in the butter and maintain a warm to hot temperature through the cooking but do not bring to the boil. Finish the sauce with lemon juice and adjust the seasoning. Set aside in a warm place.

RAZORFISH

16 razorfish hearts
250 g fine spinach leaves
zest and juice of half a lime
salt, pepper

nutmeg
10 ml olive oil
50 g unsalted butter

With a paring knife, clean the razorfish hearts of all skin and remaining shell pieces. Remove all stalks from the spinach leaves, wash thoroughly and dry well. Heat a saucepan and slightly brown 30 g butter. Add the spinach, season with salt, pepper and nutmeg and stir well. Take the spinach out and place on a towel. Heat the olive oil with the remaining butter. Season the fish with sea salt, lime zest and juice. Sear the fish in the pan for a few seconds only on each side and place on a towel.

Divide the spinach, placing it in the centre of each of 8 hot plates. Place 2 razorfish in the middle of each plate, leaning one on the other. Garnish with lemon zest. Pour the sauce around the fish and grate black pepper around the outside.

T HE FOLLOWING DISH can be made with pheasant as well as chicken.

GRAPEGROWER'S CHICKEN

4 large chicken legs
(thighs and drumsticks)
walnut oil
1 tablespoon butter
1 kg green sultana grapes to
yield 2/3 cup verjuice

1 cup fresh sultana grapes to
add to the sauce
1/2 cup jellied chicken stock
100 g unsalted butter,
cubed and chilled

Separate the thighs and drumsticks. Pick the green grapes off the stem, discarding any that are spoiled. Make the verjuice by blending the grapes to yield 2/3 cup juice. Heat enough oil and butter to just cover the bottom of a heavy-based pan and gently seal the chicken pieces until golden brown. Season the legs and discard the oil in the pan. Add the verjuice and gently braise the chicken legs. Be careful that the temperature is not so high that the skin sticks and the verjuice caramelises—if this starts to happen add a touch of stock or water. Cook for about 20 minutes until tender and then set aside, covered, for about 10 minutes. Add the chicken stock to the cooking pan and reduce the juices. Whisk in the butter to 'velvet' the sauce while it is boiling rapidly (the butter is optional in these health conscious days). Throw in the sultanas in the last few seconds and serve the chicken with the sauce. Serve with a salad and boiled waxy potatoes in their jackets.

If you wish to make this dish when grapes are out of season, take 1/2 cup raisins and soak them overnight in some medium dry sherry. Add these to the sauce in the last 5 minutes of cooking.

G UINEA FOWL MAKE great watch-dogs. I defy any person to sneak into a property that has guinea fowl in the yard. I'm sure some country people choose to have them for just this reason and enjoy the bonus of the fowl being delicious to eat and a change from mutton or chook.

In my experience, the French prefer guinea fowl to pheasant. This is a debate I prefer to stay out of, my restaurant being called the Pheasant Farm, but I know that I love to have guinea fowl on the menu. When well-cooked, it is sweet, moist and delicious and marries particularly well with orange, lemon, thyme or any fresh herb, walnuts, liver and bacon. It can be cooked and eaten with both red and white wine.

It is easy to confuse the carcasses of guinea fowl and pheasant as their skin colour and leg meat are similar. Guinea fowl can be identified by the dark black spots on the skin of the upper breast and under the wings. Its breast is whiter, and the meat more delicate in taste, texture and structure, than the pheasant's.

If you buy or are given a bird by a farmer, it is very important that the bird is no more than 14 weeks old if you plan to oven roast it—any older and it will require pot roasting. Farmers who keep only a few birds often let their flocks run together, which makes the birds' ages difficult to determine. It is also unusually difficult to determine the sex of guinea fowl, as males and females are identical to the untrained eye (and even to some very experienced eyes!). This makes keeping breeding stock rather haphazard.

A guinea fowl usually dresses out at 600 g to one kilo. You really need at least a 750 g bird to feed two people, although some farms breed 450 g birds for single serves. I disagree with this, as I find such birds immature and their flavour and texture jellyish. Incidentally, it is best to steer clear of frozen guinea fowl: although many types of game freeze fairly well, the guinea fowl has much less meat on its bones than, say, a pheasant or a chook, and so does not freeze successfully.

Don't forget guinea fowl eggs—scrambled or pickled they are a great treat. They are larger than quail eggs, yet smaller than chook eggs, and very creamy.

Very few cook books contain recipes for guinea fowl. Most chicken or pheasant recipes can be interchanged with guinea fowl, but the following cooking principles should be followed:

Use one 800 g bird for two people. Cut the spine out and squash the bird so it is 'butterflied' and lies flat in the baking dish. Brush with a marinade of olive oil and orange juice, lemon juice or verjuice. This is both for flavour and for caramelisation of the skin. If you wish, marinate the bird first and add herbs or spices of your choice.

Preheat the oven to very high (say 220°C) and roast the bird on a flat tray for 12-20 minutes. It is cooked when the thigh of the bird pulls away from the breast easily and the thickest part of the breast feels springy to the touch. At the end of the cooking period I like to turn the bird upside down in its cooking tray and leave it for about 20 minutes before I carve.

The very first guinea fowl we ever sold was to some French customers who were kind enough to pass on their method of cooking it. They made a stuffing of onions, walnuts, the livers of the guinea fowl and juniper berries. This is a dish I have reproduced many times and I love the combination of flavours. Using such a stuffing, I might then serve the bird with a red wine sauce.

GUINEA FOWL WITH RED WINE SAUCE

STUFFING

200 g guinea fowl livers (or chicken livers)	3 juniper berries, crushed
1 large onion, finely diced	salt and pepper
1 sprig rosemary	100 g coarse, roasted breadcrumbs
50 g walnuts, roasted and skins rubbed	butter

Clean the livers and cut into quarters. Sauté the onion and rosemary in a generous amount of butter. Quickly toss in the livers to seal. Add the crushed juniper berries, salt and pepper. Then add the walnuts and breadcrumbs. Stuff the bird. Cook at 220°C for 20-35 minutes and then rest for 20 minutes. I do not truss the bird.

RED WINE SAUCE

200 ml red wine	1 tablespoon Dijon mustard
50 ml port	250 ml well-reduced game stock
1 tablespoon redcurrant jelly	juice of half a lemon

Reduce red wine and port by three quarters, then add redcurrant jelly and mustard with a whisk, and lemon juice and stock. Bring to a rapid boil and reduce a little more. If you wish to 'velvet' the sauce, whisk in some butter.

If you prefer not to stuff the bird you could make some small croutons and serve a liver crostini with the bird and the sauce.

LIVER CROSTINI

200 g livers, cleaned and cut into quarters	1 tablespoon capers, drained
8 sage leaves, finely chopped	2 anchovy fillets, finely chopped
75 g butter	1 tablespoon chopped continental parsley
1 tablespoon red wine vinegar	6 croutons made from a french stick

Fry the livers and sage in butter until just pink. Add the vinegar, capers, anchovy and parsley. Serve on croutons.

THIS GUINEA FOWL recipe was inspired by a similar one in *Catalan Cuisine* by Colman Andrews. It could easily be used for chicken, pheasant or quail by adapting the cooking times.

GUINEA FOWL IN LEMON AND GARLIC SAUCE

2 x 800 g guinea fowl
olive oil
2 large onions, finely chopped
3 heads garlic, separated into
  cloves and peeled
100 g prosciutto, cut into
  5 cm julienne strips
1 lemon rind, grated

juice of 1 lemon
2 cups rich chicken stock
juice of half an orange
1 cup dry white wine
salt and pepper
paper-thin slices of
  lemon to garnish

In a heavy-based cast iron or enamel pot, brown the guinea fowl very gently in olive oil until golden brown all over. During this process I cut the skin between the breast and leg to allow the heat to penetrate more readily. (This allows for a minimum cooking time to maximise the moistness of the flesh.)

Remove and set aside. Cover the bottom of the pot with approximately 1 cm oil. Sweat the onions and garlic until wilted and golden brown. (This is called a sofregit in Catalan cooking and is usually based on olive oil, onions and tomatoes, although it can vary.)

Return the guinea fowl to the pot and add the lemon rind, lemon juice, stock, orange juice and wine. Add a quarter of the prosciutto. Season with a little pepper. Using a simmer pad to inhibit the direct heat, simmer covered for about 8 to 10 minutes. Turn the guinea fowl over and simmer for another 8 to 10 minutes. Take the guinea fowl out of the pot and cover. Take away the simmer pad and reduce the sauce for 20 minutes, adding the balance of prosciutto when it reaches the desired consistency. Cut the guinea fowl in half and serve with the sauce. Garnish with lemon slices and eat together with a green salad.

Pomegranate

POMEGRANATES ARE FREQUENTLY overlooked because people don't know how to eat them, and they are often grown just for the ornamental beauty of the trees laden with fruit in autumn.

The first time I tasted pomegranate I took one bite, spat it out and didn't try it again for years. Now I eagerly await the season to team the fruit with duck, pheasant or guinea fowl. I don't actually belong to the 'fruit with meat' school of thought but there are exceptions! Certainly, lemon and orange are ideal with game, and the old-fashioned, yet exotic pomegranate has a tartness that cuts into rich dishes extremely well. I love the crunch of the brilliant red seeds in the final texture of a dish, although some people may find it difficult as the pip is similar to that of the grape.

Pomegranates on sale attract attention just for their look— they are about the size of a quince, with a waxy skin that has gradations of colour from gold through to deep blush or rosy pink, and a crown-like calyx. You can imagine people buying them just for show, but cut in half they reveal a wonderful display of red, crystal-like seeds. These can be used in many different ways, but need first to be separated from their yellowish membranes, which give the astringency or tannin that can make a dish unpalatable. The seeds can be used simply as a dessert fruit—perhaps on a plate of autumn fruits with persimmon and tamarillo.

The pomegranate originated in Persia and most recipes for its fruit appear in Persian, Russian or Greek cookbooks. Different varieties of pomegranate are found around the world. Those from the Middle East and the Mediterranean have a sharp, acid taste that makes them particularly good in savoury dishes. I find it necessary to adjust Australian pomegranates with a little lemon unless I am using them for a fresh dessert.

Tom Stobart, in the *Cook's Encyclopaedia*, suggests a drink made from freshly-squeezed pomegranate juice, chilled and mixed with Dutch gin (I add a dash of lemon, too).

Grenadine syrup is made from pomegranates and is very popular in France with fruit salad or served with grapefruit instead of sugar. It is also used to make cordials, ices and jellies.

———

HERE IS A SIMPLE sauce created in our kitchen to team with roasted mallard duck. It has a Persian influence and can also be used with quail, chicken, pheasant or guinea fowl.

POMEGRANATE SAUCE

1 onion, finely chopped
1 pomegranate, seeded carefully
   to avoid yellow membrane
pinch cardamom
pinch turmeric
pinch pepper

touch of red wine vinegar
touch of sugar
juice of one lemon
100 ml chicken stock
touch of salt

Sweat the onion and pomegranate seeds till translucent. Add spices and continue to stir. Add sugar and vinegar and caramelise. When almost catching, add lemon juice and reduce. Finally, add chicken stock and reduce again. Taste and season with a touch of salt before serving.

———

POMEGRANATE SAUCE (SWEET)

3 pomegranates   *100 g sugar*
juice of 1/2 good-sized lemon

Cut one pomegranate in half and take membrane away from seeds. Reserve seeds in a bowl.

Cut the other pomegranates in half and squeeze them in an orange squeezer or pass through a food mill. Boil the juice along with the lemon juice and sugar in an enamel or stainless steel saucepan for 2 minutes or more to reduce a little.

Cool and add reserved seeds. Serve with desserts such as rich chocolate cake.

Pears

M Y LOVE OF PEARS stems from the tradition of the early
Barossa settlers planting pear trees on their properties to
make the well water sweet. We are lucky enough to have
three hundred-year-old trees in our garden at home.
They still bear prolifically and at the base of the most
magnificent one is a deep well that has a ledge in it
halfway up where the milk was kept cool before the days
of refrigeration. These pear trees are the size of oak trees
and we count ourselves very lucky indeed to live with
such beautiful trees. The joy extends from the beauty and
scent of their blossom in spring to the summer shade to
the autumn crop. We stack green pears into wooden
boxes and store them in the cellar to use in the winter.
The perfume in the cellar lingers long after the last pear
has been eaten.

Back in the 17th century some 300 varieties of pears
were known. In Australia there are now only a handful of
varieties readily available commercially. There is the
Duchess pear—the green pear that goes yellow when
ripe and makes good eating. The Josephine and Packham
pears are available from April right through winter.
Beurre Bosc, the small, brown, beautifully-shaped pear

which is hard to eat but cooks very well, is available at the same time. Red Sensation pears are the brightly-coloured, super-expensive ones that have been hand-picked and packed. Local folklore has it that the brightly-coloured red and green Corella pear was established many years ago here in Nuriootpa by a local orchardist. Unfortunately we don't seem to be able to buy them locally.

Eat pears fresh, dried, or pickled, or make wine or liqueur with them. Buying a perfect pear from the shop is difficult as pears are picked green and are often sold green. If you let these green pears ripen in your kitchen or in the crisper of your fridge until they give slightly around the stem, but are in no way squashy or bruised, they will be perfect for eating.

If you have your own tree, sometimes the fruit will be perfect for eating straight from the tree but more likely the fruit will drop or birds will attack if it is left to ripen naturally. The difference between a ripened juicy pear and a hard green one would seem to make them unrelated fruits. Try a good slab of cheese with a piece of pear after dinner.

Try a simple salad made with peppery herbs such as watercress and rocket, ripe pear and Parmesan or Stilton, Roquefort or a good Australian cheese. Core the pear and slice it, leaving the skin on. Dress the salad with walnut oil and a little good vinegar and add freshly ground black pepper and some oven-roasted walnuts which have been rubbed in a tea towel to shed their bitter skin. As pears will oxidise, rub the cut surfaces immediately with lemon juice or vinaigrette.

Perhaps my favourite way of preparing pears is to make a compote of pears with quince and vanilla and serve it with a vanilla crème anglaise (see page 154).

SUN-DRIED PEARS—FARM FOLLIES STYLE

Peel and core firm, ripe pears. As you go, place them in salt water for 15 minutes. Then lay them on wire racks in the hot sun. Turn them as they dry. The outside should form a skin, leaving the flesh moist inside. Store in airtight jars with silica gel (available from the chemist).

PICKLED PEARS

2 kg firm pears, as
  firm as possible
2 tablespoons allspice
1 tablespoon cloves
2 tablespoons chopped
  cinnamon sticks

2 tablespoons coriander seeds,
  dry roasted and bruised
1.5 kg sugar
1.2 litres Seppelts white vinegar

Wash and dry the fruit for any residual sprays. Tie all the spices together in a muslin bag. Boil together the vinegar, sugar and spices. Add the whole fruit and simmer until tender on a low heat. Lift out the pears and put into clean sterilised jars and then reduce the cooking liquid to a syrup. Pour the syrup over the fruit. Cover and store.

GLAZED PEARS WITH MASCARPONE
(SERVES 4)

4 medium-sized pears
200 g unsalted butter
150 g castor sugar
20 ml lemon juice

10 ml vinegar
1 halved and scraped vanilla pod
160 g mascarpone
juice and rind of 1 lemon

Melt the butter slowly in a heavy metal frypan and add the sugar, lemon juice and vinegar. Dissolve slowly and then add the peeled pears (be careful to leave the stalk on) and vanilla pod and seeds. Cook evenly and slowly over a low heat for approximately 1 hour until the pears have an even golden colour. If you have chosen ripe ones, this will take less time, but remember that the final colour is important, so be careful not to overcook them whilst colouring.

Check that the pears are done by placing a thin-bladed knife or skewer into the centre. If there is no resistance when you pull it out, then they are ready. The cooking liquid should be a light caramel colour and can be used to finish the pears off and give them a wonderful 'glistening' appearance.

Carefully mix the lemon rind and juice into the mascarpone. Don't beat it as the mascarpone will become too runny.

Put a pear on to each serving plate and pour on the caramel. Serve a dollop of the cream next to the pear and its acidic creaminess will blend perfectly with the fruity, vanilla aroma of the poached pear.

Wild Duck

AUTUMN IS THE time for wild game and wild mushrooms.
Although the wild duck season runs from mid-February to
mid-June, as the weather becomes cooler slow-cooked dishes
become more tantalising. Wild duck is a wonderful food but,
as with most game, can be very tricky to cook until you
master the principles.

One of the best food memories of my life was a wild duck
dinner cooked by my friends the Walls, of Yalumba. Both
great cooks, they well understand the principle of slow pot
roasting for many hours. In this instance, they made a liver
and sage *panade* (stuffing), wrapped it in bacon (I think—my
memory is a bit hazy), and kept it moist with stock or wine as
it cooked. It was the first time I had eaten wild duck and,
washed down with some great Yalumba reds, it was
magnificent.

It was the sort of experience that is hard to replicate—as
with so many food memories, it is linked with the people
with whom the meal is shared, the mood of the night and so
on. I mention it because of the influence of a very special
man, Alf Wark, who was Yalumba's company secretary from
1945 to 1971, and whom I was privileged to meet when we
first came to live in the Barossa in 1973.

Alf Wark had a tremendous influence both on Yalumba and across Australia. He was passionate and knowledgeable about food. His influence on the Hill Smith family—a very special wine family with a tremendous love of food who have helped South Australia develop enormously—is evident. Alf was a keen hunter and fisherman and also a conservationist, as are his son and grandson today, who are involved with the SA Field and Game Association.

The SA Field & Game Association, whose members come from all walks of life, are not only responsible hunters but committed to conservation. I was interested to learn from the Department of Fisheries & Wildlife that they have little difficulty controlling this group. In the south east of South Australia, one large landowner has undertaken a rehabilitation programme, at his own expense, of wetlands that had been drained and dried out for farming and now boast a flourishing and increasing population of many species of water birds.

Alf wrote a tiny book, *Wine Cookery*, published by Rigby Australia. With the kind permission of his family I give you his two recipes for wild duck.

WILD DUCK POACHED IN WINE SAUCE

breasts of 4 teal ducks
225 g butter
2 tablespoons
Worcestershire sauce

300 ml burgundy
4 tablespoons redcurrant jelly
grated peel of 1 orange
60 ml port wine

Melt the butter and add all ingredients except the duck, and simmer. Add the raw duck breasts, cover the pan and simmer for 20 minutes. Add seasoning to taste. (I would take the breasts out of the pan.) Add the port before serving and reduce the sauce a little.

BLACK DUCK AND ORANGE SAUCE
(SERVES 4)

2 wild black ducks, with giblets
4 oranges
4 tablespoons honey
120 ml port wine

seasoning
2 medium white onions
2 stalks celery

When cleaning the ducks, save the giblets, and make sure the inside is well cleaned of blood from shot wounds. Rub salt and pepper inside and leave for some time before cooking. Simmer the giblets with a little onion and celery pieces for stock. In the body cavity place an onion cut in quarters and a stick of celery cut in long pieces. Add 30g butter to the cavity. Close the body opening with a skewer and smear the breast of each duck with clarified butter. Cook in a pan in a moderate oven for 1 1/2 hours. In the cooking pan first pour some diluted honey and stock from the giblets and baste a few times during the cooking, taking care that the juices do not dry out.

Take the juice from 2 oranges and mix with port and the balance of the honey and when the bird is nearly cooked, baste the breast frequently to glaze it. Shred the orange rind from the other 2 oranges and cut the flesh into thin slices. When the duck is cooked (not overdone) place on a hotplate and cover to keep warm. Add the balance of the stock to the pan juices and boil until reduced to a thick consistency. Add the grated orange rind and pour over the duck. Garnish with the thin slices of orange and, with poultry secateurs, cut the birds into 4 pieces. Serve with the warmed orange slices.

A S WITH ALL GAME, it is hard to determine the age of a wild duck, so it is certainly safer to use the slow cooking methods, though I have read, particularly in American books, of spit roasting and cooking wild duck rare in much the same way as I cook pheasant. Having tested this with young mallard (grown as a domestic duck), I can assure you it is effective. The following are tests I have read about to determine the age of a wild duck:
1. The webbing on a young bird will tear as you process it.
2. The bill of a young bird is shinier.
3. The tail feathers seem to have a 'V' taken out at the end of the feather instead of being rounded like the end of a spoon (as on a mature bird).

Unless you are sure of the age, I would suggest using slow cooking methods—pot roasting, pressure cooking (with simmer pads under the pot to slow it down as much as possible), or cooking in oven bags at a very low oven temperature.

I have cooked wild duck smothered in pork back fat and stuffed with olives and thyme, or simply stuffed with onion, apple and a few herbs, using about 12 mm of stock in the bottom of the roasting pan, and a lid so that condensation helps to keep the bird moist.

If pot roasting duck in a baking dish or heavy-bottomed pan, I prefer to do it on top of the stove as I am reminded to check whether it needs more liquid, and the aroma of the food is so much greater than when enclosed in the oven—it gives a lovely feel to the kitchen. If you don't have any stock as your braising medium, try water or go for a stronger flavour such as port, though you might need to balance its sweetness with a little lemon.

Both orange and lemon marry very well with duck, as they do with most game. Tart jellies such as redcurrant, crab-apple or native currant also go very well.

One last tip with duck is to remove the 'preen glands' before cooking. In a wild duck they can impart a strong, musky flavour and in a domestic duck they can be bitter. They are located on either side of the duck's tail and are about the size of an elongated pea with the consistency of kidney.

The mallard is the most common wild duck in Europe and America and most domestic ducks are descended from this breed. In Australia the mallard has caused a problem by breeding with native ducks and 'shandying' the breeds. This is discouraged where possible.

In South Australia we have mainly black duck, teal and wood duck. The teal and black duck are considered the best eating, the teal being much smaller and the black duck much stronger. The duck's flavour is dependent on its breeding ground and, certainly in some parts of the world, can be referred to as 'fishy'. In such cases, the duck is 'pre-cooked' for a few minutes with onion in salty water to eliminate this.

In Europe, particularly, they hang their wild duck, whereas in Australia most people do not bother.

DUCK FAT

I FIRST STARTED using duck or goose fat when I collected the excess from a bird I had cooked. These days I find it so useful that I buy it in 10 kg lots from Rosina Foods of Adelaide and render it in bulk. It keeps for months and has myriad uses.

The easiest use of all is to bake slices of potato (particularly waxy potato), that have first been boiled whole in their jackets, with a little rosemary in a heavy baking pan. Heat about half a centimetre of duck fat with the rosemary before crisping the potato slices. It takes about 15 minutes in a hot oven, and the potato should be turned over as soon as the first side is a golden brown. The moment the second side is golden the potato should be slid out of the baking dish on to absorbent paper. If you wish to season it, sprinkle with a little Maldon sea salt and pepper. Eat immediately!

This is a more-ish snack and a great vegetable accompaniment to almost any dish. It cannot be done in advance and should be served crisp and straight out of the oven. There is absolutely no comparison in flavour to potatoes done similarly in oil or butter or a combination of the two. Try it!

I first heard about duck fat from Elizabeth David's books, but it was Paula Wolfert's *The Cooking of South West France* that committed me to duck fat as a cooking medium. I was so convinced about the flavour that it wasn't difficult for Paula also to convince me about its being healthier than other fats. She says that the US Department of Agriculture states that rendered poultry fat (goose, duck and chicken) contains 9 per cent cholesterol, lard contains 10 per cent, and butter contains 22 per cent. She continues, 'Since one needs less poultry fat, oil or lard than butter to sauté meat or vegetables, one will ingest far less saturated fat if these cooking media are used instead of butter. One needs less of these because butter breaks down and burns at high temperatures whereas poultry fat, lard and oil do not.'

As I have said, there is no doubt in my mind of the added flavour given when cooking in duck fat, but that doesn't mean you have to serve fatty foods when you use it. The actual flavour component in the duck fat is water-soluble and can be separated from the fat itself, so the food can be served almost fat-free yet with all the advantages of the increased flavour.

Braising meat at a very low temperature in duck fat is at the base of the cuisine of south-west France and is a technique I use with old game. I am very careful never to let the meat 'move' at anything more than a simmer and always use the heaviest pot in my kitchen (with a tight-fitting lid). I often use a simmer pad between the pot and the flame to be sure there is virtually no movement. This method means that the food being cooked is totally immersed in the duck fat.

When such low, slow temperatures are used, the cooking fats mingle but do not incorporate with the wine or juices used in the cooking, and the 'fat' is therefore easy to remove by degreasing the dish after cooking. Where possible, I chill the dish overnight to allow the fat to settle in an easily removable slab. I have always found it difficult totally to degrease freshly-cooked dishes. Flavours of slow-cooked dishes always improve by slowly reheating them the next day and, although I always degrease, I am not vitally concerned about taking out every skerrick of fat, as it is the fat that contains the flavour.

The duck fat you buy from Rosina Foods has to be rendered to enable you to use it, and the following simple method can be followed. As far as I know, you can only buy 10 kg at a time, but rendering it is like making stock, you can freeze any you don't need right at the moment and, in fact, well-covered in your refrigerator it will last for about three months. It is the sort of job that is better done in big batches once or twice a year.

Take a heavy-based stock pot or similar and place the duck fat and skin on the bottom. Some people cut up the skin into small pieces or even purée the fat and skin but, as time is the main element with us, unless we plan to use the skin for a salad, we simply add a few bay leaves and juniper berries and cover the fat with rain water. Cook slowly for about an hour until the fat turns clear, making sure that none of the skin sticks to the bottom and burns.

Strain while still hot, pour into a container and cool before refrigerating or freezing. If you wish to make the skin into cracklings, slowly reheat the pieces of skin in another pot until they turn golden brown, stirring to avoid burning. Drain and sprinkle with Maldon sea salt. Use in salads.

THE BEST-KNOWN dish made with duck fat is a confit. Here is a lesser-known but classic dish called 'rillettes'. I have adapted Paula Wolfert's recipe for duck rillettes, but you can also use rabbit, hare, pork or pigeon in exactly the same way.

RILLETTES DE CANARD (COMPOTE OF SHREDDED DUCK)

This recipe makes up to 6 cups and should be prepared one week in advance. It takes 30-45 minutes of active cooking time and unattended cooking time of 4-5 hours. The duck's breast is not used as it dries out too much for both rillettes and confit. Serve with rounds of crusty bread, cornichons, lots of pepper, and a glass of chilled sauternes.

4 duck legs (or 6 pigeon legs,
or front and back legs
of 2 large hares)
thighs, carcass, wings, etc.
of rest of duck (not breast)
1 1/2 cups duck fat, chilled
340 g pork shoulder,
cut into 2 cm cubes
salt and freshly-ground
pepper to taste

3/4 cup unsalted chicken stock
3/4 cup dry white wine
1 bay leaf, crushed
1 teaspoon fresh thyme leaves
1 large clove garlic, halved
2 shallots, peeled
1/2 teaspoon quatre épices
(recipe below)
2 tablespoons Armagnac
or brandy

Moisten the bottom of a crockpot, very heavy cast iron pot or camp oven with a little of the duck fat, place the duck legs (thigh and drumstick) on the bottom and cover with pork pieces. Chop the carcass, wings and back and add to pot, seasoning with 1 teaspoon each of salt and pepper. Add the stock, wine, herbs, garlic, shallots and quatre épices.

Cook at barely a simmer, uncovered, until the meat falls off the bone (4-5 hours). Stir from time to time to prevent sticking. The liquid in the pan will evaporate.

Strain pork and duck through a colander set over a deep bowl and let cool until you can handle it easily. Pick out all the bones and gristle, leaving aside the moist pieces of meat. Set aside half a cup of the fat that comes from the cooking.

Using a fork, shred the meat (I do not use a food processor at all for this) and add the 1 1/2 cups of chilled duck fat, the cooked garlic and shallots, and brandy. Taste for seasoning, adding more salt, plenty of pepper, thyme and quatre épices to taste. It should be very peppery.

Spoon the rillettes into clean stoneware dishes, leaving about 1 cm at the top. Seal with the reserved fat from the cooking. Chill and keep refrigerated for a few days for the flavours to develop.

QUATRE ÉPICES

THIS IS A MIXTURE used for pates, rillettes and terrines. Although meant to be made of four spices, it can be modified to suit personal taste. Spices are much better freshly roasted and used than stored for a long period.

TO MAKE ONE TABLESPOON:

10 cloves

1 tablespoon white peppercorns

1 cinnamon stick

2/3 teaspoon ground ginger

3/4 teaspoon freshly grated nutmeg

Grind all ingredients in a spice mill until powdery.

mushrooms

ONE OF LIFE'S great free pastimes in autumn is mushrooming. I have found exotic mushrooms in the Adelaide Hills and in the Mount Crawford Forest in the Barossa Valley. Mushrooming is a national pastime for the Italians, Yugoslavs, Chinese and, as Michael Dow of the *Sydney Morning Herald* says, 'especially the Russians', who, following autumn rains, take a picnic and make a day of hunting for them.

I think foraging for food is an undervalued activity. I have spoken out about the untapped resource of wild olives and I feel just as keenly that young unemployed people could be taught what to pick and how to look after, and market, wild mushrooms. So much goes to waste in the forest and it seems a great shame. We always go mushrooming on a weekday and we are the only people around. It is wonderfully eerie to walk into the woods by the long straight rows of trees. The pine needles are so thick on the ground that they cushion your feet and you feel you are walking on air, so silent you feel you are floating. The pine trees are so tall they tend to block out the sun but every now and then powerful shafts of sunlight push through and add to this ethereal effect.

You will definitely need some advice about what to pick and what to leave behind and it is important that you either gather scientific information from a book and study it carefully or find a friend who already has the mushrooming bug and become what English gastronome Paul Levy calls a 'fungi bore'.

My mushroom adviser, Peter Wall of Yalumba, as well as being a great friend and gourmet of note, has with his encyclopaedic mind made a study of mushrooms so that when our families went mushrooming, I felt very safe.

Firstly, what not to pick:
Aminata verna: Commonly called Destroying Angel. This is a pure white, stately, often large species. The best way to describe them is that they grow out of a cup which becomes visible when you brush away the grass from the stem. This egg-shaped cup called the 'volva' holds the mushroom in place. Other members of the Aminata family can also be found in Australian forests so caution is necessary.
Puffballs: Some are edible, some are not. It is best to leave these alone without an expert in tow.

What you can pick and enjoy includes far more than the common field mushroom:
Boletus granulatas: This mushroom grows in pine forests and has a reddish-brown cap with yellow pores and stalk. The upper part of the stalk is distinguished by granules. It is quite chewy or rubbery in texture. It is great sliced into salads or pickled.
Suillus luteus or *Boletus luteus:* Commonly known as Slippery Jack. The cap is slimy and pine needles stick to it easily. It is a dark, dull reddish-brown when young. The tubes are yellow and there is a ring of a purplish-brown colour on the stalk. Wipe the slime from the cap and remove the tubes before cooking. It has an excellent flavour and is perfect for using in soups and risotto. I enjoy these simply wiped and sliced and sautéed in olive oil with some fresh herbs. When we planned the Wild Mushroom Terrine (see page 186) for the Seppelts Dinner of the Year menu we had the pine mushrooms to practise with. Sadly, due to rain spoiling them, we couldn't use them on the night. As winners of the competition, obviously the substitute mushrooms were fine, but we knew the difference the pine mushrooms made to the original recipe!

It is a great shame that, so far as I know, no *Boletus edulis*, the famous porcino of Italy or cepe of France, has yet to be found in South Australia. I have heard rumours of its existence in Tasmania.

Coprinus comartus: Known as the ink cap mushroom, this is one of the best-flavoured mushrooms and is also the one most often left behind. It is often thought to be a toadstool and looks like a parasol with a shaggy white coat. As it grows older the cap dissolves into an inky mass.

Agricus campestrus and *Agricus robinsonii:* These are the common garden wonderfully tasty field mushrooms that poke through the ground from as early as April when the soil is still warm and the first rains occur. These are still most people's favourites as they are easy to recognise and don't require special knowledge in order to identify them. *Campestrus* has a white cap and *robinsonii* a browny cap. *Robinsonii* is not as intensely flavoured. Peter Wall cooks them with butter, a fresh bay leaf and a splash of champagne.

Mushrooms have so much flavour that they can be cooked very simply. A special breakfast can be made by simply frying them in butter with black pepper and serving on toast. Elizabeth David suggests that if in spring or summer you yearn for field mushrooms you can bake cultivated mushrooms in vine leaves and olive oil to give a wonderful earthy flavour. It really works!

THIS RECIPE COMES from Gerard Madani, an exciting chef I worked with at the Hotel Intercontinental in Sydney when I was guest chef there. Gerard uses button mushrooms, which can be obtained all year round, for this tasty soup.

GERARD MADANI'S MUSHROOM SOUP

1 small onion, chopped
30 g butter
1 kg cultivated mushrooms,
  sliced roughly
300 ml white wine
200 ml chicken stock
200 ml veal stock

bouquet garni (2 parsley stalks,
  2 sprigs thyme, 1 bay leaf,
  1/4 stick celery, 1/4 leek)
1 litre cream
1 teaspoon gewurtztraminer
  wine per portion

Sweat the onion and cook the mushrooms in butter without browning them. Add the white wine and the bouquet garni and reduce the liquid in the pan by two thirds. Add the veal and chicken stock and reboil. Add the cream and bring back to the boil, then simmer for 2 hours. Pass the soup through a fine strainer, skim and season. In the bottom of each warm soup bowl place some of the strained mushrooms and a teaspoon of the wine. Serve.

PIGEON AND FIELD MUSHROOM PIE
(SERVES 4 TO 6)

6 pigeons	*fresh herbs—use whatever is*
12 golden shallots	*available: thyme,*
350 g field mushrooms,	*marjoram, oregano*
thickly sliced	*1 litre reduced chicken stock*
200 g sugar-cured bacon,	*1/2 cup red wine*
cut into strips	*puff pastry*

In a frypan gently brown the pigeons with the shallots. Quickly toss the mushrooms and bacon in a little butter at high temperature. Place the pigeons, shallots, bacon and mushrooms in a pressure cooker or crockpot and deglaze with red wine. Reduce the wine quickly and cover with fresh herbs and stock. You could also pot roast slowly on the top of the stove in a heavy-bottomed pot. The cooking time will vary enormously, depending on the method of cooking. As most pigeons we buy are wild and of varying ages the 6 birds may take 6 different cooking times. The pigeon is cooked when the meat comes away from the bone but is still intact.

If you are using a pressure cooker, cook using the lowest pressure possible and check every 30 minutes. If there is a lot of liquid remaining at the end of pressure cooking, reduce to the desired consistency. A crockpot could safely be left on low overnight. A pot roast on top of the stove would have to be checked during the cooking period and perhaps more stock added. The cooking time could vary from 30 minutes to 3 hours this way.

When the pigeon has cooled, take the meat off the bones and place in the bottom of a Pyrex pie dish or something similar and spoon over the mushrooms, bacon and juices. Cut a puff pastry circle and let it rest in the refrigerator for 20 minutes before putting on the pie dish and brushing with an egg yolk wash. Bake in a very hot oven for approximately 20 minutes.

WILD MUSHROOM TERRINE

150 g guinea fowl breast
1 egg white, whipped
250 ml rich cream
500 g cepes mushrooms
500 g pine mushrooms
250 g chanterelle mushrooms
  (or others)
70 g smoked bacon

1 small onion or shallot
2 cloves garlic
salt, pepper
thyme
2 leaves sage, finely chopped
2 rosemary sprigs, finely chopped
30 g parsley, finely chopped

Put the guinea fowl breast meat through a fine mincer and pass it through a fine sieve. Cool. Add egg white slowly and season well. Fold in the cream and put aside in a cool place.

Finely chop the onion or shallot. Finely slice the garlic. Finely chop the bacon and fry until crispy. Add the onion or shallot and garlic. Sweat for 2 minutes. Add the mushrooms and fry until just brown. Season with salt, pepper and thyme. Remove mushroom mixture from the pan and reduce the juices in the pan. Add to the mushrooms and cool. Mix the mushroom and gunea fowl mixtures together with the other herbs.

Poach in a terrine dish (in a bain-marie) at 180°C for 45-60 minutes.

Persimmons

T**HE WONDERFUL** late Jane Grigson, from whose books I have learnt so much, brought to my attention this quote from the famous Japanese poet Shiki, who wrote himself an epitaph:

> *Write me down*
> *As one who loved poetry*
> *And persimmons.*

The beauty of the persimmon tree heavily laden with its autumn fruit is unquestionable—the leaves fall from the tree so that only the fruit is left. It is perfectly shaped and looks a little like a tomato with its large green calyx and vivid orange-red colour. It also feels wonderful and is so perfect it almost appears 'fake'.

The fruit itself is unknown to many and I suspect one of the reasons is that most people have tried it before it is properly ripe—it tastes so astringent it is virtually inedible. The ripe persimmon is almost rotten, although I learnt, again from Jane Grigson, that the Israelis of the Sharon Valley have developed a persimmon they call 'Sharon' that can be eaten with pleasure at the firm stage—skin, seeds and all. A similar smaller persimmon, called vanilla persimmon or fujifruit, is being grown in the Riverland.

Harold McGee, in his second book on food science and lore of the kitchen, *The Curious Cook*, has a chapter called 'Persimmons Unpuckered' which I recommend as serious reading for persimmon lovers and others interested in tannins; persimmons are astringent because of the huge amounts of tannin they contain. McGee tells that an atmosphere rich in carbon dioxide can bring about a reduction in astringency long before the fruit softens, and gives examples of simple methods to achieve this. It certainly makes fascinating reading and explains the steps that led to this discovery, with tales of boys in Chinese villages burying persimmons in the ground, smothering the fruit in covered earthenware jars along with a stick of incense, and sealing the fruit in airtight, empty Japanese sake barrels, all with the idea of depriving the persimmon of air.

The astringency can be reduced by freezing the fruit but this takes 10 to 90 days and the result is mushy.

McGee also tells us that the Portuguese love to dry persimmons, the Chinese preserve them with sugar, and that the fruit is a member of the ebony family and its wood is much sought after to make golf clubs, shoe lasts and weavers' shuttles. The persimmon is grown widely in Japan: the annual crop is approximately 450,000 tonnes (compared to 2000 tonnes in the US).

It is best to allow persimmons to ripen off the tree—the birds will beat you to them if you don't! To eat fresh persimmon, choose fruit that is so soft it is almost translucent. Cut the top off just under the green calyx and spoon out the pulp, avoiding the 4 or 5 seeds. I also like to eat the unblemished parts of the skin but that is very much a personal choice as the skin can taste very astringent. The flavour of the fruit, as with many foods, is difficult to describe accurately but is a little like a very ripe apricot.

Once you have cut off the top of the fruit you will notice a star-like pattern in the cross-section of the fruit—it is easy to imagine how attractive slices would look in a dessert or with a light vinaigrette in a cold dish or salad.

Melbourne cook, writer and teacher Penny Smith teamed some of my smoked kangaroo with persimmon for a special Australian dinner she served to some visiting African dignitaries. She tells me it was a startling success!

M arg Lehmann, of Peter Lehmann Wines, gave me the following recipe collected from a friend in the United States. It is a classic example of a recipe that is added to and improved by friends—I love all the options given to turn it out successfully. Marg says it is a taste sensation and, as persimmon is in season at Christmas in the States, it is often served flamed with brandy and surrounded by holly.

This recipe is of the 'nuts and fruits' school and opinion is divided as to the better option—plain persimmon or as described here. Simply omit the nuts and fruits if you feel they overpower the persimmon.

JANE'S PERSIMMON PUDDING

1/2 cup melted butter	*1 cup persimmon pulp*
1/2 cup chopped walnuts	*2 teaspoons baking soda dissolved*
1 cup sugar	*in 2 tablespoons warm water*
2 eggs	*1 teaspoon vanilla essence*
1 cup flour	*1 cup currants or chopped raisins*
1/4 teaspoon salt	*a dash of brandy*
1 teaspoon cinnamon	

Mix sugar, butter, walnuts and eggs. Add flour, salt and cinnamon. Add persimmon pulp, soda-water, brandy, vanilla and raisins.

Thoroughly oil an 8-cup steam mould and coat with sugar. Fill two-thirds with batter. (A 1 kg coffee tin with an aluminium foil lid can substitute.) Place covered mould on a rack in a larger pot (rack may be made of pencils or jar lids). Add water to a level halfway up the mould and cover the larger pot.

Steam the pudding for 2 1/2 to 3 hours—longer cooking won't harm it. The finished pudding will be dark, springy and may pull away from the mould slightly.

To unmould, turn upside down on a plate. If the pudding does not drop right out, shake and pound the mould vigorously, right side up, then invert it again. The next alternative is to leave the pudding inverted on a plate to drop out when it is cool. The last resort is to loosen the pudding with a flat knife. If it breaks, it can usually be reassembled.

The pudding may be frozen. To store at room temperature, pour up to 2 tablespoons of brandy over the cooled pudding and wrap it tightly in plastic wrap. Add brandy occasionally if it is to be stored for a long time.

Heat the pudding before serving and flame at the table with brandy. Serve with ice-cream or hard sauce.

HARD SAUCE

1/4 cup unsalted butter	*2 tablespoons brandy*
1/2 cup sugar	*fresh grated nutmeg to taste*

Mix together and then chill.

———

FROM THE SAME source comes a recipe for persimmon bread.

PERSIMMON BREAD

2 eggs	*1 teaspoon cloves*
1 cup sugar	*3/4 cup milk*
2 tablespoons melted butter	*1 1/2 cups persimmon pulp*
2 cups flour	*(4 medium-size)*
2 teaspoons baking soda	*1 cup raisins*
2 teaspoons cinnamon	*1 cup pecans or walnuts*
1 teaspoon nutmeg	*1 teaspoon vanilla*

Mix together eggs, sugar and melted butter. Sift flour, soda, cinnamon, nutmeg and cloves. Add milk and persimmon pulp then vanilla, raisins and pecans or walnuts.

Put in two loaf pans, place in a water bath and bake at 180°C for 75 minutes.

———

TO FINISH, HERE is a small piece out of a book I love—*Please to the Table: The Russian Cookbook* by Anya von Bremzen and John Welchman: 'To me one of the simplest and most delightful conclusions to a meal with a Mediterranean accent is a plate of lusciously ripe persimmons, peeled, sliced and garnished with mint sprigs.'

Pheasant

I N THE LATE 1970s, when we opened the Pheasant Farm, one
would rarely see pheasant on a restaurant menu, let alone in the
kitchen of a private house. Even now it is still not common.
Pheasant is a seasonal bird. It is much more interesting to eat than
chicken—sweet, moist and delicious, yet not as strongly flavoured
as duck or pigeon.

Is the pheasant fresh or hung? When someone asks this
question it usually indicates that they are from Europe. To many a
European, unless a pheasant is hung until it is so high that it
'walks away', it is not worth eating. I would have to say that given
the choice and someone else to cook a hung pheasant for me (the
smell permeates every bit of the cook's skin and clothing because
the pheasant is hung with its skin on and has not been gutted), a
hung bird would be my choice.

All game in Europe is wild and therefore to the cook it is of
indeterminate age and must be handled very carefully. Hanging
tenderises and gives the bird its high gamey flavour. If you're
given a cunning cock that has outfoxed his predators over many
seasons it would be a less exciting meal without hanging; rather
like eating a roasted old boiler.

In Australia the general public finds this idea repugnant and
this is largely to do with our weather. Late autumn is the time for

game. In the United Kingdom it is illegal to serve pheasant in a restaurant until the first of October and then for a 12-week period only. There are large fines for flouting this law and restaurants cannot serve birds that were caught in the season and frozen for later. Of course it can be hung outside in the northern autumn but an Australian autumn can be like an Indian summer and our game would go off very quickly.

So in Australia we enjoy our birds fresh in season and frozen at other times of the year. Pheasant is very simple to cook when you know how to treat it. Cooking is all about enjoying yourself in the kitchen, so forget all you've read about larding (threading the fat through the meat with a larding needle) and barding (wrapping the meat in fat), or roasting the bird for anywhere from 40 minutes to 1½ hours. No wonder people think pheasant is dry! You will find those techniques in European cookery books.

MY WAY OF COOKING PHEASANT

buy an 800 g-1 kg bird,   *6 juniper berries*
enough to feed 2   *fresh thyme*
people generously   *gin*
1 orange   *olive oil*

Cut the bird up the spine and flatten it as though you were going to put it in a frame on a barbecue.

With a sharp knife cut the tips off the wings and take the flesh off the wing joint to show bare bone. Because of the lack of fat in pheasants, the wing is not a succulent part, and if the flesh is left on this part of the wing it inhibits the cooking of the breast.

Place the pheasant in a dish with the juice and zest of the orange, crushed juniper berries and couple of sprigs of thyme. (Use this quantity for each pheasant.) If you are feeling extravagant, slosh in a little good gin as well. Leave to marinate for three hours. Then mix the marinade with some olive oil and brush this on the skin of the bird for baking. Cheong Liew gave me this recipe for his favourite marinade. It gives the skin a wonderful caramelised texture.

Bring your oven to the highest temperature it can manage, place the flattened bird on an oven tray and once more brush the marinade generously over the skin.

Bake the pheasant for 12-18 minutes in a household oven (or for 9-

12 minutes in a commercial oven) without opening the oven door.

Check to see if the bird is cooked by pulling the leg away from the breast. It should pull away easily and, while still pink, the meat should show no signs of rawness.

Turn the bird upside down and let it rest with a cover on it for another 15 minutes.

The easiest way to serve the bird is to cut it in half like a chicken and put on a plate with the juices from the pan.

Serve accompanied by roasted parsnips and a green salad.

———

THE WHOLE SUCCESS of the Pheasant Farm has been taking the direct link between the farmer and the user to the furthest point by our becoming a restaurant! Not that I would encourage every primary producer to go that far, but what has worked for us is that we are passionate about our product and that we have learnt everything we could about it by experimenting and marketing. We were accessible to feedback and were able to act upon it.

As the cook, I was able to tell Colin how I wanted the birds presented—at what age and size they were the most succulent—and even how I wanted them processed. We loved to eat pheasant; I have heard so many farmers say that they don't even like their product. How then can they truly believe in it, improve and market it?

In short, Colin raises our pheasant to suit my needs as the cook. You could hardly have a more direct line than that.

One of the reasons that pheasant are expensive is that they take 14-16 weeks to reach maturity. The birds are not given any growth hormones or antibiotics to 'rev' them up. They are free ranged and given as much green feed as possible.

Pheasants are particularly prone to misadventure in every form. That, combined with low hatchability and a long growth period, sometimes makes us wonder why we ever started breeding them. Colin had a dream of raising wild game from his days in New Zealand while taking his commercial pilot's licence. He was based in the South Island where game was plentiful and it just seemed like a good idea to him as a country boy. And so we began.

Our operation just seemed to evolve over the years and now the vision is firmly in place. Perhaps this is because the vision becomes clearer the closer you get. Our vision is a food bowl—with our property providing more and more of the essence of our restaurant.

First came the pheasants, then the vines, the quince orchard, the bees, the guinea fowl, the yabbies, the callup (also called yellowbelly), the kitchen garden and the smokehouse. So while the pheasants are our reason for being, it has now developed way beyond that.

As much as I love pheasants, just sometimes I wonder how it would be to call ourselves 'The Guinea Fowl Farm' for a change of pace! I do cook all sorts of game but about 65 per cent of the public insist on pheasant.

I am always seeking new ideas for using these birds that we raise and I try to utilise every part, from the liver for pate to the giblet and heart for confit and the head and feet for stock. I smoke the breeder birds and have even had people collect feathers for fly fishing and jewellery.

I HAVE A SPECIAL recipe for the older birds we fatten and smoke. They are so juicy that you would have no idea they would otherwise have ended up in the stockpot. The first time I assembled this recipe was when the Australian Symposium of Gastronomy was held in Adelaide in March 1990 and they organised a huge 'Market to Table Fair' in Gouger Street. The whole street was blocked off and trestle tables stretched the length of the street. About 25 restaurants participated, many of them cooking in the street. There was a queue from the minute we set up, and I cooked about 800 serves of this dish. The queue was so long my daughters kept offering tastes of our pate to stop people from becoming restless.

It was an exhausting, exciting day cooking there in the street with my customers talking to me as they waited—a great bit of street theatre.

WARM SALAD OF SMOKED PHEASANT

mixed lettuce leaves, including	*250 g large dark*
witlof, cos, mignonette	*mushrooms, sliced*
and rocket	*18 pieces mustard apricots*
1 large smoked pheasant	*(see page 138)*
to serve 6 (a chicken would	*olive oil*
probably only serve 4)	*balsamic vinegar*

Wash and dry the lettuce leaves. Make a vinaigrette with the oil and vinegar, approximately 4 parts to 1. Carve the smoked pheasant off the bone and slice thinly. Sauté the mushrooms until cooked and then add the pheasant and mustard fruits to warm them. Toss in a little vinaigrette to coat the ingredients.

Compose the leaves on serving plates and dress them. Divide the pheasant, mushroom and apricot mixture. Serve.

PHEASANT WITH SULTANA GRAPES AND VERJUICE
(SERVES 6)

3 young hen pheasants,	*1 cup reduced veal or chicken stock*
approximately 800 g each	*(or game stock if you have some)*
1 lemon	*1 cup verjuice (see page 161)*
salt and freshly ground pepper	*2 cups sultana grapes, removed*
250 g unsalted butter, cut in cubes	*from the stem*

Remove the second joint and wing tip from the pheasants, leaving only the first joint of the wing as an exposed bone. Cut through the skin around the thigh to free the legs a little, but do not remove them completely.

Preheat the oven to 250°C.

Squeeze a little lemon juice into the cavities of the birds and season with salt and pepper. Melt a little of the butter in a frypan and brown the birds gently on all sides until they are a golden colour. Arrange them in a baking dish, allowing the legs to spread out.

Bake in the preheated oven for 10 to 12 minutes. Remove from the oven and turn the birds over, cover and rest in a warm place for 15 minutes. Meanwhile deglaze the baking dish with verjuice and boil vigorously. Add the stock and boil by half. Beat in the cold butter to finish the sauce. About 40 seconds before serving, toss in the grapes.

Olives and Olive Oil

IF I COULD PAINT and had the necessary time, I should devote myself for a few years to making pictures only of olive trees. What a wealth of variations upon a single theme.' (Aldous Huxley, *The Olive Tree*)

Not everyone shares my passion for olives and olive oil but I love everything about them, from the tree to the olive to the oil. In my restaurant days I have made many converts to olive oil, though some still resist, thinking incorrectly that it isn't good for you or that I use too much of it.

I also battle to convince my husband Colin of the beauty of the trees. He is letting me plant an olive grove for practical, agricultural reasons but I would plant them just for the wonderful landscape. Considering the bounty and beauty of the olive tree I'm surprised we don't see more of them planted in groves. They have been declared a noxious weed in some council areas where they grow wild along the roadside, which offends me greatly as I take such benefit from them. Certainly there is much competition in the Greek and Italian communities for 'known' sites. I understand that some families pay the council for the privilege of picking from the trees in the Adelaide parklands. I suppose it's a bit like blackberrying: the fruit seems all the sweeter to those who take the time and trouble to pick them.

The wild olive tree (Oleaster) grew, and still grows, in most Mediterranean countries, as does the domestic clone (*Olea europaea*) developed from it. I have always been interested in the origin of our wild olive trees. Were they brought out by early settlers or are they so hardy that they have just taken hold on many roadsides in the Adelaide Hills and the Barossa Valley?

These wild olives are perfect for pickling. When I pick for oil I separate the olives from the twigs and leaves but when I pick from the roadside for pickling I like to leave some in with the brining olives as they look so attractive on the plate when you finally serve them.

There are so many different shapes and sizes of olives, particularly wild ones. I like them all, from the tiniest to the largest; in fact, my very favourites are those that others throw away. They are tiny like the Niçoise olive and have very little flesh in ratio to seed but, when well-matured, have an intense flavour. Much to my chagrin, I threw out about ten 10-litre buckets of these olives after maturing them for six months as they still tasted bitter. Fortunately I forgot about the second batch and tried them again a year later—I can assure you they just keep getting better and better.

The Department of Agriculture has a wonderful pamphlet on the treatment of olives for pickling which is well worth searching out. I have tried the two simplest ways.

You can pack them in dry salt using equal quantities of olives and salt in a container that lets the juice flow out, such as a hessian bag. They must be weighted down and left for at least a month. This method leaves the olives fairly crinkled and salty but you can adjust this by washing them before putting them down in olive oil. I have enjoyed these immensely with drinks.

The second method we tried is one inspired by Stephanie Alexander's book, *Stephanie's Menus for Food Lovers*. It is laborious and messy but worth the result. Pick the olives and put them in large plastic crates and immerse them in rain water. Change the water every two days for a period of 40 days. After that time, drain them well and cover with rock salt for two days before washing the olives. Pack them in jars with lemon or orange and sprigs of thyme, and cover with olive oil.

We started using this method many years ago and have engaged in a fair bit of trial and error. We used to rinse them every day but found out that this wasn't necessary. Because wild olives are so much more bitter than cultivated ones, remember to be patient and keep persevering if they still taste bitter. Time will mellow them!

You don't have to resort to roadside olives—you can buy them by the half case in the markets, although you may have to order them.

At least one book has been written about the many ways to use olives. I can recommend *The Essential Olive Oil Companion* by Anne Dolamore to any serious olive lover.

Olives are great with pre-dinner drinks; they can be used in dips such as tapenade, or in pizzas, breads or polenta. You can use them in salads, such as Niçoise teamed with tuna, or with pastas, with just cream and Parmesan. Black olives complement goat's cheese, lamb, kid, duck, veal, oxtail and fish such as red mullet. The list is endless.

I am sure there are just as many uses for green olives but I must confess I know very little about them. You have to remember that they have an entirely different flavour. A very knowledgeable journalist-about-town once told me that cracked green olives with orange blossom tossed in olive oil was a taste sensation. It so inspired me that I wrote it on the back of an envelope and kept it for years, waiting for the right time of year. So far my memory and the right time of year have not connected, but it certainly sounds wonderful!

———

I SOMETIMES SERVE the following potato gnocchi with green olives studded through it, with a green olive sauce.

GREEN OLIVE GNOCCHI WITH GREEN OLIVE SAUCE

GNOCCHI
500 g cooked potatoes
2 egg yolks
1 cup plain flour
20 large green olives, stoned
  and chopped finely

freshly grated nutmeg
salt and pepper to taste

Steam the potatoes until cooked right through and mash while still warm. Allow to cool and add flour, nutmeg, salt and pepper and chopped olives.

Mix in the egg yolks until the dough is fairly firm. Knead it gently for a few minutes. While the salted water comes to the boil, shape the gnocchi dough into your desired form. Leave to rest. Gently place the gnocchi into boiling water and as they come to the surface, allow them to cook for one minute. Take out with a slotted spoon and put aside.

SAUCE

1 large onion, finely chopped	juice of 1 lemon
3 garlic cloves, finely chopped	100 ml chicken stock
1 tablespoon olive oil	200 g green olives, stoned and
100 ml cream	chopped

Sweat the garlic and onion in olive oil until wilted. Add chicken stock and cream and reduce to desired thickness. Add olives and adjust with lemon juice if necessary. Allow to cool a little and then purée in blender.

To serve, pan fry the gnocchi in some nut-brown butter and serve with heated sauce.

F INDING ONE RECIPE to encapsulate olives is difficult, but as bread is the staff of life I decided on our olive bread.

AILEEN'S OLIVE BREAD

850 g hard flour (we use Laucke's)	olive oil to fry rosemary
15 g dried yeast	—approximately 2 tablespoons
5/8 cup of pipped olives	500 ml warm water (varies every
large pinch salt	time you make it)
2 tablespoons rosemary, finely chopped	

Fry the rosemary off in the olive oil and reserve. In a large bowl mix the flour, salt, yeast and rosemary, including the little oil. Add the pipped olives and begin to pour in the warm water to make the dough.

When it reaches the desired consistency, remove dough to a floured workbench and knead until smooth and satiny to feel—at least 15 minutes by hand. Place back in the bowl smeared with a little olive oil and leave covered with a wet tea towel or plastic wrap to double in size.

Knock it down and shape into rolls or loaves as required. Leave to rise again on trays or in a greased loaf tin.

Bake at 200°C for 15-20 minutes. Turn out on to a rack to cool. Eat with unsalted butter.

OLIVE OIL

Different varieties of olive are grown for oil production and table olives. Although the best oils are made from less ripe olives, the riper the olive the more oil it produces. The green, multicoloured and black olive are one and the same, merely at different stages of ripeness. For the very best oils, the fruit is hand-picked, with the pickers returning to each tree as they ripen at different times.

Olive oil has increased dramatically in price, partly because of the incredibly high cost of producing it—it takes approximately 7 years for a tree to bear, one tree yields 15 to 20 kilos (and every second year has a smaller crop) and it takes between 5 and 10 kilos of olives to yield 1 litre of oil. In addition, a great frost in Italy (Tuscany particularly) in 1985 killed 50 to 75 per cent of the olive trees, and up to 90 per cent of those growing on hilltops.

There are many similarities to the vine. Like wine, the character of oil is determined by the type of tree, the soil, the position, the climate, and the conditions of setting of the fruit. Rain or hail at blossom time can be disastrous. In general, one in 20 flowers becomes an olive.

Traditionally, olive trees have been grown in arid lands. Certainly they can survive in the poorest of soil where their roots travel far to whatever moisture there is, but under such harsh conditions they produce a meagre harvest. As with the grape, it is a vexed question whether the 'suffering' of the tree equates with a higher-quality end product.

With so many similarities it is perhaps surprising that, unlike wine which improves with age, good olive oil is best consumed young. Although olive oil mellows and becomes more 'refined' with age it loses its flavour. In Europe many extra virgin olive oils are dated with their vintage.

Olive oil production today is a huge business requiring great capital investment for fertilisation, irrigation and pruning. Trees are pruned to allow easy access to the centre of the tree as well as more sunlight to the fruit. As the fruit spoils rapidly, it must be handled carefully and crushed within 24 hours of picking. Olives are seldom picked entirely by hand; usually they are beaten off the tree with sticks to fall into nets on the ground, or machines like cherry-pickers are used.

We are lucky to have first-class olive oil producers in South Australia—Coriole at McLaren Vale and Joe Grilli and Don Evangelista at Angle Vale, both vignerons. As our Mediterranean climate is so suitable to olive oil production, I'm sure we will see more produced here in the future despite the expense involved. However, until we get over the cultural cringe that our Australian product isn't as good as imported olive oil, development will be slow.

There is a great deal of romance in the traditional methods of olive oil production. Stainless steel equipment is the way of the future—Italy is renowned for its 'small' equipment that is so suitable for Australian production. Coriole produces a first-class olive oil employing the old style of milling, which is becoming more and more rare. The sight of the woven mats drying in the sun, the grove of wonderful, gnarled olive trees, and the vista of the Valley make you feel you could be anywhere in the Mediterranean.

In Adelaide you can take your own crop of olives to Don Evangelista of Greenfields Olive Oil Company for crushing. You can either exchange the olives for oil or, if you have enough, take home the fruit of your own labours, so to speak. Although Mr Evangelista prefers to exchange oil for olives if the customer has only a small quantity—his machinery needs a tonne an hour to work economically—he does understand the desire to have your 'very own' oil. Less than four 50 kg bags is considered a small batch.

The average yield for a 50 kg bag of olives is about 5 litres. Remember that we are talking about wild olives or olives that have not been grown for oil production, which is why the yield is so small. Greenfields have the sophisticated stainless steel Italian equipment mentioned above, and I was impressed by the quality of some olive oil that was pressed for a group of oenology students from Roseworthy Agricultural College.

How to buy olive oil? Knowing how to choose the best-quality product is very confusing when you are confronted by so many different levels. As a basic rule of thumb, cold-pressed virgin olive oil is the best you can buy. The colour in virgin oil varies from year to year, but colour is no indication of quality. Perhaps the easiest way is to trust your merchant and your own palate when tasting. Tastes range from pungent and peppery to light and fruity, with many stages in between. Tastes such as almond, passionfruit, grass or sweetness can all be detected in different oils. Olive oil tastings can be great fun—find out if your merchant has them. Take the oil and rub it in the palm of your hand and delight in the aroma, then try dipping pieces of bread into the ones you like. An apple in between to clean the palate is a good idea.

T O ENSURE WORLD-WIDE standards of olive oil, the International Olive Oil Council, based in Madrid, sits twice a year and has members from all olive oil producing and importing countries. It sets standards for all categories of olive oil but does not define cold-pressed or first pressing. The following is a discussion of the grades of olive oil as designated by the IOOC.

Virgin olive oil is the oil obtained from the fruit of the olive tree solely by mechanical or other physical means without the use of heat. The olives have not undergone any treatment other than washing, decanting or centrifuging.

The terms 'cold pressed' and 'first cold pressed' can sometimes be used on the labels of virgin oils to indicate that no heat has been used and that the oil is the result of the first pressing. These terms are being phased out, however, as pressing is tending to be replaced by centrifuging in modern olive oil factories, so the term no longer applies.

There are two types of virgin olive oils: 'Extra virgin' olive oil is olive oil of absolutely perfect taste and odour and an intense fruity flavour with a maximum acidity (in terms of oleic free fatty acid) of 1%. 'Virgin' olive oil has good flavour but a maximum acidity of 3%. Most of the virgin oils in Australia are Extra Virgin.

Refined olive oil is obtained by refining oil that is obtained from the fruit of the olive tree solely by mechanical or other physical means but which is not generally considered acceptable for consumption without further processing and blending because of its acidity or off-taste. Refined olive oil is without specific colour, odour or taste. To restore the distinctive flavour, colour and aroma, some virgin oil is blended back.

'Olive oil' is the common name of a blend of refined olive oil and virgin olive oil. The terms 'pure' and '100% pure' are often used but these terms will be seen less and less.

In Australia and the United States there are 'Extra Light' and 'Light' oils which are blends of refined olive oil and small amounts of virgin oil which give them a light, subtle taste.

Olive pomance is the residue remaining after the extraction of all oil that can be removed by mechanical or other physical means. It contains about 4-10 per cent oil, depending on the system used for obtaining the virgin olive oil, and this can be extracted with the aid of solvents. The extracted oil must then be refined. After refining, the oil is without specific colour, odour or taste. To produce a product that is generally acceptable to most consumers, the refined olive pomance oil is then blended with virgin olive oil.

'Olive pomance oil' is the common name of a blend of refined olive pomance oil and virgin olive oil. This type of oil has recently become available on the Australian market.

GREAT USES FOR OLIVE OIL

On the dinner table, instead of a plate of butter, serve a tiny jug of olive oil, perhaps with a clove of garlic and a sprig of thyme in it. Put a flat dish next to the bread and butter plates for the oil and add pepper and/or salt before dipping the bread in. Serve the oil in small amounts fresh daily, as it oxidises when in contact with the air.

Use the same system for dipping fresh vegetables such as celery, fennel or, particularly, radishes fresh from the garden. It makes a wonderful appetiser.

Bruschetta is a simple, tasty item found in cafes and on Italian menus. Toast a thick slice of bread—unsalted bread over an open fire is best of all—and rub with slightly crushed cloves of garlic. Pour over a good-quality, warm olive oil and sprinkle with Maldon sea salt. It is fabulous on its own or with slices of ripe tomato or anchovies.

Olive oil can be used in salads, when frying fish or grilling meat or poultry, making soups, bread and even cakes. It can be used as a marinade, especially on game, which tends to dry out, and for shallow and deep frying.

Olive oil is used to store preserved artichokes, wild mushrooms and onions, red peppers, eggplant and chillies. All of these foods from the summer and autumn can be held over to make winter fare more interesting. Olive oils flavoured with herbs can give added interest to your cooking. To make garlic olive oil, simply peel the garlic, cut off the ends and cover it with vinegar for 24 hours. Then place in a bottle and fill with oil for a couple of weeks. Once the garlic has flavoured the oil to your liking, remove the cloves.

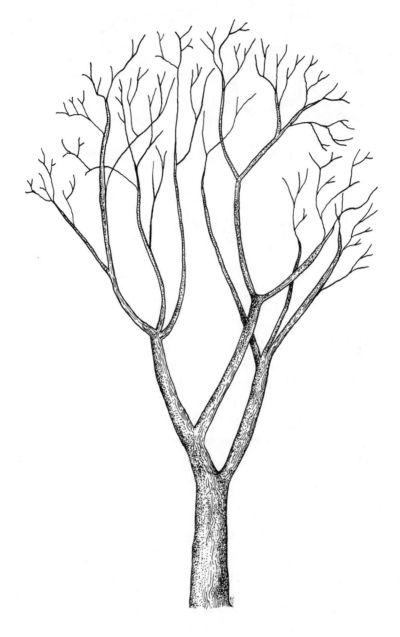

Winter

Offal

WINTER AND COLD weather make us think of hearty meals. My favourite dishes to share with friends are the one-pot type, where you just put a dish in the middle of the table and serve it with crusty bread and a salad. However, you'll have to choose your friends well for this particular topic as it isn't everyone's cup of tea. For the cheapest tasty meal, try offal.

I am so fond of offal I cannot go past it on menus and have been known to have three offal entrees for a meal instead of the more conventional entree, main course and dessert. It certainly inspires the 'hearts' of many but can be particularly divisive at a normal dinner table.

One of the regrets of my life is that I never attended one of Cath Kerry's 'Offal Breakfasts' when she was cooking at Bridgewater Mill in the Adelaide Hills. Cath still does the occasional class for Rosa Matto's 'Delicious Prospects' on King William Road, and offal lovers should put the pressure on there for some repeat performances.

Generally I find the most adventurous eaters are offal lovers. In France, offal reigns supreme as a delicacy; the French word for it is *abat*, from 'abattoir'. The French are wonderfully resourceful in using every part of the animal. Because there is only a small amount per animal and it is so highly-prized, offal is quite expensive in France whereas in Australia it is inexpensive.

Your attitude to offal as a food will depend on your upbringing—it was the very first food I learnt to cook. Most Australians, however, shun it. I have heard over the years that the more adventurous abattoir workers understood the attraction of offal and took home special 'treats' such as sweetbreads and calves' brains. These days, things are much more regimented, supposedly for our safety, and abattoirs must have special rooms if they want to keep the offal. Abattoirs without this special room have to throw the offal away. As the whole abattoir has to be hygienic, I do not understand how offal dissected in a separate room makes it 'safer' for us.

It is a little like pig's ears no longer being legal. Why is a pig's ear any dirtier than a pig's trotter? A suckling pig at a feast doesn't look the same minus the ears and no matter what you substitute, the effect is just not the same. For our tenth anniversary party at the Pheasant Farm, I had Schulz's Butchers, of Angaston, prepare a pig for me. It was delivered as proceedings were about to begin and some deftly-draped grape leaves had to suffice for the ears.

Then there is our politeness (perhaps from the British) in calling lamb's liver 'lamb's fry' and bull's testicles 'prairie oysters'.

There are so many possibilities with offal. There is the heart, which you can stuff; the caul fat or crepinette (the lining of a pig's stomach), which you can wrap delicate food in to bake or pan fry (nature's Gladwrap, as Cath Kerry says!); kidneys, which can be grilled or roasted in their own fat; and liver, which can be sautéed or roasted whole.

Lungs and intestines are more likely to be found in Chinese food and it is a testimony to my upbringing, where authentic Chinese food was unknown, that I have never been able to say I really enjoy them.

Pig's ears, when you can get them, make the most wonderful eating, braised slowly in stock and then stuffed with sweetbreads or chicken. Pig's trotters are essential to my stock-making but I also love them slowly braised and served with lentils. Then there is my favourite offal, sweetbreads, although I prefer veal's to sheep's. I find lamb sweetbreads lack the nutty characteristics of the veal, and they are very small. Sweetbreads come from both the thymus and the pancreas, which is why you get different shapes.

Then there is tongue, which is a firm favourite on my menu. I often serve it smoked (from Schulz's Butchers), simmered gently with stock vegetables and light veal stock till it is soft to touch. I simply let it cool a little, peel and slice it while still warm, and serve with pesto or a *salsa verde*. If you want to prepare it in advance, cut it into slices and cover with plastic wrap until you are ready to use it, then toss in a tiny bit of butter in a thick-based pan. This gently caramelises the tongue as it warms and is particularly tasty.

Brains are one of the best-selling entrees on our menu. Perhaps this is because brains (and probably all offal) fall into that category of food that is not often cooked at home because not everyone likes it. Brain and walnut sandwiches were something I used to make when I wanted to show off. Cath Kerry does a marvellous brain and mushroom parcel based on this idea.

CATH'S BRAIN AND MUSHROOM PIE
(SERVES 8 AS AN ENTREE)

PASTRY

2 cups plain flour	*4 tablespoons sour cream*
250 g butter	

This pastry can be made in a food processor by pulsing only to mix. It can be used immediately, without resting.

FILLING

12 lambs' brains	*1 tablespoon chopped parsley*
1 medium to large onion	*2 tablespoons butter*
250 g mushrooms	*salt and fresh pepper to taste*

Soak the brains in lightly salted water for an hour. Bring a saucepan of water to the boil and blanch the brains in this for about 30 seconds. Drain and allow to cool. Trim off unnecessary bits.

Chop the onion finely and soften in half the butter. Set onion aside and in the same pan soften the roughly-sliced mushrooms in the remaining butter. Dice the mushrooms finely by hand or in a food processor. Combine the onion, mushrooms and parsley, with salt and pepper to taste.

Divide the pastry into two rounds, one slightly larger than the other.

Roll out the smaller piece to form a disc about 24 cm across. Spread the mushroom mixture over this, avoiding the edges. Place the brains on top of the mushrooms and season with a little salt and pepper. Cover with the other round of pastry. Seal the edges well. Glaze with egg and decorate the surface of the pie if you wish.

Bake in a moderate oven (180°C) for about half an hour or until the pastry is golden brown. Serve warm alone or with a sauce of equal parts veal or chicken stock and white wine, reduced until thickened and finished with a spoonful of redcurrant jelly and a large knob of butter.

BRAINS IN CAPER BUTTER

6 sets brains
70 g butter
30 g capers
1 tablespoon chopped parsley

1 dessertspoon lemon juice
black peppercorns
1 bay leaf

The brains should be very fresh—shiny and sweet smelling. Rinse them several hours before use. We make little parcels of brains wrapped in foil so that they keep their shape while cooking.

Poach the parcels in water with a little lemon juice added, the bay leaf and a few peppercorns. Start off the poaching in cold water and bring to a simmer. Cooking time depends on how 'done' you like then (I like them only just set). Leave the brains to cool before unwrapping. Then trim the brains and slice in half.

Put the butter into a large frypan and allow it to turn nut-brown. Seal the brains on their cut side. As soon as they brown, turn them over. Be careful not to have too many in the pan at once as it will not be hot enough and they will poach and turn soggy. Season with salt and pepper. Add capers and parsley and deglaze with lemon juice. Serve immediately.

TRIPE IS THE only food in the world that I couldn't stomach as a child. I still can't even look at it in a white sauce, which is how my mother used to cook it. As soon as I see it I immediately smell what I revolted against in my childhood. It must be an acquired taste because I love it now, cooked with tomatoes and olives in the Italian manner.

This recipe is inspired from 'Tripe Prepared My Way' by Antonio Carluccio, in *An Invitation to Italian Cooking*. It was the dish that converted me!

TRIPE WITH TOMATOES AND OLIVES

1 kg honeycomb tripe
2 carrots
3 celery stalks
3 onions, roughly chopped
2 cloves garlic
2 cans peeled Italian (Roma) tomatoes
2 sprigs fresh oregano

2 sprigs rosemary
120 g kalamata olives
2 glasses white wine
100 ml chicken stock
salt and freshly ground pepper
4 tablespoons chopped continental parsley
olive oil

Most butchers sell the tripe already partially cooked. If your tripe has not been prepared, it needs to be boiled several times in fresh water each time. I think my mother repeated this process three times—giving the tripe an hour's cooking time in total before proceeding with the recipe.

Chop the onions, carrot and celery and slice the garlic. Toss with the olive oil in a large frypan and set aside. Toss the tripe with the oregano and rosemary in the remaining oil. Add the wine and well chopped tomatoes and reduce rapidly. (Use a little of the tomato liquid later if you feel it is needed.)

Add the chicken stock and simmer quietly for about 1 hour. Season with salt and pepper and add the olives in the last few minutes. Serve with lots of freshly chopped parsley.

Root Vegetables

ROOT VEGETABLES have long been favourites of mine. Perhaps this is because of their special affinity with game but they deserve to stand on their own. They are at their very best in winter, when there is a smaller variety of fresh vegetables available.

Parsnip is a particular favourite and I use them as often as possible. I do have one, very special, regular diner, 'Sir Lunchalot Bob McLean', who hates them. I have given up trying to convert him and try to ensure he has a plate of potatoes instead. It is hard to believe that anyone could hate such a wonderful vegetable—perhaps he went to boarding school!

I don't like parsnip that much when simply steamed or boiled (unless it comes straight from the garden), but when roasted to that wonderful caramelised, almost burnt stage, they are delicious. People like me who profess not to have a sweet tooth can get all the sweetness they need from vegetables with natural sweetness taken to the 'nth' degree by 'over-roasting'.

Don't forget sweet potato and swede. Sweet potato needs to be handled carefully so it is not oversweet: I like to add a little lemon juice for balance. Swede is a vegetable that is often ignored but it is delicious when picked fresh from the ground and simply boiled and mashed with a little butter and sprinkled with freshly ground black pepper. It makes a wonderful addition to any meal, from a piece of boiled silverside to a grilled lamb chop.

Turnips are easy to grow. They are a little like radishes, as they seem to mature very quickly, or perhaps it is just that I like them fairly small (not 'baby', particularly), as their sweetness is then at its peak, especially when they are pulled fresh out of the ground.

The bonus with turnips is that turnip greens have a lovely, sharp flavour which contrasts well with the sweetness of the vegetable. Turnips have a particular affinity with duck, and of all vegetables they work best at the 'baby' stage. They look attractive whole, either caramelised or just boiled and tossed with butter and black pepper.

THIS SOUP AROSE from a Sunday in winter when I had run out of ingredients and, in desperation, turned to the greens growing in a very small vegetable patch. I made a soup of the fresh greens and used the turnips puréed in the centre instead of cream. I remember it as wonderful! Freshness is of paramount importance in this recipe, so don't try it if the turnips and their greens don't look crisp.

GARDEN GREEN SOUP WITH PURÉE OF TURNIP

1 bunch spring onions, chopped
2-3 cups turnip greens, washed
  and chopped finely
3 sprigs parsley
10 leaves sorrel
3 cups light chicken or vegetable
  stock

4 tablespoons butter, melted
salt and pepper
450 g turnips
2 tablespoons cream

Cook the peeled turnips till tender in salted water, then purée in a processor. Add cream and salt and pepper to taste.

Simmer spring onions till translucent then toss the greens in the melted butter and add chicken stock. Cook for a few minutes till tender. You could purée the greens and swirl with the turnip purée but I choose to serve this with the greens just wilted, with the purée in the centre.

A BOUT TEN YEARS ago, after author and cook Stephanie Alexander first visited my restaurant, I remember being delighted by her comment in the visitors' book, 'Parsnips were wonderful'. That day I had served Parsnip Puff, a Beverley Sutherland Smith recipe, from her book *A Taste for All Seasons*. The following is my adaptation of her recipe.

PARSNIP PUFF

6 medium parsnips 10-12 cm long pinch nutmeg
*   and 3 cm wide (unpeeled)   1 egg*
75 g butter   salt and pepper
3 tablespoons cream

Cook parsnips in salted water till tender. Drain well and purée in a blender or put through a mouli while still warm. Add the butter cut into small pieces, cream, nutmeg and egg, and adjust with salt and pepper. Spoon into a buttered ovenproof dish.

TOPPING
1 tablespoon breadcrumbs made   30 g melted butter
*   from stale bread*

Sprinkle the breadcrumbs over the top, then the melted butter. Reheat in moderate oven at 180°C for 20 minutes. This can be prepared in the morning and reheated at dinner time.

A SIMPLER METHOD is a straight parsnip purée with a dash of cream and butter. I like the texture from using the food processor but the trick is to start with good parsnips—they should be crisp, not wilted, and as smooth and creamy white as possible. I avoid really large parsnips and the woody ones found near the end of the season.

THIS IS A GREAT way to use leftover large parsnips.

PARSNIP CHIPS

Peel and cut the tops off the parsnips and slice very thinly lengthways with a sharp knife and a steady hand (or a kitchen implement called a 'mandolin'). Soak slices in cold water for 10 minutes, drain and dry very well with a clean tea towel. Heat oil of your preference to about 190°C and fry in small batches till crisp. Drain, salt and serve.

CARAMELISED PARSNIPS OR TURNIPS

500 g parsnips or turnips	*1 tablespoon sugar*
75 g butter	*1 tablespoon red wine vinegar*
juice of one lemon	*salt and pepper*

Peel the parsnips or turnips and cut into strips to suit your purposes. Melt butter, add lemon juice and vegetables and simmer gently in a shallow pan with a lid till just cooked.

In another pan, melt sugar then add vinegar, simmering gently till sugar caramelises. Add the cooked vegetable in its juices into the caramel, season, toss and serve.

Oranges

THE FRAGRANCE of oranges is enjoyable in a multitude of ways—from the traditional orange blossoms at weddings to the fragrant, juicy, thirst-quenching orange of the sports field. Whether you played hockey, football, netball or tennis, remember that squirt of juice cooling your overheated body, your nose buried sensuously in the flesh as you gulped every bit of juice, drained it and grabbed the next quarter? When I am in the kitchen zesting a juicy orange and the citrussy tang sprays in my face like champagne, I'm reminded of 'quarter time'.

Although oranges are available throughout the year, they are at their best in winter. Navels (my favourite) come on the market about the last week in May and are available until August. They are seedless and have a thick skin that makes them easier to peel, and are sweeter than the Valencia.

In Australia it is only the navels that are gassed to improve their colour and only in the first few weeks of the season. By June they are at the peak of their season.

All oranges are waxed for presentation with a food grade wax. You can use the peel without any problems. Probably nothing is as perfect as picking an orange off your own tree if you want to avoid such things as gassing and waxing, particularly as oranges can hang ripe on the tree for months without spoiling. Valencias have an extraordinary ability for this.

The Valencia arrives in August and lasts right through until the following May (its very optimum time being the first week in October until Christmas). When they come into season in the spring it is worth a trip to the Riverland not only for the beauty of the orange groves laden with fruit but also the aroma of the Valencias being harvested in their own flower-scented air.

The Valencia is the best juicing orange—it does have a seed and a thinner skin but the juice does not go sour for about 5 days. Navel juice will last only about 2 days.

As with most foods, if you buy in the peak season, the item is at its best flavour and lowest price. There is not much variation in quality of crop from year to year. Oranges are not only good for you, they are wonderful to eat and wonderful to cook with. The public will be the greatest losers if the growers have to continue pulling out their trees. We should be doing everything we can to protect our local industry. Watch that what you are buying is local and try to buy juice and cordials made from Australian and not Brazilian concentrate. Everyone's catchcry should be to buy locally and to buy in season.

Oranges are not originally Mediterranean as we might have thought, but come from China. So do the cumquat, tangerine and mandarin. Oranges arrived in Italy towards the end of the Roman Empire, brought to Europe by Arab traders along with spices.

In South Australia we don't have the right temperatures to grow a good blood orange or pink grapefruit but they are grown successfully in Western Australia. They are perfect in Maltaise sauce, which is a hollandaise with the juice of a blood orange added at the end—a beautiful accompaniment to fresh asparagus.

———

THE ALIVENESS of orange makes it a very important tool in my cooking. It marries so well with guinea fowl and of course duck. I use orange juice in my everyday marinade for pheasants and put the zest into my game pies. I make pasta with orange zest as well as salads, cakes and desserts. I have even been told about wonderful orange scones. Try this delicious recipe for chicken wings with orange.

CHICKEN WINGS WITH ORANGE PEEL

3 tablespoons orange peel
2 kg chicken wings
1 tablespoon finely minced garlic
1 teaspoon minced ginger
2 shallots, crushed
2 tablespoons soy sauce

1/4 cup peanut oil
1/4 cup sesame oil
2 teaspoons Sichuan peppercorns,
*   roasted in a dry skillet until*
*   fragrant and pulverised in*
*   a mortar and pestle*

Mix all the ingredients together and leave the chicken wings to marinate for 4 hours. Roast the chicken wings in a hot oven until cooked, being careful they don't burn.

ORANGE AND ALMOND TART

pastry for 25 cm tart base (see Sour Cream Pastry, page 60)

150 g castor sugar
200 g butter
150 g ground almonds
50 g plain flour, sifted

zest and juice of 1 orange
2 tablespoons lemon juice
8 egg yolks

Blind bake the pastry shell. Roast the almonds to release the flavour and grind them in a food processor. Make sure the almonds are cool before proceeding with the recipe. Cream the castor sugar and butter until very creamy and then add the almond slowly with the mixer on medium speed. Add the flour, orange zest and juice. Then add the lemon juice and one egg yolk at a time. Pour the mixture into the pastry shell and bake for 30 to 45 minutes at 200°C. The mixture should still be a little wobbly when taken out of the oven.

Y FAVOURITE marmalade is made with a recipe given to me by an old friend with whom I've lost contact. A very special friend, who worked with me for years, still sees that my larder is well stocked with it. This is Hilda's version of Marmalade-à-la-Lizzy. It's the nicest way to start the day!

MARMALADE-À-LA-LIZZY

6 oranges	*900 g sugar*
3 lemons	*1 cup whisky*
8 cups water	

Finely cut the fruits and combine all the ingredients except whisky. Boil until the jam is ready. Cool and add the whisky. Stir well and store in glass jars sealed with wax.

ORANGE PASTRIES

PASTRY

250 g unsalted butter, very cold	*3 to 4 dessertspoons sour cream*
250 g flour	

Process the butter and flour together, leaving the butter in large chunks about the size of olives. Add the sour cream and process until just incorporated. The mix should still have patches of cream and butter.

Turn on to a well floured area and press the dough into a rectangle using a rolling pin. Lift the pastry up and dust underneath and on top with more flour. Begin to roll the pastry into an elongated rectangle. Fold into thirds. Turn the pastry around so that the open side is closest to you. Roll again. Continue this process, removing any pieces not incorporated and dust away the excess flour. Fold at least three times.

The dough is ready when the chunks of butter are hardly visible and the pastry is quite pale. Rest the dough in the refrigerator for 15 to 20 minutes. Roll out again to about 5 mm thick and cut into 5 cm squares.

Place the pastry squares on a baking tray and score the tops with a sharp knife. Make a glaze of egg white and a little cream. Be careful that the glaze does not drip over the side as this will impede the pastry from rising and flaking. Rest again for 20 minutes and then bake in an oven preheated to 230°C. Towards the end of the cooking time, remove the pastries from the oven and split them in half. Check to see that all the pastry is cooked. Scrape out any uncooked pastry and return them to the oven to dry out.

CARAMEL

1 cup sugar   *1 cup freshly squeezed orange juice*

Boil sugar and orange juice together until the caramel is quite dark. Remove from the heat and arrest the cooking by placing the saucepan in a sink of cold water.

FILLING

6 large navel oranges, peeled and   *300 ml mascarpone, whipped*
cut into 5 mm slices   *with orange zest to taste*

Fill the pastries with the mascarpone and oranges. Pour the caramel over the filling before putting on the top half of the 'sandwich'. Dust with icing sugar and serve immediately.

Risotto

I WAS NEVER KEEN on rice until I tasted risotto. Although it is not often seen on restaurant menus, it is a very special dish to cook at home. Risotto is a northern Italian speciality that can best be described as rice cooked by the absorption method. Risotto is a sensational dish that can be made with the simplest and cheapest of ingredients or it can be extravagant.

The two characteristics that make risotto special are the rice used and the cooking method. The arborio rice required is available at gourmet delicatessens. Originating from the Po Valley in Northern Italy, it is a wide-grained, round rice with a pearly white spot on it. It has distinctive large, rounded grains which respond well to slow cooking. It should be cooked until al dente and not soft or mushy. In a true risotto the grains of rice are firm in the middle and can be bitten into, while the outside of the grain is very creamy.

Risotto is a wonderful carrier of other flavours and textures. It can be the beginning to a meal, a main course or a meal in itself with salad. There are so many possibilities with this one dish. It probably lends itself more to winter as the cold weather makes us search for filling foods but a crab risotto in summer with a green salad takes a lot of beating.

It is of great importance to have a large, heavy-based pot,

preferably with a rounded bottom, in which to stir the rice and its liquid with a wooden spoon.

A good stock is essential—choose whichever kind of stock will complement your main ingredient. I make my mushroom risotto with chicken stock but it could just as well be made with vegetable stock. I have had a wonderful risotto made from just chicken stock, champagne and the best Parmesan cheese. Another great experience is risotto made from a full flavoured fish or crab stock. If you don't have seafood to hand or you are on a tight budget you needn't feel compelled to add seafood as well. The most extravagant and wonderful risotto I have ever eaten was last New Year's Eve with our friends Doug and Marjorie Coats who run our local Vintners Restaurant. Marjorie used fresh truffles in her generous style and the risotto set the pace for the whole evening and indeed for the whole year.

The basic cooking principle is carefully to coat the onions and the rice by turning them in the butter with the wooden spoon before adding any liquid. The hot butter opens the pores of the rice so that the flavours seep into the grains of rice as the stock is added. The stock should be in a pot on the stove, already heated, so that as you add it you do not interrupt the cooking process with cold stock.

If you are going to use wine (and I certainly do) then it should be added as soon as the rice is coated and the onions translucent. Add the wine with a flourish and as it hits the pot it will cause a vapour, steaming the rice slightly. Begin to add the hot stock, a ladleful at a time, when the rice just starts to stick to the bottom of the pan. Add only as much stock as the rice absorbs and continue to stir until the rice appears to be cooked. This will take about 20-25 minutes.

Just before serving, remove the pan from the heat and stir in a large knob of butter to give the dish a wonderful consistency. The rice should still be firm to bite. At this stage add the Parmesan if you are going to use it.

It is best not to attempt this dish for a lot of people unless you are very skilled and have the right large equipment (the rice will expand to three times its volume once it has absorbed the liquid), and it is not a dish to cook all the way through and hope to heat and serve the next day. I learnt this to my cost when I tried to cook for a large group of friends and it went gluggy when I tried to finish what I had three quarters cooked the day before.

I talked about the perils of risotto with my colleague Urs Inauen, formerly of the Hyatt in Adelaide. He told me that his way of dealing with preparation is to take the risotto to a first stage by sweating the rice and onions in butter, then adding an equivalent measure of stock and letting that evaporate entirely before spreading the rice mixture thinly on a tray to cool. The risotto then will not take as long to reach its final stage of perfectly cooked rice in a delicious stock.

I HAVE GREATLY enjoyed the book *Risotto* by Constance del Nero—a book devoted entirely to this subject—and it inspired me to cook the following:

RISOTTO WITH MUSHROOMS

12 large mushrooms, stems removed and caps sliced
6 cups chicken or vegetable stock
8 tablespoons butter
1 onion, finely diced

2 cups arborio rice
3/4 cup dry white wine
3/4 cup freshly grated Parmesan
2 tablespoons chopped parsley

Add the stems of the mushrooms to the stock, bring it to the boil and let simmer for 30 minutes. Then keep the stock over a gentle heat while making the risotto.

Melt 6 tablespoons of the butter in a large cast iron or enamel pan. Add the onion and cook gently, stirring, until translucent. Turn up the heat, add the rice and stir well to coat with the butter. When the rice glistens, pour in the wine. When the alcohol has evaporated, stir in a ladleful of the hot stock, and stir until it is absorbed. Continue to add ladles of stock for another 10 minutes. Then fold the sliced mushrooms into the risotto. Continue adding stock and stirring for another 10 minutes, until done. The rice should be al dente and there should still be a little liquid left. Take the pan from the heat and stir in the cheese, butter and parsley.

Serve with green salad and a dry white wine.

Risotto with Chicken Livers

<table>
<tr><td>8 tablespoons butter</td><td>1/2 cup Marsala</td></tr>
<tr><td>2 onions, finely diced</td><td>3/4 cup freshly grated Parmesan</td></tr>
<tr><td>1/2 kg chicken livers, trimmed</td><td>2 tablespoons chopped parsley</td></tr>
<tr><td>2 cups arborio rice</td><td>6 cups chicken stock</td></tr>
</table>

Have the chicken stock warm as outlined above. Melt 6 tablespoons butter in a heavy pan. Add one onion and sauté until translucent. Then toss in half of the chicken livers until they are almost cooked. Remove with a slotted spoon and set aside. Repeat for the next half and set aside. Add the other onion, adding a little extra butter if required.

Turn up the heat and add the rice. After a minute of cooking and stirring the rice gently in the butter, add the Marsala. When absorbed, add a cupful of the warm stock and stir frequently until absorbed. Repeat and stir every so often as the rice swells and the liquid bubbles. Do this for 20 minutes until the rice is nearly done—almost tender but still firm. Stir in the chicken livers. Remove the pan from the heat and add the cheese, parsley and butter. Rest before serving.

THIS RISOTTO would be excellent with kid or as a side dish for something simple such as a roasted poussin (baby chicken) rubbed with a little oil and lemon juice with some oregano in the cavity.

Risotto of Pickled Lemons, Artichokes and Olives
(TO SERVE 4 AS AN ENTREE, OR A SIDE DISH FOR 8)

<table>
<tr><td>1 litre vegetable stock</td><td>1 large preserved lemon, skin</td></tr>
<tr><td>2 onions, finely diced</td><td>and pulp cut into pieces</td></tr>
<tr><td>1 tablespoon olive oil</td><td>4 to 5 small preserved artichokes</td></tr>
<tr><td>70 g butter</td><td>juice of 1 lemon</td></tr>
<tr><td>1 cup arborio rice</td><td>60 g chopped parsley</td></tr>
<tr><td>15 kalamata olives, stoned</td><td>salt and pepper to taste</td></tr>
</table>

Have the vegetable stock hot on the stove. Sweat the onions in the olive oil and butter until translucent. Add the rice, making sure there is enough butter and oil to coat the grains. Deglaze with lemon juice. Add the carefully seasoned vegetable stock a ladleful at a time until it is all absorbed. Keep a close eye on the temperature, maintaining a simmer, and don't go too far away from the stove. After about 15 minutes, when the rice should be close to finished and most of the stock is absorbed, stir in the preserved lemon, artichokes and olives for the last 5 minutes of cooking. The rice should be creamy, yet still have a bite at the centre of the grain. Add a little extra butter in the last few minutes if you wish, and add the parsley just before serving. Check for seasoning. The pickled lemons are salty, so a little pepper should suffice.

Crabs

A TRIP AWAY sometimes makes you realise just how wonderful things are at home. There are so many things I've become aware of—the incredible bargains to be had here, the value for money that we take for granted, the quality of our produce. The raw product, particularly seafood and meat, that we have in Australia now is so superior to that in England and the non-specialist shops of America that it is not hard to see what could be achieved by rounding off some rough edges, and encouraging our farmers and producers to even greater heights.

How does all this relate to crabs? In New York recently we were unable to get blue swimmers for a recipe and had to use instead Dungeness crabs, the famous Californian variety. These crabs looked spectacular and were easy to peel, yet the flavour had none of the sweetness and intensity of our blue swimmers from the Gulf where recreational fishermen can spend an afternoon or evening crabbing on the tidal beaches near Adelaide and then cook the catch, in situ, to enjoy one of the best meals of their lives.

The crabs swim in as little as 30 cm of water in sandy or weed-covered areas and can be found at night by the light of a lantern using nets or rakes to scoop them into a floating baby's bath. They can also be caught from a boat in deep water using drop nets.

Blue swimmer crabs will never taste as good away from the shore, as attested to by Stephanie Alexander in her book *Stephanie's Australia*. We arranged a crab expedition for her at my husband's family shack at Port Parham. Stephanie declared she had never eaten better crab in her life.

Once you have caught the crabs, remember to bring back some sea water to cook them in—have a bucket handy at the shore to remind you. We have a copper set up in the back yard of the shack and our first job is to get the fire started, to bring the sea water to the boil. The crabs are then thrown in, about 25 at a time, and boiled for 3 minutes only. They are then scooped out and thrown on to an old wire mattress frame kept solely for the crabs to cool down before eating. They are turned upside down, with the white underside of the carapace showing, so that all the juices are retained. The crabs are allowed to cool just enough to be able to pick them up—they are at their very best when warm. No matter what accompaniments you have prepared for them—mayonnaise, vinaigrette or lemon wedges—they will be superfluous. The crabs are wonderful just as they are.

One of the food delights of New York was a visit to a fish market where, for the first time in my life, I saw soft shell crabs for sale. I had read about these crabs for years—they are a great delicacy in America, particularly in Louisiana and in the crab restaurants of Chesapeake Bay. We arranged a detour to Chesapeake Bay just to eat in a crab house, hoping to try the famous soft shell variety. Unfortunately we were just a week short of the fresh crab season and had to make do with frozen crab, which fell far short of our expectations.

Soft shell crabs are available, of course, anywhere in the world at the time when the crabs shed their shells (in South Australia, between the full moons in November and December). At this time, the crabs can be eaten whole as the new shell is gelatinous and totally edible.

An enterprising fisherman based at Whyalla has been attempting to 'farm' soft shell crabs. If he succeeds there will certainly be a ready market, both locally and for export.

Soft shells aside, the flavour of the blue swimmer is so wonderful that it is well worth the trouble to pick them. I think the flavour is even better than crayfish.

Michael Angelakis wrote his first article for the *Advertiser* on blue swimmer crabs, and we recently discussed the problem of what seems to be a glut on the market, with large numbers of crabs being tossed out. This is bad enough in itself, but an added insult is that commercial fishermen are being allowed to fish the recreational waters to such an extent that the locals and visitors who have delighted in crabbing all their lives are now finding their usual spots denuded.

Crabs have to be treated very carefully to make the most of them and if you cannot catch and cook them live yourself then buy ready-cooked rather than 'green' ones at the market. Smell them first, though, to make sure they do not smell of ammonia, as this is a sign that they are old and unusable both for flavour and safety. Crabs begin to decompose the moment they die. You will never get the intensity of flavour possible from crab by buying from a fish merchant!

COMING ORIGINALLY from New South Wales, the 'beach' at Port Parham was a great shock to me, as the tide is often kilometres out. However over the years I have learnt that in perfect conditions Parham can feel like the Greek Islands, and with a meal of crabs on the beach and a bottle of white wine, you can feel at peace with the world. 'Perfect conditions', by the way, mean the tide in at sunset, the water warm enough to wade in, the sun on your back and no one else around—it doesn't happen often but is such a delight when it does that it makes up for all the times you visit in the heat of summer and find there is nowhere to swim.

PORT PARHAM CRAB SANDWICH

80 g per person of freshly-picked blue swimmer crab meat (approximately one average-sized crab per person); leave one crab claw per serve for garnish

MAYONNAISE
This was inspired by Stephanie Alexander's idea of using the 'mustard' (innards) of the crab to enhance the mayonnaise.

2 duck egg yolks
1 1/2 cups best olive oil
3 tablespoons crab mustard

juice of one lemon (more if necessary)
salt and pepper

Place egg yolks, crab mustard and lemon juice in food processor and blend well. Begin pouring oil in, as slowly as possible for the first half cup, then allow to flow a little faster making sure the oil is completely absorbed as you go. Check for salt and pepper and extra lemon juice if needed.

(The best mayonnaise is made by hand, and you can begin with the food processor and continue by hand. If your processor is a 'Cuisinart', you can buy a small plastic tube with a hole not much bigger than a pin, that controls up to half a cup of oil at a time dripping into the bowl.)

MUSTARD BREAD

150 g cracked wheat	*380 ml warm water*
1 tablespoon olive oil	*4 scant tablespoons top quality*
350 g wholemeal flour	*grain mustard*
150 g white flour	*1 teaspoon sea salt*
60 g fresh yeast (or 30 g	*1 teaspoon sugar*
dried yeast)	*1 tablespoon maple syrup*

Soak wheat in half a cup of tepid water. Activate yeast if fresh with sugar and 80 ml of the water. Stir activated yeast into the flour and salt. If using dried yeast, mix yeast and sugar with flours. Add the soaked wheat. On the stove warm the olive oil, mustard and maple syrup. Gradually pour the liquid into dry ingredients and mix with a wooden spoon. It will resemble the consistency of scone dough. Turn out and knead on a floured board. Leave to rise and then separate the dough into desired shapes. Leave to rise again.

Bake in a hot oven for 45 minutes for loaves, or 25-35 minutes for rolls or miniature loaves.

Make the sandwich by slicing a small loaf of mustard bread diagonally in two. Place the picked crab meat (being very careful that there are no pieces of shell) on one side and the crab mayonnaise on the other. Serve with a wedge of lemon, a crab claw and, for those who must have it, some chilli jam. I usually serve some peppery greens with this such as mustard cress or rocket.

Rabbit

R ABBIT IS ONE of the cheapest and most nutritious meals one could have. It is also one of the dishes many cooks seem to ruin. It is harder than turkey to cook properly and certainly more difficult than pheasant. The most common mistake is overcooking the rabbit until the meat is dry and stringy.

A recent newspaper article with the heading 'Vermin to some but still big business' set me thinking about rabbit. It is a delicious irony that an enterprising South Australian company is now exporting what is vermin to us back to the country from which they were introduced. The domestic rabbit in Europe has little flavour so the 'wild rabbit' is much sought after.

At the restaurant it is surprising how popular rabbit is. Those from the country love to eat the food of their childhood (no one cooks it quite like their mother!) and Europeans love the 'wild' flavour.

Rabbit was the survival food of the depression. My husband's grandfather was a butcher and during the depression became a rabbit trapper at Mannum in order earn a few shillings to feed his family.

My mother-in-law has often talked about grilling rabbit livers over hot coals and remembers her father grilling rabbit kittens over an open fire after the coals had died down. Even though she ate rabbit every day for many years, she still loves me to cook it for her.

To cook a rabbit perfectly, it is actually best to dissect it and treat the front legs, back legs and saddle as different cuts, all requiring different cooking times and methods. (The exception to this is the rabbit kitten barbecued whole.)

Dissect the rabbit with a sharp knife by first cutting off its front legs and then the back legs. The remaining piece is the saddle. This has a silvery sinew covering it which will drastically interfere with the cooking if not removed.

There are three ways of removing the sinew. Firstly, you can run a sharp knife along the spine and around the ribs to free a fillet from each side of the spine. The fillets will still have sinew on the outside and should be trimmed in the same manner as a fillet of beef. A thin, flexible fish filleting knife is best for this job.

These fillets can be sealed in foamy golden butter and literally just turned over before turning off the gas and letting the residual heat in the pan finish off the cooking.

The second way to handle the sinew is to seal and bake the saddle and then carve off the fillets and trim the sinew after cooking.

The third and, to my mind, most successful way is to remove the whole sinew with a filleting knife before you cook the saddle to avoid any shrinking or toughness during the cooking. The saddle can then go to the table whole with a sauce.

Rabbit bones are best discarded—they can turn a stock bitter if cooked for a long time.

If the thought of dissecting a rabbit is too difficult for you, you can buy specific portions from butchers and specialist suppliers.

I cook the saddle of rabbit by browning it on both sides, taking care that the butter stays golden, and then placing it in a small baking dish in the oven for 5 minutes at a high temperature. I remove it from the oven and let it rest under cover for 10 minutes before carving the meat off the bone.

If you want to make pasta or risotto using rabbit, you could cook in this fashion and then carve off the meat for tossing in the dish.

The kidneys, on the underside and encased in fat, will cook together with the saddle. Toss the liver quickly in some butter to seal each side and leave it to rest before serving.

One of the simplest ways to serve the saddle would be to make a sauce of reduced white wine, chicken stock and cream with some basil leaves thrown in for flavour.

The front legs are the sweetest meat of all. I often pot roast them in a heavy pot on top of the stove with some stock, fresh rosemary and baby pickling onions. I cook them very slowly and turn them several times during cooking until the meat readily comes away from the bone. This meat is also perfect in sandwiches and for rillettes as it is very moist and sweet.

The back legs I cook in a pressure cooker or crock pot with carrots, onions or leeks and celery, and some chicken stock. When the meat is cooked so that it comes away gently from the bone, I use it as a casserole or make a small pie of rabbit pieces and prunes. The cooking liquid is reduced and the pieces of meat are tossed with pitted prunes and rendered bacon to taste.

Rabbit is marvellous when marinated in olive oil, lemon juice and marjoram before cooking. Rabbit also has a good affinity with mushrooms.

Nicola Cox's book *Game Cookery* has more interesting information and recipes for rabbit.

All of my recipes call for wild rabbit as distinct from the farmed rabbit available in Western Australia and the eastern states. I have cooked farmed and wild rabbit side by side and have to say that I prefer the flavour of the wild. Wild rabbit is inexpensive, nutritious and I feel a much under-utilised food. But farmed rabbit is much easier to handle and is more forgiving in the cooking. Farmed rabbits are all grown to the same age whereas wild rabbits are of indeterminate age and cooking them is more difficult.

Because the farmed rabbit is a much larger animal (almost the size of a hare), it makes it easier to manage portion sizes. Whereas it would take a whole medium wild rabbit, dissected and using the best pieces, to feed one person, it is possible to serve two people from a farmed rabbit.

I LIKE TO SERVE rabbit rillettes with cornichons (baby dill pickle prepared in the French manner, available from specialist delicatessens), together with crusty bread and lots of salt and pepper. Prunes soaked in tea or brandy, whichever is your tipple, and then puréed to a thick paste with a little grain mustard goes well, especially in concert with the crispness of the cornichons.

RABBIT RILLETTES

2 kg rabbit legs, front and back (if you have a choice, use all front legs as they are the sweetest— leave the saddle for other dishes as it overcooks easily and is wasted in rillettes)
1 kg belly pork (with the rind and bones removed)

500 g pork fat
1 cup duck fat
salt
1 clove garlic, crushed
bouquet of fresh herbs
pepper
stock or water

Rub the pork and fat well with salt and stand overnight in winter, and for 4 to 6 hours in summer. Cut the pork into thick strips along the grooves where the bones were, and then again into small strips shorter than a match and about twice as thick. Cut the pork fat into small pieces.

Leave the rabbit on the bone and put it into a heavy ovenware dish together with the pork strips and pork fat. Bury the crushed garlic and herbs in the centre, season with pepper and add a soup ladle of stock or water. Cover the pan and cook in a very low oven for about 4 hours. The rabbit meat should be soft and falling off the bone. Taste to see if more salt and pepper are needed. Rillettes are insipid if not seasoned properly.

Turn the contents of the pan into a wire sieve set over a large bowl so that the fat seeps through. When well drained, remove the rabbit bones. Using two forks, pull the meat off the rabbit and pork in fine shreds. Put the meat into a jar. Strain the fat from the cooking pot and pour into the jar, or use melted duck fat if you prefer. Rillettes will last for ages if they are sealed properly. If you intend eating them soon after making them, use less salt in the first stage.

RABBIT RISOTTO

3 rabbits, or 6 saddles including fat and kidneys	3 tablespoons olive oil
4 oranges	3 cloves garlic, finely chopped
3 medium onions	60 g butter
425 g arborio rice	1³/4 litres chicken stock
3 tablespoons pine nuts	fresh thyme
3 tablespoons black olives	3 bay leaves (fresh if possible)
	pepper

Cut the rabbit into strips 4 cm long and 1/2 cm wide. Toss in a bowl with the olive oil, finely chopped garlic, plenty of thyme and black pepper. Shave the peel from one of the oranges, making a few long curls. Bury the peel in the rabbit and add 2 bay leaves. Cover and leave in the refrigerator for at least one hour.

Half an hour before you plan to serve the risotto, finely chop the onion and soften it in three quarters of the butter. Bring the stock to simmering point in a separate pan. Stir the rice into the softened onion, add the juice of the three oranges and cook gently, stirring occasionally, until the rice absorbs most of the juice. Add a generous ladleful of the hot stock, the zest from two oranges and a bay leaf. Continue cooking gently, stirring lightly and adding another ladleful of stock each time the previous one has been absorbed. After 15 to 20 minutes of cooking time the rice should be ready—creamy and tender with just a hint of bite at the centre of each grain.

While the risotto is cooking, lightly toast the pine nuts in a dry frypan and set them aside. Heat the balance of the butter in the frypan and add a dash of olive oil. Remove the rabbit from its marinade and sauté over a moderate heat for about a minute, shaking and stirring as necessary to cook the meat and slightly brown it. Only cook a small amount at a time so as not to poach the meat.

When the rice is cooked, season the rabbit with salt and tip the contents of the pan into the risotto. Use a spatula to ensure you scrape in every drop of the flavoursome rabbit juices. Add the pine nuts and olives. Mix well, check the seasoning and serve immediately with a crisp, green salad.

Celeriac

HAVE YOU EVER wondered about that prehistoric-looking vegetable at the market—the one that is roughly the shape of a large turnip, the colour of a dirty parsnip, and has hairy roots and leaves darker and coarser than celery?

It is celeriac, a versatile vegetable available from late autumn right through winter. Celeriac is as old a vegetable as celery so its lack of success is hard to understand, although it is much more popular in Germany. I prefer the mild 'celery' flavour of the celeriac. Cooked and puréed, it is the natural accompaniment to game.

A bunch of celeriac will have about four large bulbs and will cost somewhere between $5 and $6. As it has a convoluted or rough surface, it is best to choose the smoothest you can find so that you don't lose too much of the vegetable in the trimming.

As celeriac discolours on cutting, it is best to put it in a bowl of acidulated water (water with lemon added) while preparing to cook it. If you are going to eat it raw, just rub the cut surface with a lemon as you would for an artichoke. Sliced finely, celeriac gives a lovely crunch to salads.

Celeriac cut thickly and roasted to a golden brown in olive oil can be added to a dish of chicken or guinea fowl, often served by Urs Inauen, the very talented chef, formerly of the Hyatt in Adelaide.

CELERIAC CHIPS

With a firm hand and a sharp knife or on a mandolin or Japanese shredder, peel and cut the celeriac crossways into thin pieces 2 cm thick. Soak in acidulated water for 10 minutes, then drain and pat dry. Deep fry in your favourite oil until golden brown. Drain on absorbent paper and sprinkle with a little salt.

THIS CELERIAC PURÉE can also be made with just potatoes added or just apples, depending on what you have to hand and what you are serving it with. Celeriac with apple goes well with pheasant and celeriac with potatoes is wonderful alongside the best sausages you can buy.

PURÉE OF CELERIAC TO ACCOMPANY GAME

1 large celeriac	*50g butter*
2 granny smith apples	*150 ml cream*
1 medium potato	*salt and pepper*

Peel, core and slice the apples, potato and celeriac into large slices. Boil the potato and celeriac in salted water until tender, adding the apples after 5 minutes. Drain well and then purée in a mouli. Whisk in the butter and cream to make a fluffy purée. Season to taste.

BRAISED CELERIAC

Simply peel and cut the celeriac into slices of desired size. Use 250 ml chicken stock and 1 tablespoon butter to braise the celeriac for about 20 minutes until tender. Strain and reduce the remaining stock to pour over the celeriac with freshly chopped parsley, salt and pepper to taste.

THE FOLLOWING PIE is a very favourite dish inspired by Nicola Cox in her book *Game Cookery*—an excellent book for anyone interested in game.

PHEASANT AND CELERIAC PIE

450 g cubes of cooked pheasant, rabbit or chicken, well trimmed	225 ml milk
	1 tablespoon Dijon mustard
35 g butter	375 g cooked, cubed celeriac
1 small onion, finely chopped	salt and pepper
1 small carrot, finely diced	200 g puff or shortcrust pastry
35 g flour	egg wash
300 ml game or chicken stock	

Melt the butter in a saucepan and gently soften the diced carrot and onion. When soft, add the flour and stir over moderate heat for 1-2 minutes, then draw the pan from the stove and wait for the sizzling to cease. Add the milk to the pan, stirring with a wooden spoon. Cook gently for 15 minutes. Add stock to thin the mixture. Simmer for 2-3 minutes. Stir in the mustard, season with salt and pepper and fold in the meat and celeriac. Place in pie dish and allow to cool.

Roll the pastry thinly and cut a 1-2 cm strip around the edge. Moisten with cold water and set in place around the rim of the pie dish. Then moisten this with cold water and set the pastry cover in place. Trim the edges, knock them up and decorate the pie. Paint with egg wash and cook in a hot oven at 220°C for about 10 to 15 minutes until a good brown colour and then lower the temperature to 180°C and continue cooking for a further 10 to 15 minutes until the pie is heated through and the pastry is crisp.

WHEN WE WERE in France last year we were served this delightful salad. It goes well with smoked or salted meats such as prosciutto or smoked chicken or pheasant.

CELERIAC WITH REMOULADE

1 large celeriac
juice of one lemon
1 to 2 tablespoons olive oil
salt and freshly ground pepper

1 cup remoulade (mayonnaise)
celery leaves (the inner apple-green
 leaves from the celery put into
 icy water to crisp)

Peel the celeriac and cut into julienne or put through a coarse vegetable grater. Add lemon juice and stir in the oil. Season with a little salt and freshly ground pepper to taste. Stir in the remoulade and serve with chilled celery leaves.

ANOTHER PREHISTORIC vegetable that you have might only have seen in a book rather than a greengrocer's is salsify. To my knowledge no one in South Australia is growing it in commercial quantities. This is a vegetable we should all be demanding—it has a wonderful oyster flavour and is known by some as the oyster vegetable.

Salsify and scorzonera have much in common. They are distinguished vegetables which have not caught on with the general public. They belong to the same family and are shaped like a long carrot. Salsify is whitish in appearance, like a fresh parsnip, and scorzonera is a brownish black. Like celeriac, they have hairy roots that resemble those of ginseng.

I have grown salsify very successfully and last year I bought some scorzonera from a local grower but it wasn't as good as I had hoped—I think they left it too long in the ground. Those in the know say that scorzonera has the edge over salsify but salsify has been a winner for me. This year I will try them both again. Sowing time is in spring, for harvesting in late autumn to winter. Autumn sowing is supposed to be better for hot climates. Cultivation is similiar to carrots.

Cut the tops off the salsify as you would a carrot and scrub the soil away under running water. They can be peeled and tossed in acidulated water to keep them white, but I just leave them whole, with the skins on, and either steam or cook them in salted water. When tender, pass them under running water again and slip the skins off. I like to serve them on their own with simply a little butter and black pepper. You could make a purée of salsify although I would leave out any potato or apple as in the celeriac recipe. French and Italian dishes often team salsify with chicken and it makes a terrific soup.

The flowers of the salsify are also edible. The buds taste a little like asparagus. They can be pickled: put alternate layers of the flowers in a jar with layers of sugar and pack down firmly. Cover with cider vinegar that has been boiled and cooled. Leave to mature for a week. Use in salads.

ONE OF THE best entrees I can remember was one featuring a combination of oyster flavours and centred around the salsify from our garden. I steamed salsify, tossed abalone or oyster mushrooms quickly in butter and black pepper and warmed some Coffin Bay oysters for a few seconds in the juices of the mushrooms and salsify. The dish was served with a champagne sauce.

SALSIFY WITH COFFIN BAY OYSTERS AND OYSTER MUSHROOMS WITH A CHAMPAGNE SAUCE

2 salsify per person

3 large Coffin Bay oysters per person (preferably unopened with their juices)

3 medium to large oyster (abalone) mushrooms per person

butter

salt and freshly ground pepper

1 lemon

Cook the salsify in acidulated water with a pinch of salt until tender. Drain and let cool a little to slip the skins off the salsify. Cut in half lengthways. In a large pan toss the oyster mushrooms in butter, allowing them to go nut-brown (do not poach them as they go grey), and toss in the salsify to both warm and gently brown. Grind a little black pepper to taste. At the last minute open the oysters and slip them into the pan with the juices. Toss for just a few seconds and then strain the juices from the pan into the champagne sauce and finish quickly by whisking in the unsalted butter (see below). Sauce the plate first and then place the salsify pieces stacked on top of each other with the oyster mushrooms on top and the oysters cascading over.

CHAMPAGNE SAUCE

375 ml bottle Yalumba Brut de Brut Champagne

250 ml rich cream
80 g unsalted butter

Reduce the champagne to about 100 ml and add the juices from the mushrooms and oysters. Add the cream and reduce to desired consistency. Have the butter cubed and sitting in the fridge ready to use at the last moment.

Pigeon and Squab

THERE IS OFTEN confusion about the difference between squab and pigeon. Squab is baby pigeon before it leaves the nest. It is large and very tender. Squab is reared by some farmers in Australia especially for the table and is expensive. Pigeon, on the other hand, is caught anywhere and is of indeterminate age. It is inexpensive but erratic in its availability and quality. With wild pigeons you need also to consider whether they have been feeding on 'sprayed' crops.

More than ten years ago I remember becoming excited by a phone call from Adelaide offering me hundreds, even thousands, of pigeons. I was delighted at such a find until it became clear to me that not only were the birds still alive but I would have to go and trap them. The call was from an enterprising member of the Adelaide City Council who thought it a perfect solution to both the council's problems and mine. I refused the kind offer.

I have no preference between squab and pigeon. I use them in totally different dishes and prefer not to compare them. Pigeon makes the best pie I have ever eaten and is also great in ragouts or pasta dishes. Squab can be used elegantly with only a game jus, grapes and verjuice, or it can be barbecued and made into a warm salad. It can also be used in all the same ways as pigeon, although I find that a little too extravagant.

Squab, though expensive, is well worth the cost. It is very easy to prepare and should be seriously considered for special occasions. It is always handy to know how to make a really spectacular dish with next to no effort.

The differences in taste and texture between squab and pigeon are enormous. Tasting them side by side you could be forgiven for thinking they were entirely different poultry. Both require very specific cooking methods. Once you understand the principles, cooking them is simple.

The meat of the squab is thick and buttery and should be served fairly rare, though not necessarily 'blue', as it often is. I insist on my squab being quite pink as I find that 'blue' has a more limited taste. It should be tender, moist and delicious.

Squab is best cooked very quickly at a high temperature with a long resting time. It can be teamed with simple or extravagant accompaniments and either a game jus or a warm vinaigrette-style sauce.

Pigeon, on the other hand, has to be cooked very slowly until the meat almost falls off the bone. The flavour is strong and gutsy and the texture fine when it has been cooked with loving attention. I prefer to use a crock pot or pressure cooker for pigeon, or the 'confit' method, where I cook the bird in duck fat at barely a simmer for the whole cooking process. This can take 1 to 4 hours, depending on the age of the bird.

The flesh of the pigeon can be dry if cooked conventionally, which is why I use the slower cooking methods. It should be cooked so slowly that each quarter seems just to 'lift off' the carcass. Even so, I am very careful, after having lifted the meat off the bone, to make sure that it is immersed skin side down in some cooking liquor. I then make a well-reduced pigeon glaze with the chopped-up bones of the carcass, extra chicken bones chopped up raw, normal stock vegetables and veal stock.

Chestnuts are a wonderful accompaniment to pigeon. If I can't get fresh ones, I buy dried chestnuts from an Italian grocer and reconstitute them in pigeon stock, overnight, before cooking with them. I have found canned chestnuts unsatisfactory.

The piquancy of pickled walnuts is very good with pigeon. First cook the pigeon gently in some stock, with just a dash of pickled walnut juice, up to the stage of taking it off the bone and making the sauce. Reduce the pigeon sauce, adjust it very carefully with some more pickled walnut juice, then cut the walnuts crossways and add to the sauce in the last few minutes, with a little cream. (Commercially-pickled walnuts will disintegrate very quickly.) Rosemary complements these flavours.

Another favourite idea for good-sized pigeons is to stuff them with some sausage mince, perhaps studded with olives, to help keep them moist during cooking. Add some good-quality tinned, peeled tomatoes, lots of herbs and some chicken stock and cook in a pressure cooker or crock pot. When the pigeons are cooked so that the meat is just coming away from the bone, transfer them (upside-down to retain moisture) and cover to keep hot. Reduce the cooking liquid, then toss some more olives in at the last moment and serve with polenta (see page 99).

Squab is particularly popular in France and I found it impossible to resist when on the menu of any serious restaurant we visited. The best of all was at Jamin, a Paris restaurant run by chef Joël Robuchon. These were the notes I wrote after that night, 'Pigeon presented in flambé dish and then carved at the table using wooden board with deep ring around for juices. Fresh pepper ground. Hearts and livers spooned out on to a crouton. Finely-cut crisp game chips served with sauce "just a jus". MAGNIFICENT.'

VIGNERON'S SQUAB

6 squab (450 g each)
salt and freshly-ground black
  pepper
1/2 lemon
1 tablespoon butter
stock vegetables: 2 brown onions,
  unpeeled and cut in half;
  2 small carrots, 1 stick celery,
  piece of parsley and thyme

100 ml verjuice (see page 160)
500 ml reduced veal stock
bunch fresh, large seedless grapes
  (or muscatels dried on the
  stem if out of season)

GARNISH (OPTIONAL)
6 slices french stick
4 tablespoons butter
squab liver

2 tablespoons champagne or wine
salt and freshly-ground black
  pepper

Heat the oven to maximum for household ovens (250°C). Salt and pepper the cavity of the birds and squeeze a little lemon juice inside. In a frypan, seal the birds with the butter to a gentle golden brown, turning on all sides. Sit them in a baking dish with the juices from the pan and roast at very high temperature for 8-12 minutes (depending on the heat of the oven). Check them after 8 minutes. Take the squab from the oven and turn them upside-down to rest for a good 15 minutes before carving. After carving off the frame, set the squabs aside, cut side down, on an enamel tray with just enough of the cooking juices to keep them moist.

Drain the fat from the baking dish. Roughly chop the stock vegetables and brown them in the baking dish, being careful not to burn. Chop up the carcass and add to caramelised stock vegetables. Deglaze with verjuice (or wine and a little lemon juice), add veal stock and cook vigorously until the sauce reduces (about 20 minutes). Strain and add the grapes just before serving.

Croutons: Using half the butter in a heavy-bottomed frypan, fry bread to golden brown on both sides. Drain on to absorbent paper. Sauté liver in a little of the butter, add champagne and flame. Mash the liver and juices with the rest of the butter, softened, and season. Spread on croutons. Drink the rest of the champagne!

Snails

IN ONE OF OUR first years at the vineyard, we experienced a snail plague. I remember us, in our rubber boots, collecting about a bucket per vine. Because we were still in our 'romantic' early stage and didn't let nature's disasters worry us, I thought how wonderful it would be to utilise the sudden feast. It remained as nothing more than an idea when we began the restaurant—it seemed just too difficult.

I really enjoy eating snails and I remember a meal of fresh ones at Stephanie's Restaurant in Melbourne. She had an army of youngsters collect snails for her and painstakingly prepared them for a special banquet at the Symposium of Gastronomy. The difference between these and the tinned variety imported from France was startling!

I buy my snails from Merle and Brian Authers who have a business called Ozcargots in Kangarilla. The snails they breed are the *Helix aspersa*, or common brown snail, called 'petit gris' by the French. While smaller than the Burgundian snail, they are much sweeter. If you wanted to, you could gather those snails attacking your garden and prepare them for your own table. However, you should consider what pesticides have been used in your garden before you proceed and be prepared for a great deal of tedious work.

Ozcargots is happy to post snails to individuals. There are two price ranges—one for prepared and cooked snails and the other for live snails by the dozen.

The farming of the snails is managed by an 'oasis' that consists of the cut-off bottom of a rain-water tank, partly filled with soil, with roofing tiles placed around it for the snails to gather under. A sprinkler system sprays the oasis six times a day, which keeps the snails active. While they are active they are feeding and, therefore, growing. The whole oasis is covered with cloth, both to shade the snails and keep out the birds. Other than birds, predators include mice, spiders and some kinds of worms.

For commercial farming, snails require a constant temperature and a humidity of 85%, so they have erected a polyweave tunnel 6 m wide and 9 m long. This is a controlled atmosphere and is costly to maintain, but it prevents the snails aestivating (or hibernating) and thus ensures a supply all year round.

This enterprise is not unlike other sorts of farming. They hatch approximately 150 snails a day and, the day we spoke, collected 400 eggs. The eggs look like roe, so you could say snail farming is like pheasant farming in miniature! All mating snails are noted and marked. Those which appear to be laying are marked and, later, the eggs removed, counted and put in special containers. These are monitored to see when and how many hatch.

The snails are fed daily on a special mixture of high-protein grains, and are given salad twice a week. All feeders are cleaned daily.

When preparing an order the snails are placed in purging bins and fed on a bland mash for seven days, then cooked in boiling water with vinegar and lemon juice. Next they are shelled, then cooked again in boiling water, white wine and lemon juice. They are carefully rinsed in cold water, then packed in containers in a marinade of white wine, light oil and slivers of garlic.

They should be eaten within 7 to 10 days, but may be frozen. The cooking time for this preparation is 8 to 10 minutes, but the snails will need further cooking in the recipe of your choice. Be adventurous about timing, though: some recipes call for up to 2 1/2 hours. For most requirements, further cooking of 5 to 15 minutes is adequate.

This recipe is from my former supplier Margaret Adams.

SNAILS STUFFED IN THE BURGUNDIAN STYLE

1 large bunch parsley	500 g unsalted butter, softened
5 cloves garlic, peeled	4-6 dozen snails
60 g shallot or onion, peeled	breadcrumbs
4 level teaspoons salt	white wine
2 level teaspoons ground black pepper	

Put first five ingredients in a blender until well-chopped. Gradually add the butter. Remove the snails from the shells. Put a dab of butter mixture in each shell, replace and cover snails liberally with more butter mixture. Place snails in an ovenproof dish, sprinkle with breadcrumbs and a teaspoon of white wine per snail.

Cook in a hot oven till bubbling and browned (about 10 minutes). Serve sizzling hot with plenty of fresh, crusty bread, large serviettes and finger bowls. A variation on this recipe is to cut rounds of bread to fit small, ovenproof dishes. Cut a small hole in each round of bread, place a snail on each and cook as above.

For a change from garlic butter, snails may be simmered in olive oil, tomato purée and fresh rosemary or mint.

———

THIS IS THE traditional dish served on Midsummer's Eve in Rome.

CASSOLETTE OF SNAILS WITH ROQUEFORT

4 dozen snails	1 teaspoon gravy (reduced stock)
4 mushrooms	50 g Roquefort cheese
8 tiny pickling onions	50 g butter
4 slices thin lean bacon	2 egg yolks
1 teaspoon Madeira	500 g puff pastry

Drain snails and sauté with butter, onions, mushrooms and bacon sliced into tiny cubes. Add Roquefort, Madeira and stock and leave to cook for a few minutes.

Into each of 4 small, ovenproof dishes, place 12 snails, 2 onions, one mushroom, bacon and sauce. Cover each dish with a round of puff pastry, glazed with egg. Cook in a hot oven (200°C) for 15 minutes.

Kangaroo

KANGAROO HAS BEEN available for human consumption in South Australia and the Northern Territory for many years. In early 1994, after a great deal of discussion on the issue, New South Wales and Victoria brought in new legislation in line with this as well. Whilst it is legal to *eat* kangaroo in the other states, by 1995, following mutual recognition legislation passed federally, restrictions to the sale of kangaroo in restaurants and other food outlets will be removed. In the very early days it was legal to 'give it away' and I was often asked to present my smoked kangaroo at special functions interstate.

Kangaroo is such a tasty meat, low in cholesterol and fat and of course unique to Australia, so interstate and overseas visitors are particularly keen to try it. It has a much looser texture than beef and some say its flavour is closest to young venison.

When roo first became available we used to buy a whole saddle and spend hours trimming and stripping sinew. Things are much simpler now and the meat can be bought as fillets, legs or tails. For normal home cooking or barbecuing, fillet is the most convenient and inexpensive cut as most pieces of fillet approximate a serve. I have not cooked legs of kangaroo but I am told they are very good when baked in a Weber. You can use kangaroo tail for soup as well as a great stew in the oxtail mould. The Regency Park School of Food and Catering in Adelaide has done a great deal of work with kangaroo and is a good source of advice.

Smoked kangaroo is my favourite. In the Barossa Valley I have a wealth of food tradition to draw upon, and the smoking of products is one of the strongest. Smoked roo has a denser consistency and it can be sliced paper-thin, like prosciutto. It is particularly good in snacks or nibbles before dinner as well as in salads and pastas.

W HEN COOKING KANGAROO fillets, either on the stove or for the barbecue, place them on a tray with just enough olive oil to moisten them, sprinkle with freshly-cracked black pepper, and allow to marinate, covered, for about an hour. Don't be tempted to use a red wine (or any other) marinade for roo—it will disturb the natural flavour of the meat. The very best result is gained if you buy only enough meat for your proposed meal. Kangaroo oxidises on contact with the air more than any other meat I have dealt with!

To cook, simply seal the fillets quickly on both sides in a very hot pan (the oil around the roo is usually sufficient) and then place the pan in a very hot oven (250°C) for 4 to 5 minutes. Take out the pan, turn the fillet over, cover the meat and let it rest for at least 10 minutes before carving and serving. As with all game, the resting period is very important. Kangaroo should be served rare or at the most medium-rare—well-done kangaroo is tough and tasteless.

If you are barbecuing, throw the meat on to a very hot barbecue and cook for about 2 to 3 minutes each side or even less if the fillets are thin. Once again *it is important to rest the meat* for at least 5 minutes on the side of the barbecue before serving.

Serve the meat simply with something like an olive and anchovy butter or, as Chris Manfield (ex-Adelaide, now owner-chef of The Paramount Restaurant in Sydney) showed me, a wonderful wasabi butter. If my memory serves me correctly, this was made with lots of greens—parsley, spring onions, perhaps some sorrel—puréed with a dash of lemon juice and soft butter with wasabi (Japanese horseradish) powder to taste. Serve with a salad.

For other ideas for kangaroo you could follow recipes for venison in game cook books. If you want to serve roo more formally, an excellent method is to make a rich red wine and port glaze, toss in some thinly-sliced pickled quinces, and serve with creamy mashed potato. Kangaroo marries with Asian flavours and you can substitute it for beef in most dishes. I've had wonderful kangaroo dishes with black bean sauce at Nediz Tu in Adelaide, for example, and stir-fry kangaroo is quick, easy and tasty. I remember a kangaroo dish at Ann Oliver's Mistress Augustine's restaurant that was brilliant and kangaroo with couscous at The Running Man.

SALAD OF GUM-SMOKED KANGAROO
(SERVES 6)

300 g thinly-sliced smoked kangaroo	*100 g Keta caviar*
3 generous witlof bulbs	*balsamic vinegar*
1 mignonette lettuce	*virgin olive oil*
1 butter crunch lettuce	*1 teaspoon finely-chopped garlic*
1 bunch rocket	*sun-dried tomatoes (optional)*

Make a vinaigrette of olive oil and balsamic vinegar at approximately 4 to 1, depending on personal preference. Add freshly-chopped garlic.

Prepare lettuces and arrange. (The witlof is particularly important to the dish. Gum-smoked kangaroo is very successful as an appetiser with only witlof, but is a delicious entree with the combination of lettuces listed.)

Drape the sliced kangaroo through the salad and strew sun-dried tomatoes. Dress the salad and place generous amounts of caviar on each dish.

Sugar-Cured Kangaroo, Barbecued

2 kg kangaroo back strap,
  sinews trimmed
25 g black peppercorns, coarsely
  crushed

125 g coarse sea salt
125 g sugar
8 juniper berries, bruised
100 g fresh thyme

Mix the salt, sugar, peppercorns, juniper berries and thyme. Evenly spread the fillets with the mixture, place in a plastic tray and seal well. Weight the tray down with a similar size tray inserted as a lid with weights, and leave in the refrigerator overnight.

Take the fillets from the tray and wipe off any excess moisture. Brush with olive oil and bake on a very hot grill. Cooking time will depend on the thickness of the fillets and may be as little as 4 minutes but no longer than 10 minutes. After the fillet is cooked it is essential to rest the meat for at least 15 minutes before serving.

Serve with horseradish cream and a salad of bitter lettuces.

BIBLIOGRAPHY

Stephanie Alexander, *Stephanie's Australia: Travelling and Tasting*, Allen & Unwin, Sydney, 1991

Stephanie Alexander, *Stephanie's Feasts and Stories*, Allen & Unwin, Sydney, 1988

Stephanie Alexander, *Stephanie's Menus for Food Lovers*, Methuen Haynes, Sydney, 1985

Colman Andrews, *Catalan Cuisine*, Headline, London, 1989

The Barossa Cookery Book, Tanunda Soldiers' Memorial Hall Committee, Tanunda, 1917

Beeton, Mrs, *Family Cookery*, Ward Lock, London, 1963

Frances Bissell, *Cook's Calendar: Seasonal Menus*, Chatto & Windus, London, 1985

Georges Blanc, *Ma Cuisine des Saisons*, Macmillan, London, 1987

Antonio Carluccio, *An Invitation to Italian Cooking*, Pavilion, London, 1986

Arrigo Cipriani, *The Harry's Bar Cook Book*, Smith Gryphon, London, 1991

Claire Clifton, *Edible Flowers*, Bodley Head, London, 1983

Nicola Cox, *Game Cookery*, Victor Gollancz, London, 1989

Constance del Nero & Rosario del Nero, *Risotto*, Harper and Row, New York, 1989

Anne Dolamore, *The Essential Olive Oil Companion*, Macmillan, Melbourne, 1988

Lois Dribin, Denise Marina & Susan Ivankovich, *Cooking with Sun Dried Tomatoes*, Fisher Books, Arizona, 1990

Jenny Ferguson, *Cooking for You and Me*, Methuen Haynes, Sydney, 1987

Carol Field, *Celebrating Italy*, William Morrow, New York, 1990

Theodora Fitzgibbon, *Game Cooking*, Andre Deutsch, London, 1963

Patience Gray, *Honey From a Weed*, Prospect Books, London, 1986

Jane Grigson & Roy Fullick (eds.), *The Best of Jane Grigson*, Michael Joseph, London, 1992

Jane Grigson, *Fruit Book*, Michael Joseph, London, 1982

Jane Grigson, *Good Things*, Penguin, Harmondsworth, 1973

Jane Grigson, *Vegetable Book*, Atheneum, New York, 1979

Marion Halligan, *Eat My Words*, Angus & Robertson, Sydney, 1990

Marcella Hazan, *The Classic Italian Cookbook*, Macmillan, London, rev. ed. 1987

Aldous Huxley, *The Olive Tree*, Ayer, USA, reprint of 1937 ed.

Jennifer Isaacs, *Bush Food*, Weldon, Sydney, 1987

Madeleine Kamman, *In Madeleine's Kitchen*, Atheneum, New York, 1984

Max Lake, *Scents and Sensuality*, Penguin, Melbourne, 1991

Deborah Madison, *The Greens Cookbook*, Bantam Books, New York, 1987

Harold McGee, *The Curious Cook*, Northpoint Press, San Francisco, 1990

Harold McGee, *On Food and Cooking*, Unwin Hyman, London, 1984

Perla Meyers, *The Seasonal Kitchen*, Simon & Schuster, New York, 1989

Richard Olney, *Simple French Food*, Atheneum, New York, 1980

Elise Pascoe, *Four Seasons of Food and Wine*, Macmillan, Sydney, 1984

Angelo Pellegrini, *The Food Lover's Garden*, Lyons and Burford, New York, 1970

Jeremy Round, *The Independent Cook*, Barrie & Jenkins, London, 1988

Time Life Fruit Book, Time Life, Amsterdam, 1983

Tom Stobart (ed.), *Cook's Encyclopaedia*, Papermac, London, 1982

Beverley Sutherland Smith, *A Taste for All Seasons*, Lansdowne, Sydney, 1975

Michael Symons, *One Continuous Picnic*, Duck Press, Adelaide, 1982

Anya von Bremzen & John Welchman, *Please to the Table: The Book of Russian Cooking*, Workman, USA, 1990

Alf Wark, *Wine Cookery*, Rigby, Adelaide, 1969

Alice Waters, *Chez Panisse Menu Cookbook*, Chatto & Windus, London, 1984

Alice Waters, Patricia Curtain & Martine Labro, *Chez Panisse Pasta, Pizza and Calzone*, Random House, New York, 1984

Stafford Whitaker, *The Compleat Strawberry*, Century, London, 1985
Paula Wolfert, *The Cooking of South West France*, Dorling Kindersley, USA, rev. ed. 1987
Paula Wolfert, *Mediterranean Cookery*, Ecco, New York, 1977

INDEX OF RECIPES

INDEX